The Excellence of the Arabs

Letter from the General Editor

The Library of Arabic Literature makes available Arabic editions and English translations of significant works of Arabic literature, with an emphasis on the seventh to nineteenth centuries. The Library of Arabic Literature thus includes texts from the pre-Islamic era to the cusp of the modern period, and encompasses a wide range of genres, including poetry, poetics, fiction, religion, philosophy, law, science, travel writing, history, and historiography.

Books in the series are edited and translated by internationally recognized scholars. They are published as hardcovers in parallel-text format with Arabic and English on facing pages, as English-only paperbacks, and as downloadable Arabic editions. For some texts, the series also publishes separate scholarly editions with full critical apparatus.

The Library encourages scholars to produce authoritative Arabic editions, accompanied by modern, lucid English translations, with the ultimate goal of introducing Arabic's rich literary heritage to a general audience of readers as well as to scholars and students.

The Library of Arabic Literature is supported by a grant from the New York University Abu Dhabi Institute and is published by NYU Press.

Philip F. Kennedy
General Editor, Library of Arabic Literature

About this Paperback

This paperback edition differs in a few respects from its dual-language hardcover predecessor. Because of the compact trim size the pagination has changed. Material that referred to the Arabic edition has been updated to reflect the English-only format, and other material has been corrected and updated where appropriate. For information about the Arabic edition on which this English translation is based and about how the LAL Arabic text was established, readers are referred to the hardcover.

The Excellence of the Arabs

by

Ibn Qutaybah

translated by

Sarah Bowen Savant and Peter Webb

foreword by

Jack Weatherford

volume editor

Michael Cooperson

NEW YORK UNIVERSITY PRESS

New York

NEW YORK UNIVERSITY PRESS
New York

Library of Congress Cataloging-in-Publication Data
Names: Ibn Qutaybah, ʻAbd Allāh ibn Muslim, 828–889? author. | Savant, Sarah Bowen, translator. | Webb, Peter, 1978– translator. | Cooperson, Michael, editor.
Title: The excellence of the Arabs / by Ibn Qutaybah ; translated by Sarah Bowen Savant and Peter Webb ; foreword by Jack Weatherford ; volume editor, Michael Cooperson.
Other titles: Faḍl al-ʻArab wa-al-tanbīh ʻalá ʻulūmihā. English
Description: New York : New York Univeristy Press, 2019. | Includes bibliographical references and indexes. |
Identifiers: LCCN 2019017348 (print) | LCCN 2019017757 (ebook) | ISBN 9781479859764 () | ISBN 9781479863334 () | ISBN 9781479899265 (pbk. : alk. paper)
Subjects: LCSH: Islamic civilization—Early works to 1800. | Islamic Empire—Intellectual life—Early works to 1800.
Classification: LCC DS36.85 (ebook) | LCC DS36.85 .I28 2019 (print) | DDC 909/.0974927—dc23
LC record available at https://lccn.loc.gov/2019017348

New York University Press books are printed on acid-free paper, and their binding materials are chosen for strength and durability.

Series design and composition by Nicole Hayward
Typeset in Adobe Text

Manufactured in the United States of America

10 9 8 7 6 5 4 3 2 1

Contents

Foreword

JACK WEATHERFORD

The Excellence of the Arabs offers us two valuable books in one. The first presents an ethnic and cultural evaluation of the Arabs compared to their Muslim neighbors, particularly the Persians. The second presents summaries of a list of traditional Arab intellectual achievements.

Ibn Qutaybah addresses social issues of the ninth century, but he speaks with a voice that is modern about topics that could easily be lifted from today's news headlines or heated internet websites. He provides an ethnic map, looking outward from the Arab center. In addition to Arabs, Persians, and Turks, he locates the Greeks. Copts, Armenians, Nubians and "Children of Israel" around him. Interestingly he offers an ethnically cross-cultural psychological typology as well, delineating the different emotions with particular emphasis on pride and envy. He offers perceptive observations that vary from philosophically and psychologically astute to glib generalizations worthy of a modern psychologist talk-show host. Whether we like what he says or not, we can easily recognize ourselves, or at least our own attitudes towards others, in many of his timeless comments.

In his analysis of Arab fields of learning, the second part of *The Excellence of the Arabs,* Ibn Qutaybah presses some well-trodden themes of bravery, hospitality, self-sacrifice, love of horses, and the Arab rise from poverty to preeminence; yet his copious documentation of these traits shows how deeply imbedded these cultural themes have been, even before the rise of Islam. Ibn Qutaybah emphasizes nomadic traditions such as oral poetry, horsemanship, reading the stars, predicting the future from stones, and others that are often dismissed by scholars as mere skills, customs, or superstition, not rising to the higher ranks of intellectual achievements. He raises these to a level commensurate with more prestigious forms of knowledge. In a crisis moment of battle being able to read a face or interpreting gestures can be more important than having studied a text on warfare.

Ibn Qutaybah frames his book in terms of the specific Arab versus Persian cultures, but his analysis presages the work of fourteenth-century Ibn Khaldun who generalized similar observations to a more abstract level of the tension between the cultures of nomadic and sedentary civilizations. Some of what Ibn Qutaybah describes as the Arab genius is generally characteristic of equestrian nomads, including Turks, Berbers, and Huns, as well as the Mongols and Manchus, who represented the final wave in a three-thousand-year phase of nomadic conquests of urban and agricultural civilizations. For both pre-Islamic Arabs and the Mongols, their traditional ways of life necessitated a keen ability to understand animals, to navigate by stars, to read topography, to interpret the faces of strangers, and to memorize oral literature. Even the emphasis on hospitality to guests seems part and parcel of all horse and camel nomad culture.

Other aspects of culture—such as the stress on personal honor and reputation based on adherence to a specific chivalrous code of conduct in battle, sexual segregation, and genealogical purity—are more specific to the Arabs. Pre-Islamic Turks, and later the Mongols, prized victory in battle no matter how achieved. There were no rules of combat, and often the more devious or surprising one was to the enemy, the better. Eurasian nomads also imposed fewer social restraints on women, and even the highest leaders, such as Genghis Khan, explained away female infidelity and allowed the incorporation of children into the family as equals no matter who fathered them.

The Arab emphasis on spreading the use of their language, customs, dress, and religion lacks parallel in the Hun-Turco-Mongol steppe nomads of Eurasia. Writing *The Excellence of the Arabs* derives from this Arab sense of pride. For Muslims—whether Arabs or converts from other ethnic groups—the divine revelation of the Qur'an was inextricably tied to Arabic, which held a unique prestige and contributed to its spread within the Umayyad and Abbasid caliphates as a language of religion, scholarship, and administration. The Mongols, on the other hand, forbade foreigners from using their language, from following their customs, or from wearing their dress. Just as Genghis Khan allowed no images to be made of him and did not permit his name to be inscribed on coins or monuments, he would never have allowed a book such as *The Excellence of the Mongols* to be written. Anyone who did so would be a traitor revealing the knowledge that made the Mongols successful. The first book about their history was not written until after Genghis Khan's death, and as shown in its title, *The Secret History of the Mongols,* it was carefully hidden from the public.

Mongols distinguished themselves from other ethnic groups through their accomplishments, notably victory in war, not through writing. Ibn Qutaybah intended his work to distinguish Arab values and intellectual achievements from those of Persians, but it is also helpful to us in understanding the differences between Arabs and other nomadic conquerors. It also contributes greatly to the broader discussion of nomadic conquest dynasties and sedentary civilization.

Ibn Qutaybah's outsider perspective as a non-Arab writing in Arabic gives his work added authority and a clearer, crisper vision than an insider might have. Like Tacitus among the Germans in the first century, Alexis de Tocqueville among the Americans in the nineteenth, or even the less scholarly Marco Polo among the Mongols and Chinese in the thirteenth century, the author's slight detachment from his subject, despite obvious biases, makes it a timeless text able to speak to scholars across generations and disciplines.

Ibn Qutaybah's voice in *The Excellence of the Arabs* is that of a sophisticated observer describing the Arabs through their literature, but he also unashamedly advocates a particular perspective of support for the Arabs of his time over the rising influence of Persians within the world of Islam. Clearly, he was writing for readers of that time and not for us; yet, that makes his work all the more valuable for modern scholarship. He presents an idealized picture that helps understand the values that motivated the Arabs of his time, how they wished to see themselves, and how they wished to be seen by others. His explication helps us to interpret the events of the era—without an understanding these values, it is extremely difficult to interpret the history.

The usefulness of this book and its application to a range of scholarly issued is increased by Ibn Qutaybah's clear prose backed by careful thought and a strong literary training. The accessibility is accentuated by the careful work of the editors and translators, James E. Montgomery, Peter Webb, and Sarah Bowen Savant. They render the text highly accessible, leaving more detailed information for their well- documented notes, and they write in a clear, contemporary style avoiding the twin dangers of either awkward anachronistic phrasing of a time long past or sinking into modern jargon or clichés. They write to be understood.

In the final analysis, Ibn Qutaybah offers us the most authoritative vision of how the Arab elite wanted to be pictured in the ninth century. He fulfills his goal admirably, and we are fortunate to now have such readable English-language access to *The Excellence of the Arabs*.

Jack Weatherford
Tur Hurah, Mongolia

Acknowledgments

I would like to thank the many persons who have read and critiqued my translation of *Arab Preeminence*—starting with Riḍā al-ʿArabī (Cairo University). In addition, I thank John Hayes (University of California, Berkeley), James Montgomery, Michael Cooperson, the anonymous reviewers of the Library of Arabic Literature, and also its editorial staff, including Stuart Brown and Allison Brown. I would also like to thank Chip Rossetti and Gemma Juan-Simó for their patience and faith in the project. All faults of course remain my own. Roy Mottahedeh (Harvard University) first introduced me many years ago to *Arab Preeminence* and Shuʿūbism, and to him I express special gratitude.

Sarah Bowen Savant

In editing and translating *The Excellence of Arab Learning*, I incurred substantial intellectual debts owed, in the main, to James Montgomery and Michael Cooperson for the reviews, revisions, and the insight they imparted; material debts were generously alleviated by the British Academy whose grant of a postdoctoral fellowship afforded me the time and means to complete this edition. All are gratefully thanked.

Peter Webb

Introduction

The spirited defense of the Arabs that unfolds in Ibn Qutaybah's *The Excellence of the Arabs* addresses us from an intellectually fertile but politically and socially precarious moment of early Islam. The old order of the caliphate was being challenged by political instability from which it would never fully recover, yet scholars were spearheading an unprecedented period of book production that yielded many classics of Arabic literature. This book is the product of one of the most prolific scholars of that age, and it addresses one of the central questions confronting his writerly community and its elite patrons.

The lifespan of the author, Abū Muḥammad ʿAbd Allāh ibn Muslim ibn Qutaybah (213–76/828–89), coincided with a changing of the guard in the Abbasid Caliphate. At the time of Ibn Qutaybah's birth, the caliphate had just emerged from a war between the two sons and joint heirs of the Caliph Hārūn al-Rashīd (r. 170–93/786–809), which resulted in the sack of the caliphate's capital, Baghdad, considerable damage to the Iraqi heartland, and a reorganization of power under the victor, the Caliph al-Ma'mūn (r. 198–218/813–33). Al-Ma'mūn and his successors edged out the Arab noble families who had enjoyed preponderant power in the caliphate since its inception, as they replaced Arab military elites with Turkic and other mercenaries imported from outside the imperial borders. Al-Ma'mūn's immediate successor, al-Muʿtaṣim (r. 218–27/833–42), moved the capital from Baghdad to the new palace city of Samarra, where the Turkic generals and personal retainers from various backgrounds, notably eastern Iranians, established new cliques and personal networks of power. By the time Ibn Qutaybah was in his thirties, the Turkic generals had seized opportunities for personal gain, and instability, intrigue, and regicide followed. Five caliphs in succession were murdered between 247/861 and 256/870; the wider Iraqi economy deteriorated; and caliphal central authority declined sharply as many regions of the empire, including North Africa, Egypt, Arabia, and eastern Iran, asserted increasing local autonomy.

The last nineteen years of Ibn Qutaybah's life, however, held some promise of an upturn. A new caliph, al-Muʿtamid (r. 256–79/870–92), curbed the power of the Turks, returned the capital to Baghdad, and survived a twenty-one year reign without any recorded attempts on his life, and while in hindsight this Abbasid revival would be short lived, Ibn Qutaybah died before the onset of the next wave of difficulties. Perhaps Ibn Qutaybah's last years thus afforded some moments of optimism, though the negative opinions he expresses of some of his contemporaries suggest that the political and economic decline during his lifetime made him aware that the "good old days" of Abbasid power were past. Ibn Qutaybah was a state-appointed judge and moved in courtly circles; the sense of loss and whatever prospects of renewal that accompanied al-Muʿtamid's reign were therefore in his full view. From that context, Ibn Qutaybah emerges as a man who considered himself a bastion of knowledge, piety, and good sense, which he dutifully shared in a large number of books penned in efforts to combat what he perceived as a "dumbing-down" in the court culture of his day.

If we distance ourselves from Ibn Qutaybah's particular worldview and consider Iraq's cultural scene in the latter half of the third/ninth century more broadly, the situation seems somewhat brighter, as there was much intellectual growth across diverse fields of learning, from philosophy and mathematics to history and jurisprudence. Scholarly endeavors were augmented by a rapidly expanding industry of book production, and Baghdad remained the preeminent cultural capital of the Muslim world, despite the political instability and fragmentation. We can thus appreciate that Ibn Qutaybah and his peers would have lamented the disintegration of the caliph's power and yearned nostalgically for what they perceived to be the better times of the past two centuries, yet the remarkable books they wrote established a new legacy that would influence centuries of subsequent Muslim intellectual growth. From our perspective, therefore, Ibn Qutaybah's lifetime represents not the end of the road, but rather the first fruits of what we identify as classical Muslim civilization. This was an era when the manifold ideas circulating in earlier generations were distilled, assimilated, and disseminated in new ways that survived the test of time. This book is an important marker in the emergence of that Arabic tradition: its subject was of central importance, and its argument both looks backward to those "better days" and points forward to the new ways Muslims interpreted Arab culture and the origins of Islam.

Virtues of the Arabs and Arabic in the Third/Ninth Century

The Excellence of the Arabs is one of the most explicit, sustained, and detailed descriptions of Arab identity written before modern times. We do not know precisely when Ibn Qutaybah wrote it, though it was probably toward the end of his career, that is, during al-Muʿtamid's caliphate, since the text refers back to several books of Ibn Qutaybah's own oeuvre. The book's purpose is to extol the virtues of the Arabs and to explain their preeminence among all peoples of the world. Such ideas about Arab identity and the merits of the Arab people were very much at the center of third/ninth-century political, social, and intellectual concerns.

Arab history is the subject of much debate. Most modern European writers have treated "the Arabs" as a homogenous group of predominantly Bedouin people inhabiting the Arabian Peninsula since antiquity. But recent inquiry into Arab archetypes reveals this approach to be misleading, and the Arab story to be more convoluted. From the ninth century BC, various Middle Eastern peoples used words resembling "Arab" to describe nomads and sometimes settled groups, but the terminology exclusively connoted the idea of distant outsiders and never referred to one specific ethnicity. It appears that people only began to call themselves "Arabs" and to use the term to express group solidarity after the dawn of Islam.[1] Evidence suggests that the Muslim faith originally spread among different groups living in what is now the Arabian Peninsula, Syria, and Iraq, and that the very first Muslims saw themselves as a broad-based faith community, rather than one interrelated ethnic group. But the situation soon changed: over two or three generations, the Muslim conquerors sought to maintain their distinctiveness from subject populations by developing strategies to segregate themselves, including the creation of a novel sense of belonging to an "Arab" community. In the early second/eighth century, Arab identity became widely invoked to connote an elite, conqueror status and, since very few of the conquered peoples converted during Islam's first century, it also laid claim to Islam as the "Arab faith." Many urban Iraqis identified themselves as "Arabs" by claiming lineage (real or perhaps imagined) to Arabian tribes. Specialists of Arabic poetry, genealogy, and history such as al-Aṣmaʿī (d. 213/828), Abū ʿUbaydah (d. 210/825), and Ibn al-Kalbī (d. 204/819) began the process of creating a sense of pan-Arabian, pre-Islamic Arab identity, and repackaged a vast lore from pre-Islamic times into an imagined origin story about the Arabs.

Ibn Qutaybah wrote *The Excellence of the Arabs* some 150 years after Arab identity had been well established, and he drew most of his source material from the opinions and anecdotes from these late second/eighth century specialists. He wrote it just as many of his contemporaries began to drop the sense of Arabness from their identity. They spoke and wrote in Arabic, but they were dissociating themselves from a sense of Arab community. Instead of counting themselves as members of an Arab race (expressed in terms of Arab *ummah*, *jīl*, or *nasab* [Arab "people" or "kin"]), the majority of Iraqis were choosing instead to identify by their locale, profession, or sectarian affiliations—or, more upsetting to Ibn Qutaybah, by Persian and other ethnic affiliations.[2]

The reasons behind the changes in self-perception and presentation were manifold: Iraq was a cosmopolitan place, and the mixing of populations in its great cities, especially Baghdad and Basra, would have made it difficult to maintain pure tribal/racial lineages for long. Baghdad in particular had expanded massively since its founding in the 760s; by the time Ibn Qutaybah wrote *The Excellence of the Arabs*, many of these immigrants had little or no sentiment of Arabness. Ibn Qutaybah's contemporaries also lived at least a generation after the official termination of the *dīwān al-ʿaṭāʾ*, an official state stipend which the caliphate had paid to the descendants of the original Muslim conquerors of the Middle East. Since the Umayyad era, the stipendiary payment had bestowed an economic advantage to members of Arabian tribal groups, and the status and wealth associated with the stipend played a substantial role in maintaining the sense of Arab identity in urban Iraq. As long as the caliphate paid the stipend, being "Arab" paid dividends. But the system broke down at the dawn of the third/ninth century. Thus, the fall of Arab political factions, increased migration to Iraq, the disintegration of the caliphate into more regional blocs, and the underlying process of cosmopolitan assimilation in Iraq's towns made it difficult and impractical to preserve a unified sense of Arab identity across the Muslim world.[3]

In an intriguing contrast to political and social factors that were eroding the value of Arabness as a social asset, intellectually the star of Arabic was rising. Abbasid-era Muslim identity was underwritten by distinctly Arab cultural capital: the Qur'an was in Arabic, Ibn Qutaybah's peers firmly believed that Muḥammad was an Arab prophet, and they memorialized early Islam as a movement that established a simultaneously Arab and Muslim rule over the Middle East. Such historical projections of Islam's roots in Arabness were further augmented by the remarkable spread of the

Arabic language. Arabic notionally became the official language of all caliphal administration during the reign of the Umayyad ʿAbd al-Malik (r. 65–86/685–705), and in the ensuing 150 years, Arabic supplanted most of the Middle East's pre-Islamic vernaculars, namely Greek, Middle Persian, and Aramaic dialects. Ibn Qutaybah and most of his contemporary Iraqis did not, therefore, claim direct kinship with the early conquerors of Iraq. But by virtue of their speaking Arabic, by their learning of the Arabic language and Arabic poetry, and by translating the philosophical, medical, and scientific traditions of other peoples into Arabic, Iraqi writers of the third/ninth century could cement their culture in a firmly Muslim identity. It hardly mattered that Ibn Qutaybah's own father hailed from Merv (in modern Turkmenistan) or that he reckoned himself a non-Arab. Arabicization had become the marker of Islam: in a cosmopolitan world where individuals came from multiple and mixed backgrounds, Arabic as a lingua franca offered a means for cultural production to unify in an otherwise socially and politically fragmenting time. By extolling the virtues of the Arabs, Ibn Qutaybah was perhaps most concerned to establish that Arab culture constituted a worthy heritage and that the Arabic language was a preeminently worthy language of which a Muslim of any background could be proud.

Arabs and Non-Arabs

The Excellence of the Arabs can productively be read as a circling of the wagons to defend the social prestige of Arabness in the waning political system of the centralized Abbasid caliphate. In the earlier period of substantial political unity and tremendous economic opportunity, the political structure had been dominated by Arab groups. The association of current decline with the rise of the Turks, and the commensurate association of bygone prosperity with the old Arab elites, would have weighed on the minds of Ibn Qutaybah, his peers, and perhaps even the Caliph al-Muʿtamid himself. If the caliphate was to be revived, was a return of the Arab elites necessary?

One of the most interesting aspects of Part One of *The Excellence of the Arabs* is the contempt Ibn Qutaybah expresses for Persians, compared to the generally favorable treatment he gives to other peoples from the eastern reaches of the caliphate—including Turks, who posed a very real and visible threat. Persians were a meaningful presence at court and in cultural circles running back to the mid-eighth century or even before. The early Abbasids valued many aspects of the pre-Islamic Sasanian model of kingship and hired Persian courtiers, who transmitted knowledge about statecraft and Iranian history. *Kalilah and Dimnah*, a collection of animal fables likely originating in the Sanskrit *Panchatantra* tales, had been transmitted a century earlier through Middle Persian into Arabic and enjoyed great popularity. Baghdad had long been a major center for translations into Arabic from Persian and other languages. Since the Persians were hardly parvenus, what, then, accounts for the vitriol against them? The answer is likely threefold. Ibn Qutaybah sensed the increasing cultural confidence of his Persian colleagues and perceived this as a disregard for the proper place of Arabs and Arabic. His manual for court secretaries, *Instruction for Court Secretaries* (*Adab al-kātib*), in which he instructs courtiers on the proper pronunciation and writing of Arabic, says as much. It would take another century for Persian literature to begin its ascent, but Persians were beginning the long process of writing themselves into the story of Islam, and were increasingly asserting themselves on political and cultural fronts too. Secondly, one could critique current society by casting aspersions against Persians without fear of the same sort of reprisal that one might face from Turks, who held military power. Thirdly, it is likely that Ibn Qutaybah blamed Persians for opening the door to what the scholar Ignaz Goldziher over a century ago termed "the foreign elements in Islam."[4]

Ibn Qutaybah's favorable treatment of Khurasan—a region in what today comprises eastern Iran and contiguous territory—gives a good sense of the fine political line he walked. Ibn Qutaybah treats its inhabitants as a distinct group, quoting sayings of the Prophet

Muḥammad that anticipate the great partnership between the Arab caliphs and the Khurasanian allies that helped bring the Abbasids to power. Among Khurasanians, Ibn Qutaybah singles out ethnic Turks with a widely circulated hadith in which Muḥammad is reported to have said, "Leave the Turks alone so long as they leave you alone." He also gives Khurasanians credit for prophetic statements about Persians. For Ibn Qutaybah, when Muḥammad says, "If faith were hung from the Pleiades, the Persians would be able to reach it," he meant the Khurasanians. He supports this improbable interpretation by arguing that at the dawn of Islam, the Persians were the Muslims' implacable enemies, and that for the Arabs, Persia and Khurasan "were one and the same thing because they share a border and also a common language, namely Persian." The Arabs, says Ibn Qutaybah, "therefore refer to both peoples as 'Persians.'"[5] He accordingly places the history and culture of Khurasan in a most favorable light, speaking at length about the forbearance of the pre-Islamic Khurasanians in the face of Sasanian treachery, and about the great learning of the region's scholars after the coming of Islam. He writes: "In general, man's desire for virtue, knowledge, and culture tends to wane and decline, but among the Khurasanians it increases and is constantly renewed."[6]

Ethnicity in the Abbasid Iraqi Context: Terms and Concepts

Ibn Qutaybah addresses his book to the Abbasid elites, for whom the people, places, and cultural references he makes were familiar and required no explanation. For readers today, however, it is important to draw attention to two key terms he uses when referring to non-Arabs.

The Bigots

Ibn Qutaybah never names his opponents individually, choosing instead to label them all "Shuʿūbīs," a term which we render in English, for reasons that will become clear, Bigots. The Arabic term al-Shuʿūbiyyah ("Shuʿūbism") and the related term "Shuʿūbī," or partisan of Shuʿūbism, have exercised the imagination of scholars. Scholars of the nineteenth and early twentieth centuries saw Shuʿūbism as a form of premodern Iranian nationalism. Hamilton Gibb, acknowledging the shortcomings of the nation-state as a prism for analyzing medieval Iraq, proposed that the Shuʿūbist "movement" was in fact a reflection of competing cultural values and a struggle over the "inner spirit of Islamic culture." In Gibb's influential interpretation, the Shuʿūbīs were a group touting egalitarianism, while at the same time seeking to promote Sasanian institutions and values as models for the caliphate to emulate.[7] In the sources, the label Shuʿūbism is applied mainly to Abbasid insiders living during the late eighth and early ninth centuries—but it is applied retrospectively, including by other Abbasid insiders, to persons they considered bigoted (thus prompting our use of the term "Bigots"). Lexicographers repeat the statement that a "Bigot" [Shuʿūbī] is someone who belittles the significance of the Arabs and who does not see them as having precedence over others.[8] Following such interpretations, many scholars have read Ibn Qutaybah's work as evidence for the existence of an active and indeed popular Shuʿūbī movement, but a close reading of *The Excellence of the Arabs* and its context should prompt circumspection. The identity of Ibn Qutaybah's living opponents is, after all, elusive, and the ideological content of Shuʿūbism as described in the sources is quite vague. Whereas the premodern biographers do say, for instance, that the Shuʿūbīs insulted Arabs, they give no indication that the Shuʿūbīs specifically promoted Persian culture. Neither do the biographers characterize Shuʿūbism as a cultural phenomenon in any meaningful way, such as by attributing to it an agenda, proponents, or a public profile.[9] Shuʿūbism was evidently an emotive idea for Ibn Qutaybah, but the precise parameters of its significance remain a subject of debate. Therefore, given Ibn Qutaybah's tenor in *The Excellence of the Arabs,* we have chosen to use "Bigots" for "Shuʿūbīs" and "Bigotry" for "Shuʿūbism"; we recognize that elsewhere, the term might warrant a different English translation.

Easterners

We are on somewhat firmer ground with "ʿAjam." Etymologically, it is related to words for an incomprehensible sound, or silence. When Ibn Qutaybah and his contemporaries marshalled the word, they often had in mind peoples possessed of *ʿujmah*, that is, a confused and unclear way of speaking. As this was usually intended as contrast to the clear eloquence of Arabic speakers, ʿAjam thus at times conveyed a pejorative sense. From the contexts in which he uses it in *The Excellence of the Arabs*, Ibn Qutaybah seems primarily concerned with peoples from further east, whom we might call "Iranians," though this was not a term Ibn Qutaybah himself would have used since the parameters of "Iranian" identity were the product of much later times. On occasion, he specifies the people of Fārs (i.e., "Persians" from the southwest quadrant of the Iranian plateau, the traditional homeland of the pre-Islamic Sasanian Empire) as being included among the ʿAjam; elsewhere he extends the term's ambit to the northeastern Iranian region of Khurasan, although he also notes the inhabitants of Khurasan should not be confused with Persians. While the precise boundaries (and subdivisions) of the ʿAjam community are therefore ambiguous, the divide between ʿAjam and Arab was stark, and the contrast runs through his book.[10] We use "Easterners" in our translation and hope the choice conveys Ibn Qutaybah's own ambiguity.

Contents

Ibn Qutaybah's book is divided into two parts. The first part, *Arab Preeminence* (*Faḍl al-ʿArab*), takes the form of an extended, somewhat meandering argument for Arab privilege that is defensive in tone. The second part, *The Excellence of Arab Learning* (*Al-Tanbīh ʿalā ʿulūmihā*), contains descriptions of the fields of knowledge in which Ibn Qutaybah believed the pre-Islamic Arabians excelled, such as horse husbandry, astronomy, divination, wisdom, and poetry.

Ibn Qutaybah begins *Arab Preeminence* by accusing the Bigots of being envious of the blessings that God, in His wisdom, has bestowed upon the Arabs, going so far as to say that by opposing the Arabs, they oppose God Himself. He exemplifies their slanderous behavior by invoking Abū ʿUbaydah Maʿmar ibn al-Muthannā (d. 210/825), a leading scholarly figure of fifty years earlier. Abū ʿUbaydah (like Ibn Qutaybah) did not claim to be an Arab, but he was nonetheless an important early Arabic philologist. Ibn Qutaybah alleges that he distorted and misrepresented the virtues of the Arabs. When Abū ʿUbaydah ridiculed the famous bow of Ḥājib, for example, his ridicule completely missed the point, namely that Arabs place a high premium on weapons because they are seen as the repository of a man's glory and nobility. Ibn Qutaybah also asserts that Abū ʿUbaydah and his ilk cannot take any pride in Persia's royal past, in spite of their claims to the contrary. They do not, after all, have any genealogical relationship to any of its kings, fiscal administrators, state secretaries, chamberlains, knights, or other elites. "What business does a member of the vast rabble of the Easterners with no recognizable genealogy or famous forefather have with Khosrow's throne, crown, silks, and fineries?" Ibn Qutaybah asks.[11]

Arab Preeminence is written as a rebuttal though it is not clear of whom, since Ibn Qutaybah never identifies his opponents (Abū ʿUbaydah, for example, was long dead), nor does he go deeply into their positions. His assumptions about his readers' familiarity with these opponents' arguments suggest either that Ibn Qutaybah's text originally also included the arguments he is rebutting, or that he is responding to a pamphlet or other piece of writing that circulated in his own day. A fourth/tenth century Andalusian text by Ibn ʿAbd Rabbih, *The Unique Necklace* (*Al-ʿIqd al-farīd*), which includes excerpts from *Arab Preeminence*, also excerpts statements attributed to the Bigots that may very well have been the material to which Ibn Qutaybah was responding.[12] These excerpts are brief, but give a sense of what so exercised Ibn Qutaybah. For example, so-called Bigots are quoted as saying:

> If the non-Arabs were to ask you whether you consider the basis for glory to be kingship or prophethood, what would

> you say? If you were to claim it is kingship, we would say to you that all the kings on earth have been from us—pharaohs, Assyrian kings and Amalekite kings, khosrows and caesars. Can any Arab claim anything like the reign of Solomon, to whom mankind, jinn, birds, and the winds humbled themselves? . . . And if you were to claim, instead, that the only basis for glory is prophethood, we would say that without exception all prophets and messengers beginning with Adam were non-Arabs, except for four—Hūd, Ṣāliḥ, Ishmael, and Muḥammad; and we would say that this world's "chosen ones,"[13] Adam and Noah, were also from us—they are the two roots from which mankind branches out. This makes us the root and you the branch. You are merely one of our branches.[14]

In *Arab Preeminence* Ibn Qutaybah dismisses these ideas as nonsense. He maintains that the bonds between the Arabs and prophets run deep—indeed, to a time before the Arabs even spoke Arabic.[15]

Ibn Qutaybah would defend the superior status of the Arabs as the natural order of things—just like other forms of differentiation and hierarchy that keep the world going. Humans have natural inborn qualities that differentiate them, and so, too, do peoples—most notably the Arabs, whose virtues of hospitality and courage distinguish them. The Quraysh, in particular, deserve special respect because of their connections to the sacred territory of Mecca prior to Islam and because of their maintenance of the "original monotheism" they inherited from their forefather Ishmael, the son of Abraham.[16] After God brought Islam, He blessed the Arabs, generally, and the Quraysh specifically. As Ibn Qutaybah sees it, it was God Himself who gave power to the Arabs when He endowed them with the caliphate.[17] In the present scheme of things, the Arabs' partners are, as already mentioned, the Khurasanians.

Ibn Qutaybah devotes a sizeable part of *Arab Preeminence* to countering specific slights to Arab culture by asserting the Arabs' innate sense of self-sacrifice and generosity. For him, reports about

Arabs eating repulsive dishes such as bloodied fur and snakes, or consuming drinks such as the stomach juices and blood of camels, point to their poverty and desperate times. The Arabs' comparative deprivation only goes to show their innate merits. Whereas Persians had the benefit for wealth, weapons, and the leadership of a king, the Arabs fought bravely without any such benefits; their successes, well attested in the poetic tradition, show just how fierce and intrepid they are.

Toward the end of *Arab Preeminence*, Ibn Qutaybah gets around to mentioning the Qur'anic verse from which the term "Shuʿūbism" was said to derive. The full verse reads: «We have . . . made you into peoples [*shuʿūb*] and tribes [*qabāʾil*] so that you might come to know each other. The noblest of you in God's sight is the most pious.»[18] Ibn Qutaybah would have us believe that the "Bigots" used this verse to cite not just the equality of the Persians, but their superiority too, since they, as one of God's "peoples" (*shuʿūb*) are mentioned before the Arabs, or God's "tribes." To this, Ibn Qutaybah replies that "a thing may be mentioned first but this does not mean that it has priority in merit."[19] What's more, Ibn Qutaybah asserts, the term *shuʿūb*, as "peoples," can just as well apply to Arabs as to their opponents.

Throughout, Ibn Qutaybah supports his arguments with citations from the Qur'an and prophetic hadiths, often widely reported ones appearing in the contemporaneous canonical collections. When citing hadiths, he occasionally cites chains of transmission, but does not systematically provide these. He also quotes poetry, proverbs, and something he characterizes as one of the Easterners' own books. He is also very interested in pre-Islamic lore, whether Arabian or Iranian.

In *The Excellence of Arab Learning*, the second part of *The Excellence of the Arabs*, Ibn Qutaybah presents the body of evidence upon which he rests his case for the Arabs' superiority. He opens with a general statement, which flows naturally from the first part of the book, namely that the Arabs are a very learned people whose intellectual tradition is as venerable as, and even richer than, those of other peoples. Lest his declaration be discounted as mere bombast and partisanship, he provides a long list of empirical examples of Arab intellectual prowess, which he classifies according to an array of fields of knowledge, each of which, he argues, is unique to the Arabs.

The flow of the argument is now straightforward: each section opens with a brief description of the nature of the specific field of learning in question, followed by examples demonstrating the Arabs' cultivation of it and their wide expertise. Some of the examples take the form of short anecdotes and prose statements, but the majority of the evidence consists of lines of poetry. This was a common approach developed by Arabic writers, who considered poetry, as "the archive of the Arabs" (*dīwān al-ʿArab*), the most truthful and most bountiful source of Arab knowledge. Poetry also had a distinct empirical appeal; stories were accepted as definitively true only if they were corroborated by poetry. Much of classical Arabic literature has in fact been prosimetric, that is, consisting of a mixture of prose and accompanying poetic corroboration. Ibn Qutaybah's book is thus an excellent introduction to a style of early Arabic discourse in which writers follow statements with a selection of verses intended to prove the veracity of the author's position. Seldom does Ibn Qutaybah provide definitive conclusions in *Excellence of Arab Learning*; rather, he assumes that readers will find the poetry to be sufficient proof. His editorial comments in this second part of the book, much like those of many of his contemporaries in their works, are relatively sparse.

Readers accustomed to encountering stand-alone poems may find unusual Ibn Qutaybah's adducing of two or three verses in support of his points. Arabic poems could be very long, often running into dozens of lines, but in the second part of the book Ibn Qutaybah is concerned not with the complete poem as a work of art, but rather with the evidence that can be deduced from individual lines. The quoted verses rarely reveal any overt clues about the intended context, but Ibn Qutaybah and most of his readers would likely have known most, or at least many, of these verses, having acquired them during the course of their education (a literary and ethical learning known as *adab*). We are left to commend the erudition of readers in his day, and this is part of the charm of encountering the period's literature.

Notwithstanding the brevity of Ibn Qutaybah's comments and the seemingly scattergun approach that results in peppering *The Excellence of Arab Learning* with isolated lines of poetry, the message is clear. The proof adduced for the Arabs' mastery over each of the fields of knowledge Ibn Qutaybah enumerates is the existence of a specialist vocabulary, preserved in Arabic poetry, for each field—something the Arabs could only have developed over a long period of time and as a result of long-standing and close attention to the cultivation of knowledge. Add to the poetry, the prose anecdotes and the specialized vocabulary found in their aphorisms, and we have further proof of the Arabs' independent, native intellectual prowess, which Ibn Qutaybah hopes to demonstrate was not innate among other peoples.

It is noteworthy that Ibn Qutaybah's evidence for his arguments comes almost exclusively from poetry and prose expressed by peoples who lived long before his own time. The most recent anecdote (§2.7.8) refers to the time of al-Maʾmūn (r. 198–218/813–33), an Abbasid caliph whose reign ended when Ibn Qutaybah was but a young child; moreover, the vast majority of material dates to the pre-Islamic and Umayyad eras. Likewise, Ibn Qutaybah does twice cite the poetry of the early third/ninth-century poet Abū Tammām (§2.8.2), but those two poems specifically describe the past. Ibn Qutaybah's sense of Arab merit is decidedly rooted in the past, as is also the case with his contemporary al-Jāḥiẓ.[20] This perspective is perhaps a reflection of the troubled times in which Ibn Qutaybah lived. It would seem that Ibn Qutaybah intended his readers to see that the heyday of the Arabs was past, and that they were a worthy people whose greatest achievement was to carry Islam from Arabia to the world.

This projection of Arabness into the past and the distancing of Arab achievements from Ibn Qutaybah's own society are matched by a tendency to view Arab achievement as a function of desert life. For Ibn Qutaybah, the "sciences of the Arabs" (*ʿulūm al-ʿArab*) are horse husbandry, observation of the stars and other physical phenomena, the use of natural ingredients in medical practice, and the composition of poetry, oratory, and wisdom in an oral environment. These are not the province of urban folk, with their bookish culture, but of the Arabian desert nomads. Ibn Qutaybah accordingly constructs a temporal and spatial barrier between his contemporary urban Iraq and the desert Arabia of the past where "proper" Arab traits were developed. The purpose of *The Excellence of Arab Learning*, then, appears to be to create a stereotyped projection of Arab-Bedouin identity in order to characterize the rise of Islam as a uniquely "Arab venture." Ibn Qutaybah was not an Arab, but he invites his readers to appreciate the contribution of this ancient desert people in shaping a new world order, one in which he was an appreciative resident.

Note on the Text

We have aimed to render Ibn Qutaybah's writing in the clearest English possible, as his Arabic would have been considered relatively straightforward for educated readers in his own day. We sought to reproduce his sentences in an equivalent English register and syntax, rather than replicating Arabic phrasing. At the same time, we acknowledge the cultural specificity of metaphors and many turns of phrase with more literal translation. Since Ibn Qutaybah's argument hinges on the richness of the Arabic lexicon, he does use some Arabic terms that would have been obscure for his own audiences, and in these cases, we sought equivalents in English wherever possible, but we have often used a single term in English when the Arabic uses synonyms for reasons of style.

Some of the ancient Arabic prose anecdotes that Ibn Qutaybah quotes pose problems for comprehension: he often cites them out of context, and they are so brief as to cause possible confusion. We have interpreted the stories as best we could, and always searched for fuller citations of the anecdotes in other sources contemporary with Ibn Qutaybah. We have sought to translate these passages as clearly as possible, and where we deemed background context absolutely necessary for comprehension, we have added explanations in the endnotes and glossary.

A large number of names appear in the stories, most often merely in passing. Ibn Qutaybah's readers would likely have known all (or most) of them, and hence could fill in missing context with extensive background knowledge. Rather than augment the translation with footnotes or in-text hints, we direct readers to the glossary, which includes everyone appearing by name in *The Excellence of the Arabs*.

The Excellence of the Arabs also contains a large number of verses. As with the anecdotes, Ibn Qutaybah often cites them in abbreviated form, relating just the individual line pertinent to his argument, and omitting the rest of the poem: readers thus encounter the verses out of context. We have refrained from providing that context (unless absolutely necessary for the meaning) in an effort to present an English translation as reflective as possible of the flow of the Arabic discourse. In translating the poetry, we have sought an appropriate poetic register but we have not rhymed, as rhyming can force the English translation into something that neither resembles, nor rhymes like, the original Arabic. We have also aspired to remain as faithful as practicable to the Arabic words, refraining from undue use of English euphemisms and metaphors.

For Qur'anic passages, we have relied on the translation of Maulana Wahiduddin Khan. Dates are cited by Islamic Hijri year followed by the AD equivalent, e.g., 181/797.

Notes to the Introduction

1 The use of words resembling "Arab" in Assyrian, Greek, biblical, and south Arabian records have engendered many varied theories about the origins of Arabness as the identity of a specific group of people. Some recent commentators suggest the evidence is so obscure that it is anachronistic to label any pre-Islamic populations as "Arabs" (Donner, *Muhammad and the Believers*, 217–20; and Millar, *Religion, Language and Community in the Roman Near East*, 53, 154–58). For a review of earlier theories and a narrative of Arab ethnogenesis synthesizing pre-Islamic evidence with the Muslim-era Arabic material, see Webb, *Imagining the Arabs*, 23–156.

2 For Persian identity in the Abbasid Caliphate, see Savant, *The New Muslims of Post-Conquest Iran*. For the changes in senses of Arab identity, see Webb, *Imagining the Arabs*, 240–49, 270–78.

3 The retreat from Arab identity in urban Iraqi society is further detailed in Webb, *Imagining the Arabs*, 270–78, 294–319.

4 Goldziher, *Muslim Studies*, 1:140; and Goldziher, *Muhammedanische Studien*, 1:151.

5 See §§1.13.2–1.13.3.

6 See §1.13.2.

7 Gibb, "The Social Significance of the Shuubiya," 66.

8 Al-Azharī, *Tahdhīb al-lughah*, s.v. *sh-ʿ-b*, 1:442; Majd al-Dīn ibn al-Athīr, *Al-Nihāyah fī gharīb al-ḥadīth wa-l-athar*, s.v. *sh-ʿ-b*, 2:223; and *Lisān al-ʿArab*, s.v. *sh-ʿ-b*, 3:440.

9 See Savant, "Naming Shuʿūbīs." In contrast, modern scholars have labeled many later figures as Shuʿūbīs and extended the geographical

scope of the movement beyond Iraq to include figures whose milieu was Iran and Transoxiana, for example, al-Bīrūnī (d. after 442/1050). Their citation of sources is highly selective and disregards the silence in our sources about Shuʿūbism.

10 On these terms, see Savant, "'Persians' in Early Islam."

11 See §1.15.3.

12 Ibn ʿAbd Rabbih, *Al-ʿIqd al-farīd*, 3:403ff. The text begins: "From the Shuʿūbīs' argument against the Arabs . . ."

13 The phrase comes from Q Āl ʿImrān 3:33.

14 Ibn ʿAbd Rabbih, *Al-ʿIqd al-farīd*, 3:404–5.

15 The process by which third/ninth and fourth/tenth century Muslims constructed a history of Arab prophets and prophecy before Muḥammad was protracted and contested; see Savant, *The New Muslims of Post-Conquest Iran*, esp. 31–60; Webb, *Imagining the Arabs*, 205–22; and for Ibn Qutaybah and his contemporaries' role in particular, see Webb 207 and 215–21.

16 See §§1.10.5–1.10.6.

17 See §§1.11.1–1.11.2.

18 Q Ḥujurāt 49:13.

19 See §§1.14.1–1.14.3.

20 Al-Jāḥiẓ, *Al-Bayān wa-l-tabyīn*, 3:366.

Book One: Arab Preeminence

In the name of God,
the Merciful and Compassionate
May God bless and keep Muḥammad and his progeny

Abū Muḥammad ʿAbd Allāh ibn Muslim ibn Qutaybah writes: May God make us grateful for His blessings, patient in the face of trials and tribulation, and satisfied with the benefaction He grants us. May He protect us from the discord of partisanship, the zealotry of the pre-Islamic era,[1] and the prejudice of the Bigots, whose hearts are so full of envy and ill will that they deny the Arabs every virtue and ascribe to them every vice. Exceeding all bounds in their censure, they are guilty of gross exaggeration. They slander, lie, and dispute plain facts, very nearly abandoning their faith, at which point only fear of the sword keeps them in check. They resent the Prophet so much that they can hardly bring themselves to mention his name—it sticks like a bone in their throat and makes their eyes smart and sting. They are as far removed from God as His chosen Prophet is close to him. Their lack of restraint will be their downfall, and their recklessness in matters of religion will be their doom. Envy is an incurable disease. It was the first sin in heaven and on earth—the first act of disobedience to God. Anyone who impartially examines the issue of envy will come to the unavoidable conclusion that it consists of anger directed at the Grantor of Blessings and resentment of the Bestower of Virtues. God Himself says: «It is We who distribute among them their livelihood in the life of this world, and raise some of them above others in rank so they may take one another into service.»[2] He, blessed and exalted, is the Provider of Subsistence, the Controller of Fate, 1.1.1

and the First Benefactor. He is envied for His ability to give things then take them away, and for always having more of the thing He has given you than you will ever receive.[3]

1.2.1 Ibn Masʿūd once said: "Do not spurn the blessings of God." When he was asked, "Who spurns God's blessings?" he replied: "Envious people." In one of the scriptures[4] God says: "The envier is hostile to my blessing, resentful of my decree, and dissatisfied with the lot I apportion."[5] Ibn al-Muqaffaʿ said: "The envier constantly finds fault with God's blessings, which he thinks should never cease. These feelings become a source of personal disquiet, and thus he finds it impossible to appreciate what he has. He is continually resentful of anyone who will not humor him and is vexed over what he cannot obtain. Eaten up with repressed anger, he is thrown into turmoil over every imagined slight, and takes his frustration out on others by treating them badly. Ironically, he ends up acting like someone who was never given anything in the first place and goes through life embittered and resentful. He is not content with his share and cannot control what is not his share. The man he envies, on the other hand, is free to enjoy God's bounty as he pleases and to delight in his happiness. He can enjoy it at his leisure, without worrying that others may bring it to an end."[6]

1.2.2 It would be far better instead for such an envious person to conceal his sadness and to bear his affliction with patience, because when he growls and barks like a dog, God chases him away with stones; and when he tries to snuff out God's light, God makes it burn more brightly: «God seeks only to perfect His light, no matter how those who deny the truth may abhor it.»[7] The following verses express the point admirably:

When God wants a virtue proclaimed
    He makes it an object of envy:
Fire burns what it touches—
    whence sandalwood's lovely scent.[8]

In the case of the Bigots of our day, I find that the displays of the deepest-rooted animosity toward the Arabs and the most intense hatred for them come from the lower classes of society, the Aramaic-speaking riffraff and the sons of farmhands. The Easterners, however, who are nobles, persons of substance, or faithful Muslims, know their duties and obligations. In their eyes, noble status constitutes the surest genealogy. One of them once remarked to an Arab: "True genealogy is nobility. The nobles of one people share the same genealogy as the nobles of all peoples." 1.3.1

The lower-class Easterners are so fervently censorious of the Arabs because of who they themselves are. Some of these Easterners have simply assumed the trappings of learning and keep the company of the nobility. Another group has acquired distinction through positions in the bureaucracy and so moves in circles close to the seat of power. They take pride in their learning but feel inadequate because of the baseness of their birth and the wretchedness of their nature. Others establish ties of allegiance to the Easterners' nobility and claim descent from their kings and cavalry. In so doing they enter a wide-open field that has been left completely unguarded, since their genealogical system is extensive but unmonitored. There are others who claim nobility for all Easterners so that they can be noble themselves and overcome their own ignoble origins. These people deride the Arabs with plain hatred, as they go to great efforts to revile them, draw attention to their vices, and distort accounts of their virtues.[9] They do this in the Arabs' very own language, owe whatever it is that lets them put on airs and graces to the Arabs' accomplishments, and wage their war with the Arabs' own learning. If they learn anything good about the Arabs, they conceal it. If it becomes public knowledge, they belittle it. If it is susceptible of interpretation, they give it the most reprehensible one they can devise. But if they hear something bad about the Arabs, they spread it far and wide. If what they hear is not actually bad, they avoid it like the plague. And if they cannot find anything bad, they make it up. They are as the poet said: 1.3.2

They conceal the good they know and spread the bad,
making it up if they must.[10]

1.4.1 Let me ask you (God have mercy on you): Who is spotless and pure, who has nothing to be ashamed of at all? Someone asked a wise man: "Can there be a person who has nothing to be ashamed of?" and he replied: "No, because the one who has no faults is He who never dies."[11] A faultfinder finds fault with other people because his own faults are so serious. He attributes defects to other people to the extent that he himself suffers defects, and exposes others' private shortcomings to avoid being singled out for his own. A miscreant loves nothing more than to see a scholar slip up, just as common folk love nothing more than to see a nobleman stumble. As the poet has said:

He infers other people's faults from his own.
Easy for him, since his own are so clear.[12]

Another poet said:

Of backbiters and faultfinders, the most outrageous I have seen
are themselves the greatest offenders.[13]

1.4.2 In the face of mounting criticism against Ziyād ibn Abī Sufyān and Muʿāwiyah because of Ziyād's claim of descent from Abū Sufyān, Ziyād produced a book on defects and vices for his descendants. In it he says: "If anyone reviles you, upbraid him for his own shortcomings; if anyone defames you, catch him out for his own vices. Evil is the best defense against evil: only iron can break iron."

1.5.1 No one took pleasure in abusing people or relished the vices of the Arabs quite as much as Abū ʿUbaydah Maʿmar ibn al-Muthannā. We are loath to go into his situation in detail—his own genealogy (including the man most likely to be his father) is a subject we are reluctant to discuss[14] lest we be guilty of not heeding our own advice. Though his situation is well known, we prefer not to see it recorded in books and immortalized for posterity, particularly since he is recognized as a reliable source of knowledge, and someone whose statements on the Qurʾan are adduced as authoritative.

Can anyone be more vexatious and annoying than someone who distorts absolutely everything, turning good things into bad, making vices of virtues, and expressing falsehoods as truths? For example, Abū ʿUbaydah will single out points of pride, such as Ḥājib's bow,[15] and then will disparage them, pointing out in this case that it was made of cheap wood. But if we were to consider this case in light of how merchants ordinarily behave in the marketplace when making pledges and exchanges, the person shamed by the exchange would be the one who accepted it, not Ḥājib who offered it. When someone makes a pledge, he always tries to pledge an item of lower value in return for one of higher value. To be tricked into accepting a trifle in exchange for something valuable is to be duped. In this case, Ḥājib promised that the Arabs would cause no trouble in Khosrow's kingdom if they were permitted to dwell there until the drought was over. To back his promise, he gave Khosrow a pledge. The bow he gave was better for both parties than a hundred thousand heads of sheep, since a man's honor resides in his weaponry, and it is always better to surrender property than to surrender one's honor. A man might pledge his ring, his mantle, or his cloak for a matter of some consequence, but he would not surrender them for fear of criticism or in order to avert shame. 1.5.2

Abū ʿUbaydah reported that when the Caliph Sulaymān was on the hajj in Mecca, he heard the news that Qutaybah ibn Muslim al-Bāhilī had been killed in Khurasan by Wakīʿ ibn Abī Sūd of the Tamīm tribe. Sulaymān then preached a sermon in the mosque at ʿArafāt in which he denounced the Tamīm[16] for their treachery, their eagerness to stir up discord, and their defiance of his authority. Upon hearing this, al-Farazdaq rose, loosened his cloak, and said: "Commander of the Faithful! If the Tamīm disobey you, take this cloak of mine!" Later, when Wakīʿ's oath of loyalty to Sulaymān was announced, al-Farazdaq said: 1.5.3

My cloak was ransom enough for the swords of Tamīm,
though their swords had proved too much for Ahātim's nobles.[17]

By "Ahātim" he meant al-Ahtam ibn Sumayy al-Tamīmī and his kin.

1.5.4 In another instance, Sayyār ibn ʿAmr ibn Jābir al-Fazārī promised a king a thousand camels as blood payment for his father and gave his bow as a pledge. The king accepted it from him on those terms and Sayyār handed the camels over.[18] A poet composed a verse to commemorate this incident:

We gave the bow as our pledge; al-Fazārī alone
redeemed it with one thousand beasts.[19]

This Sayyār is the ancestor of Haram, before whom ʿĀmir and ʿAlqamah disputed their case.[20]

1.5.5 Similarly, we have the words of Jirān when he refers to meeting some women with whom he was on intimate terms:

They took away my toothstick, and I said:
It will be found in your possession and recognized.[21]

Anyone unfamiliar with this anecdote will suppose that the women had taken the toothstick from him, that he held this against them, and that he told them it would be found in their possession and recognized as his on account of the value placed on it, and because the desert Arabs are attentive to paltry trifles and things of little consequence. But how could anyone suppose this to be the case with the parties involved? After all, Najd is covered in many types of trees from which to make toothsticks. Why, with the women he desired, would he be stingy with the kind of wood one might toss into a campfire or an oven? If he needed a toothstick, he could easily take one from a nearby tree. Jirān al-ʿAwd had something else in mind. The various soils of Najd produce different trees—the *isḥal*, the *arāk*, and the *bashām*—all of them good for making toothpicks. The people of each district would clean their teeth with sticks made from whatever trees grew nearby. Now Jirān al-ʿAwd was notorious for his intimacy with the women in the poem. He would visit them surreptitiously in far-off places, and during his visit would clean his teeth with a toothstick made from trees that grew in his own area but not in theirs. When, as lovers do, they took his stick as a souvenir, as something to cherish him by, he said: "It will be found among you, and when it is, they'll recognize its wood as from my area, so they will realize that I visited you."

Abū ʿUbaydah also singles out the following verse for attention: 1.5.6

> Daughter of ʿAbd Allāh and daughter of Mālik,
> daughter of the man with the two mantles and the reddish bay.[22]

He pokes fun at this verse, making light of the two mantles and the reddish bay, contrasting them with the possessions of the kings of Persia, who have thrones and crowns. He notes that Khosrow Parviz kept nine hundred and fifty elephants in his stables, that the cushion from which he looked down on supplicants was worth a thousand gold vessels, and that he was waited on by a thousand slave women. Abū ʿUbaydah has no idea what the poem means, and his comparison is entirely mistaken. His boastfulness is based on something he has no right to be proud of since it has nothing to do with him.

Consider the meaning of this verse. Abū ʿUbaydah says that 1.5.7
al-Nuʿmān ibn al-Mundhir brought out the two mantles of "the Burner," that is, ʿAmr ibn Hind, when the Arab delegations had gathered at his court, and declared: "Let the delegate from the mightiest Arab tribe rise and take them!" ʿĀmir ibn Uḥaymir ibn Bahdalah arose and took hold of them, wrapping one around his waist and draping the other over his shoulders like a cloak. "What makes you the mightiest of the Arabs?" asked al-Nuʿmān, and he replied, "Among the Arabs, might and strength of numbers belong to the Maʿadd, then to the Nizār, then to the Muḍar, then to the Khindif, then to the Tamīm, the Saʿd, the Kaʿb, and the ʿAwf, and finally to the Bahdalah. Let any Arab who denies this contend with me."[23] No one spoke. Al-Nuʿmān then said: "This may be true for your clan, as you claim. But what about you—how great is your household? How strong are you physically?" He answered: "I am the father of

ten sons, the paternal uncle of ten men, and the maternal uncle of ten more. I can depend on them all, young and old alike." Then he placed his foot on the ground, and said: "And here is the evidence of my strength. I will give a hundred camels to the man who can move my foot." Not one person stood up to oppose him, so he took the two mantles and earned the name, "the man with two mantles." Al-Farazdaq said:

> No youth of the Saʿd or of the family of Mālik becomes a man
> unless it is said that he is descended from Bahdalah.
> Al-Nuʿmān gave them the two garments belonging to "the Burner"
> because of the glory of Maʿadd and strength of numbers manifest.[24]

1.5.8 Consider the reddish bay mentioned in the poem. Horses are the strongholds of the Arabs, the root of their might, their means for climbing to glory. Horses are how they feed their households, exact blood revenge, and hunt wild animals. In fact they would rather feed milk to their horses than to their own children. In readiness to give chase or to take to flight, they would tie up their horses right outside their tents. When the prophet Solomon, as God recounts in His Book, says: «I have put the love of good things above the remembrance of my Lord until it»—that is, the sun—«disappeared behind its veil,»[25] by "good things" Solomon means horses, because of the good they represent. So Solomon is saying that horses distracted him from prayer until sunset.[26]

1.5.9 Ṭufayl declaimed:

> Horses have victory days.[27] He who waits patiently for them,
> and can recognize their good days, will succeed.[28]

Another poet said:

> Horses, not clay walls, are our strongholds,
> our shields against death. This I know.

Horses are might manifest. They help us escape
from battle's murk, and dispel the dark.
They are the night guard on the frontier where all feel fear.
The outlaw knows they are the rich man's wealth.
Other men are crushed at night by their bloodwite—
a hard-running stallion settles mine.[29]

By "bloodwite" he means blood. He means that other men cannot exact their revenge, and so the weight of blood is heavy on their shoulders, whereas he exacted his revenge on horseback.

Muḥammad ibn ʿUbayd told me that Sufyān ibn ʿUyaynah cited Shabīb ibn Gharqadah, who cited ʿUrwah al-Bāriqī, who said: "I heard the Prophet say: 'Goodness is braided into the forelocks of horses until the Day of Resurrection.'"[30] 1.5.10

No one has horses to match the thoroughbreds of the Arabs, and the Arabs are unrivaled in their knowledge about them—I will touch on this subject below, God willing.[31] An Arab would achieve great renown for owning a prized thoroughbred, bearing a name like "Mighty," "Overtaker," "Kicker," or "Roan." This is no more untoward than the Easterners boasting about the throne of Khosrow, and etching images of it in solid rock and on mountain peaks.[32] 1.5.11

When you find Arabs using something basic and trivial as a name, it is because it has noble associations. A good example is their referring to Hunaydah bint Ṣaʿṣaʿah, the paternal aunt of al-Farazdaq, as "the woman with the long veil." If you do not know why the long veil is included in her name, you might think she was the only woman in her tribe to wear one and that this is the reason for the association. But, as Abū ʿUbaydah notes, she was called "the woman with the long veil" because she once said: "My father is Ṣaʿṣaʿah; my brother, Ghālib; my maternal uncle, al-Aqraʿ ibn Ḥābis; and my husband is al-Zibriqān ibn Badr. If another Arab woman can match my four with four male family members close enough to her to see her face,[33] then I will give her my herd of camels." Abū ʿUbaydah continued: "Hind ibn Abī Hālah, the stepson of the 1.5.12

Prophet, used to say: 'I am the noblest person of all because of my connection to four people: my father, the Messenger of God; my mother, Khadījah; my sister, Fāṭimah; and my brother, al-Qāsim.' These four put her four to shame." Furthermore, Abū 'Ubaydah was mistaken to compare Khosrow with "the man with two mantles" because the latter was not in fact the king of the Arabs, making the comparison inapposite.[34] No one has ever claimed that the Arabs could approach the sovereign majesty, tributes, equipment, weapons, silk, and fine stuffs of the Persian realm. This is to say nothing of Parviz's elephants, slave women, and furnishings. The Persians did possess all of these, as Abū 'Ubaydah says. But then God gave them to the Arabs, who plundered the Persians, stripping them of their riches like bark from a tree. Just as a revelation that overrides an earlier one is better, so too it is with peoples.[35]

1.5.13 Abū 'Ubaydah boasts about something he has no right to be proud of. You can boast of the kings of Persia only if you are descended from them, or from their fiscal administrators, state secretaries, chamberlains, or knights. What business does a member of the vast rabble of the Easterners with no recognizable genealogy or famous forefather have with Khosrow's throne, crown, silks, and fineries? A man like this has not set eyes on such regalia or even been anywhere near it! If he retorts, "It is because I am an Easterner and so is Khosrow," then he should say hello to the clichéd proverb: "I am the son of the carpenter's neighbor."[36] He might as well say, "Because I am a human being, and Khosrow is a human being too." It basically amounts to the same thing and would give him no greater entitlement to the connection he alleges since Arabs are also human beings!

1.5.14 Abū 'Ubaydah said: "Once during a horse race, as one of the horses emerged in the lead, a spectator began to jump for joy, praising God. This prompted his neighbor to ask: 'Young man, is the horse in front yours?' 'No,' the man replied, 'but the bridle is!'" Al-Mas'ūdī tells a similar story: "I was conducting trade with the desert Arabs. I would give them credit and attend to their needs until their money came in. Once a group showed up. 'Give us a dinar! God bless your dear old dad!' they would say to me when they needed money. I was getting a bit fed up with running myself ragged after them, so finally I said: 'What does my father have to do with any of this?' 'He once haggled with us over a she-ass,' they replied. 'Did he buy it from you?' I asked. 'No,' they said. 'Thank God!' I said. 'What do you mean?' they asked, and I replied, 'If he had bought it, we would practically be related!'"

Once upon a time, the Easterners covered the face of the earth, from east to west, on land and sea, with the exception of the Maʿadd settlements and Yemen. Were all of them nobles? What happened to the downtrodden and the lowly, to the street cleaners, cuppers, tanners, wine merchants, lowlifes, and lackeys? Don't you think that the nobility would have been as lost among all that lot as a speck on a camel's hide? And what about the children of ordinary people? Did they all die childless, leaving no survivors, while only the sons of kings and noblemen survived? 1.5.15

Abū ʿUbaydah's claims all pale into insignificance when compared with the Bigots' claims of a relationship to Isaac, son of Abraham, and with their boast, aimed at the Arabs, that Isaac was born from Sarah, a free woman, whereas Ishmael, the father of the Arabs, was born from Hagar, a slave.[37] Their poet recited: 1.6.1

In a land where ʿUkl, ʿAkk, and Hamdān
    have never tied a rope or pitched a tent,
A homeland to neither Jarm nor to Bahrāʾ:
    the land of the sons of the free,
Where Khosrow built his shrines,
    where the unclean woman has no sons.[38]

According to this view, the "sons of the free" are the Easterners, descended from Isaac, since Isaac was born of Sarah, a free woman. The sons of the "unclean woman" are the Arabs because they are descendants of Ishmael, and Ishmael was born of Hagar, a slave. They say, "The Arabs apply the adjective 'unclean' to a female slave."[39]

1.6.2 The people who make these claims should be ostracized and made to suffer for showing such hostility to God's intimates and for assigning such profane names to His chosen one, Muḥammad! Their interpretation of the term is based on an error: the Arabs do not regard every slave woman as unclean. Rather, the adjective "unclean" is used only for menial servants who look after camels, gather firewood, draw water, do the milking, and perform similar chores. The word "foolish" is likewise used to describe slave women, but they are not all foolish. The epithet "unclean" is used only when they stink. In correct Arabic usage, one says, "The water jar smells unclean," when it begins to stink.

1.6.3 Now, God cleansed and purified Hagar of every impurity and filth, and favored her as a lawful spouse for Abraham, the chosen companion of God, and as a mother to her pure offspring, Ishmael and Muḥammad. So is it even remotely acceptable for a Muslim, let alone an apostate, to call her unclean? The mere fact that the king of the Copts gave Hagar—his most precious slave and favorite—to Sarah is evidence that she was not unclean. On the contrary, if it were permissible to refer to all slave women as unclean, then you could apply the phrase "this is the son of an unclean woman" to any nobleman born of a slave woman and you would mean "this is the son of a slave woman." Yet slave women have given birth to caliphs and to good and pious men. Think, for example, of ʿAlī, son of al-Ḥusayn, son of ʿAlī ibn Abī Ṭālib; al-Qāsim, son of Muḥammad, son of Abū Bakr al-Ṣiddīq; and Sālim, son of ʿAbd Allāh, son of ʿUmar ibn al-Khaṭṭāb.

1.6.4 I cite Sahl ibn Muḥammad, who cited al-Aṣmaʿī, who reported that the people of Medina used to dislike using slave women to bear their children until these three individuals grew up among them and surpassed everyone in religious learning and piety. That is why they developed a preference for concubines as mothers.

1.6.5 The genealogists quite simply do not include the people of Persia or the Aramaeans in any genealogy for Isaac or Abraham. Isaac married Rebecca, the daughter of Nahor, son of Terah, Terah being the same person as Āzar—Rebecca is therefore Isaac's cousin, since she is the daughter of his paternal uncle. For her part, Rebecca bore Isaac the twins Esau and Jacob. Jacob is Israel, the forefather of the tribes, that is, the twelve men whose children are collectively called the "Children of Israel," who are all People of the Book. It follows therefore that the Children of Israel have absolutely no kinship ties with the Persians or Aramaeans.

Esau is the father of al-Rūm, who was a man so pale he looked white. On account of that, his descendants, the Romans, have been called "the pale man's progeny." Genealogists have established that al-Rūm's mother was the daughter of Ishmael, son of Abraham, and that al-Rūm in turn had five children who are the ancestors of everyone who lives in Anatolia today. The children are also referred to as the descendants of Esau, since Esau was pushed aside by his brother Jacob, who received from their father Isaac the blessing of prophecy. Jacob then prayed that Esau would be fruitful and multiply.[40] Some people claim that the people called the Ashbān are also his descendants. As for the Aramaeans, they reportedly had a forefather named al-Nabaṭ who was the son of Serug, son of Reu, son of Peleg, son of Eber, son of Shelah, son of Arpachshad, son of Shem, son of Noah. It is also said that this al-Nabaṭ was the son of Mash, son of Shem, son of Noah. The people of Persia are reportedly the descendants of Lud, son of Aram, son of Shem, son of Noah. This Lud settled with his many children in Persia—all Persians therefore are his descendants. 1.6.6

Genealogy thus disproves the claim of a genealogical bond between Isaac, son of Abraham, and the Persians and Aramaeans, except via Shem, son of Noah. All humans are anyway connected insofar as they share descent from Seth, son of Adam, and descent from Noah, after which humans diversified, since Noah had four children: Shem, Ham, Japheth, and Yām. 1.6.7

Yām perished during the Flood, leaving no descendants. He is the one Noah addressed, saying: «My son! Embark with us instead of joining the deniers!»[41] Cursed by his father, Ham became a 1.6.8

slave to both his brothers. As a result, his progeny are lowly and of little renown: the Nubians, the Fazzān, the Zaghāwah, the various peoples of the Sūdān and Sind, and the Copts. His brother Japheth received their father's prayer that he be fruitful and multiply. He is the progenitor of the Slavs,[42] the Turks, the people of Gog and Magog, and the peoples in the eastern regions of the earth, who are as numerous as sand and stone. As for Shem, it was he who received the blessing of his father, Noah, and so became the ancestor of all noble peoples, including the ʿAmālīq, the Jabābira, the pharaohs of Egypt, and the kings of Persia. His descendants also include all the prophets after Noah—Hūd, Ṣāliḥ, Shuʿayb, Abraham, and the others up to our own prophet, Muḥammad.

1.6.9 In sum, all this means that in terms of shared origins, the Arabs and the Persians are equal but, if you look further down the genealogical chain, the Arabs are superior because they descend from Ishmael and thus are more closely related to Abraham, the chosen companion of God. Furthermore, the Arabs and the Persians are comparable insofar as both ruled over kingdoms, but here too the Arabs are superior because the basis of their sovereignty is prophethood, whereas the Persians based theirs on plunder and force. Moreover, the Arabs are superior because their sovereignty abrogated[43] that of Persia and will endure until the Day of Judgment, whereas Persian sovereignty has already been supplanted. Finally, the Arabs are superior because their sovereignty extends to the horizons of the earth, whereas Persians' sovereignty was confined to a fraction of the earth: they controlled Syria, the Jazīrah, Khurasan, and Yemen (but only during the reigns of Wahriz and Sayf ibn Dhī Yazan).[44]

1.7.1 It is hard to credit the Easterners' inclusion of Adam in their boasts against the Arabs. The Prophet says: "Do not prefer me over Adam; I am but one of his many blessings." They also lay claim to the prophets, saying that only four of them—Hūd, Sāliḥ, Shuʿayb, and Muḥammad—were Arabs. This claim is an empty boast: it has no substance and is a flagrant injustice to the Arabs. Their arguments are built on falsehood and delusion and can therefore be knocked over with a feather. Such unjust claims against the Arabs are truly obscene. Adam! As if the Arabs were not also Adam's descendants! And then to say that Moses, Jesus, Zechariah, John the Baptist, and other Children of Israel are theirs! As I have already explained to you, there is no genealogical bond between Persia and the Children of Israel.

This boast denies the Arabs close relationship to these prophets, 1.7.2
when in fact the Arabs are their nephews and agnates. By consensus, the Arabs are the sons of Ishmael, son of Abraham, which makes them the nephews of Isaac. This gives them a stronger claim to share Isaac's lofty rank and to boast of kinship with Moses, Jesus, David, Solomon, and all of the other prophets descended from Abraham and Isaac. As the Qur'an explains: «God chose Adam and Noah and the family of Abraham and the family of ʿImrān above all his creatures.»[45] The "family of Abraham" here means the descendants of Isaac and the descendants of Ishmael. The Qur'an goes on to speak of «offspring of one another,»[46] meaning that in terms of genealogy the Arabs and the Children of Israel are one.

Consider God's revelation to Moses: "Verily, I will appoint for 1.7.3
the Children of Israel from their brothers someone like you, in whose mouth I will place My speech."[47] He means that he will raise up one of the Arabs—our Prophet Muḥammad—to prophesy to them. This is one of His signs and a decisive proof against the People of the Book, taken from their own scriptures. If they respond by saying "What this means is that He will appoint a prophet like Moses from among the Children of Israel" and "The Children of Israel are brothers, one to the other," scrutiny will bring their lies to light. If God had meant that, He would specifically have said to them "one of their own" or "one of them." To take an analogous case: if someone intended to dispatch a messenger from the Khindif clan, he would not say, "I will choose one of the *brothers* of the Khindif as messenger."

1.7.4 They may try to deny that Ishmael's descendants ever interwove their genealogy with Isaac's descendants because Ishmael settled in the Sacred Precinct of Mecca and married into the tribe of Jurhum. But blood ties and genealogies cannot be severed simply because people live scattered in different campsites, or because a man marries into a distant tribe or has children with slave women. Ishmael may have spoken Arabic, but a difference in languages between peoples does not rule out kinship between their fathers, brothers, and tribes. Isaac's descendants include Syriac speakers, who speak a different language than Hebrew, as well as the Greeks, who turned from God—thereby severing the ties they had contracted through marriage—and who shunned the language of their forefathers in favor of Byzantine Greek.[48] But none of this invalidates their descent from Isaac. In any case, Ishmael was not even the first person to speak Arabic: he merely learned it. The origin of Arabic lies, rather, in Yemen, since the people there are the descendants of Yaʿrub ibn Qaḥṭān, who was the first person to speak Arabic when the world's languages were thrown into confusion at Babel. Yaʿrub traveled from Babel and settled in Yemen with his children and certain members of his household. His language was adopted by Thamūd, who went forth and settled in al-Ḥijr.

1.7.5 Abū Ḥātim informed me, citing al-Aṣmaʿī, who cited Abū ʿAmr ibn al-ʿAlāʾ, who said: "There are nine ancient tribes: Ṭasm, Jadīs, ʿUhaynah, Ḍajm (or Ḍaḥm), Jaʿm, ʿAmālīq, Qaḥṭān, Jurhum, and Thamūd." Abū Ḥātim also informed me, citing al-Aṣmaʿī, citing Ibn Abī l-Zinād, who said that a man from Jurhum told him: "We are the beginning of creation. No one shares in our genealogy." The man was speaking about the ancient Arabs, whose tongues God loosened so that they were able to speak our language. Their prophets were Arabs: Hūd, Ṣāliḥ, and Shuʿayb.

1.7.6 ʿAbd al-Raḥmān told me that ʿAbd al-Munʿim cited his father, who quoted Wahb ibn Munabbih, who when asked, "Was Hūd the progenitor of Yemen?" replied: "No, but in the Torah he was the brother of Yemen. The Yemenis claimed Hūd so that they too could have a prophetic progenitor when tribal partisanship broke out among the Arabs and Muḍar boasted of their progenitor Ishmael."

Shuʿayb's ancestors were believers who had followed Abraham to Syria, but no genealogical connection has been established between the Children of Israel and Shuʿayb's kin. The name Madyan refers not to a tribe, but rather to the community to whom Shuʿayb was sent. 1.7.7

God sheltered Ishmael as a child in the Sacred Precinct and made the well of Zamzam flow for him. Then a company of travelers from Jurhum arrived and noticed something unusual about Ishmael. Hagar informed them of the boy's lineage, his situation, and what God had commanded the boy's father, Abraham, to do with her and the child. The Jurhumīs regarded the place as blessed, settled there, and admitted Ishmael into their community. He grew up among them and their sons, married one of their daughters, and learned to speak their language, "Yaʿrubiyyah."[49] The letter "*ya*'" is added to the proper noun, but omitted when used to denote kinship,[50] just as verbal augments and other affixes are elided, and just as things can be altered and changed from their original form. The proof that the Arabic language originates in Yemen is that the people of Yemen are called "Arab Arabs," whereas others are called "Arabized Arabs," that is, those who were assimilated to the Arabs and learned from them. One commonly adds "-ized" to words. Thus, when a man joins the Nizār tribe he is said to be "Nizārized," when he joins the Muḍar tribe he is said to be "Muḍarized," and when he joins the Qays tribe he is "Qaysized." 1.7.8

On this point, a poet has said:

> And Qays ʿAylān and those who were Qaysized.[51]

Were it the case that a person relinquishes his genealogy when he learns how to speak a language different from the language of his people, then any Easterner who speaks Arabic must necessarily be reckoned an Arab!

1.8.1 I shall discuss nobility with as much fairness as possible and will clarify its causes without overstepping the proper bounds or giving anyone less than he deserves. The fact that I myself am descended from Easterners shall not prevent me from rebutting the claims of crass and ignorant Easterners or from reining in the audacity of the riffraff. I shall be brief and shall confine myself to quoting major sources and pithy anecdotes. I shall avoid long, detailed discussions of the speeches that the Arabs have delivered, listing their battles before Islam, describing the Arab nobles who were delegates to the Easterner kings and their declamations. This sort of material can be found in countless books and has become tiresome and studied to the point of tedium, especially since most such accounts lack any means of authentication and have not been transmitted from trustworthy or recognized authorities, giving the impression that they have been deliberately fabricated. I hope that intelligent and insightful people will not think that I am tendentious or intend to misrepresent. Besides, I do not declare my work to be free of slips or mistakes. Only God permits me to achieve my goal—He alone can do so.

1.8.2 The fairest thing that can be said about nobility is the following: We were all born of two parents. As we were formed from dust, so will we return to dust; all of us were conceived in urine and born in filth. This then is our true pedigree, and it should suffice to deter any intelligent person from self-aggrandizement and conceit. We will all return to God, where our social ties will be severed and our personal worth count for nothing, unless it arises from piety toward God and derives its strength from obedience to Him.

1.8.3 In purely genealogical terms, some people do have precedence over others. God created Adam from a handful of earth[52] that combined all the different kinds of soil: sandy and rocky, red and black, noxious and beneficial. Adam's children exhibit all the elemental natures of the earth, which produce differing dispositions. As God has said: «Vegetation grows in abundance from beneficial land by the will of its Lord, but grows only scantily from noxious land.»[53]

One person may be brave, another cowardly; one miserly, another generous; one diffident, another brazen; one patient, another rash; one mild-tempered, another severe; or one grateful, another ungrateful. The presence of these elements likewise produces differences in color and appearance: some people are white, others black, some brown, others red, some bright red, others comely, some amiable, others boorish. Some people are much loved though they have not done any good deeds, while others are loathed for no good reason. It is these elements that produce the variety in men's yearnings and desires: some are naturally inclined to seek knowledge, others prefer wealth, others pleasure, others women, and yet others horsemanship.

The same trait may manifest itself differently in different people. 1.8.4
Consider knowledge. There are some people who readily understand jurisprudence but who are slow at arithmetic, some with an aptitude for medicine but none for astrology, and others for whom subtle, obscure subjects are easy to comprehend whereas they find straightforward ones difficult. There are likewise people who learn a scientific discipline so thoroughly that it becomes deeply rooted in their hearts as if carved in stone, but when they learn something less demanding, it disappears like writing on water. Some who seek wealth do so through trade, some through salaried employment, others in the service of rulers, and still others by alchemy, squandering their capital in vain pursuit of unrealizable riches. Or take women. Some men desire a slender woman, others a sturdy one, some want a young, inexperienced girl, others a voluptuous, mature woman. Most remarkable of all are men who go in for old women. As one poet says:

Old she may be, but she's feisty still!
Will a crone like her do me in?
If all the water in the world belonged to her,
she'd never let me enter into her waters.[54]

1.8.5 Consider also perverse dispositions. There are people who love to be disparaged much as others love to receive praise, and who delight in defamatory poems just as the latter do in eulogies—men eager to criticize their own people, insult themselves and their ancestors, and vilify their tribe. In this vein, ʿAmīrah ibn Juʿal al-Taghlibī declared:

May God cover both clans of Taghlib bint Wāʾil
in lingering contempt, slow to disappear![55]

Or al-Ḥirmāzī, who declared:

The Ḥirmāz knuckle under to everyone
Though they play the lord at home.
To disgrace them,
Send them a poet who knows what I know.[56]

Or al-Naḥīf, who said this about his mother:

I wish our mother would just die
and go to Heaven or to Hell.
Hajar cannot satisfy her appetite,
nor can Dhū Qār slake her thirst.
She gorges herself on a camel-load of supplies, still fastened and tied,
her face like it's been coated in tar.
She's a fool—no sense for what's good,
though an adept at harming family and neighbor.

1.8.6 Or consider al-Ḥuṭayʾah, who insulted his father, his mother, and himself. He composed the following about his mother:

Away with you—far from me!
May God free the world of you!
I hate you—don't you get it?
No, you'll never be clever enough to see.
Why don't you keep any secret in your trust,
why do the gossips flock to you?[57]

To his father he said:

God curse you! God curse you as a father!
God curse you as an uncle!
Look at how rotten and shameful you are,
look at how rotten your noble deeds!
You're a combination of vileness, foolishness, and error.
I wish God would end your life!

Of himself, he said:

My lips insisted on speaking evil today.
I didn't even know to whom I was speaking!
God gave me a foul face, I think.
What an ugly face, what an ugly person!

Once, al-Ḥuṭay'ah came to ʿUyaynah ibn al-Nahhās al-ʿIjlī to praise him. ʿUyaynah said to his agent: "Go with him to the market. Buy absolutely anything he points to or bargains for." But al-Ḥuṭay'ah showed no gratitude to his host, saying: 1.8.7

You gave, but so little that I cannot say
whether it's blame you deserve, or verses of praise.

On the subject of vile dispositions, there are people who prefer the smell of toilets[58] to the smell of aloe wood, the smell of outhouses to the smell of roses. They are aroused by ugly, smelly women, but remain unmoved by beautiful, perfumed ones. Similarly, some people may experience ease after distress or enjoy abundance after scarcity, but find their new condition to be boring, and shun it in favor of their former sorry state. 1.8.8

A desert Arab who had come to town and was prospering said:[59]

When afflicted by satiety in town, I say
"Can't I return to a land of hunger?
A land where there is no food,
where hunger hurts so much it splits your head?"

Perverse temperaments such as these are common in all peoples.

1.8.9 These elemental natures lead some men to rise and others to fall. A man who is ambitious by inclination aspires to noble deeds and shuns dishonorable ones. He risks his greatness in pursuit of a great goal and in his quest for honor treats his honor lightly. He confronts fear, and journeys far into the night. He plumbs the depths but his very being will insist on ascending until he satisfies his ambitions, possesses what he desires, and wins renown for himself and his progeny. The man without ambition is a stay-at-home, with no get-up-and-go. He ekes out a modest life and is content with very little because he enjoys taking things easy. If he is destitute, he will even beg. A coward will abandon his mother, father, partner, and children, whereas a brave man is passionate about protecting his neighbor and comrade and will even take up arms on behalf of strangers. A miser is stingy and will deny himself what little he has, whereas a generous man gives liberally to people he does not even know. As Almighty God says: «He who purifies his soul will indeed be successful, and he who corrupts it is sure to fail.»[60] He means here that a person who has cultivated and nurtured his soul with righteousness will prosper, whereas a person who has demeaned and smothered it in immorality will fail.

1.8.10 A man might differ from his father in his moral sensibilities, personal qualities, ambitions, or in all three, because of traits inherited from his mother's or his father's side. A poet declared:

> You take after your grandfather, who was the worst.
> When least expected, breeding will prevail.[61]

1.8.11 There is the nobleman who is reputable, that is, someone who adds his own good qualities to those of his forefathers; and there is the nobleman who is not reputable, that is, someone who is ignominious; and finally the individual who is neither noble nor reputable—that is, someone ignoble in his own being, with ignoble ancestors.

1.8.12 Qays ibn Sāʿidah alluded to this when he said: "When I judge Arabs, I stick to a principle that I originated and that will stand the test of time. When a man is accused of acting ignobly and subsequently does a noble deed, I deem him noble. Similarly, when a man claims to be noble but has acted basely, I deem him devoid of nobility." In other words, a man is best defined by his own qualities, so it does him no harm if he is himself noble of spirit and his ancestors are base—he should still be counted noble. By the same token, ancestry will do him no good if he is ignoble of spirit. There is a similar statement by ʿĀʾishah: "A person of breeding who acts basely is a base person, while a low-born person who acts well can be reckoned high-born." A poet makes the same point:

> Look at what you see a man do
> judge him not by his line,
> Valor outshines a lowly birth,
> while baseness dries the vine.

The term "repute," *ḥasab*, is derived from the notion of counting expressed by the verb *ḥasaba*, as when you say, "I reckoned something" or "I made a reckoning of it," meaning that you counted it up. A man of honor reckons the glorious deeds of his forefathers, counting them up, man by man. Likewise, someone is called "a man to be reckoned with," meaning that his forefathers can be counted and their virtues enumerated. (The verbal noun from the root *ḥ-s-b* is *ḥasb*, with no vowel on the *s*, whereas ordinarily the noun is vocalized *ḥasab*, with a following vowel. The root *h-d-m* follows a similar pattern: when you say, "I pulled the wall down," you use the verbal noun *hadm*, with no vowel on the second letter, whereas the word for the thing that falls to the ground (that is, the rubble) is *hadam* with a vowel.) 1.8.13

The same is true of all peoples, including the Arabs, who were reared and nurtured on nobility. Thus in pre-Islamic times, they urged mutual respect, self-restraint, and the living of a blameless life. They would reproach one another for being cheap and for backstabbing and reckless behavior as they sought to rise above shameful and unworthy ways. They were trained to show fortitude and to 1.8.14

be intrepid and courageous. They adhered scrupulously to the rules relating to people under their protection and would observe their rights, even above and beyond the obligations that they owed to their blood relations and close kin. Thus they would give up their lives for those under their protection, and expend their resources to protect the resources of others. They were also prepared to die for the sake of their families.

1.8.15 Consider Kaʿb ibn Māmah. When someone's dependent died under his protection, he would pay him the blood price, and if a guest's camel or sheep died, he would replace that too. Or take ʿUmayr ibn Salmā l-Ḥanafī, an Arab legendary for keeping his word. ʿUmayr's brother Qurayn tried to take away the wife of a man under his protection. The man did his utmost to protect his wife, but ʿUmayr's brother killed him. ʿUmayr was away at the time, but when he returned and was told about what had happened, he turned Qurayn over to the dead man's legal representative, who killed him. He asked his mother's forgiveness and admitted his crime was heinous, but she rejected his plea, saying:

You give me excuses for your crime
but there's no pardon for fratricide.[62]

1.8.16 One of the strangest things we have heard on the topic of protection is the story of Abū Ḥanbal Jāriyah ibn Murr. When locusts landed near his house, the tribe set out to chase them away. Seeing the commotion he asked people where they were going. They said: "We're here for those neighbors of yours." "Which neighbors do you mean?" he asked, and they replied: "The locusts." Then he said: "Now that you've called them my neighbors, by God, I won't let you near them," and fended off the people until they gave up and left. A member of his clan made the following boast:

Ours is the stronghold, ours is the rise
where our lances led us up.

We seized that hill when time began,
in the dawn of Noah, the dawn of ʿĀd.
Ibn Murr, who saved the locusts,
was one of us;
So was Zayd, and Ḥātim too,
who fed the world when the hard years came.[63]

Qays ibn ʿĀṣim described his people as follows:

They're slow to reproach a neighbor
but quick to spring to his side.[64]

Miskīn al-Dārimī said:

I share my fire with those I protect:
the pot is placed in front of them first.
They are not harmed
even if I know their secrets.[65]

Al-Ḥuṭay'ah composed the following verses on the good qualities of his people:

If they build, they build well. If they swear an oath, they honor it,
and if they make a pact, they are true to it.
They requite all favors done to them
and bestow them freely and easily.
They rule commendably, with patient restraint,
but if angered, they are men to be reckoned with.
Stop criticizing them, you nobody,
or go and try to take their place.[66]

Hospitality is common and widespread among all the Bedouin, as 1.9.1
is a sense of self-sacrifice and generosity with whatever they have. The most commendable form of giving is the self-sacrifice of a man of modest means. ʿUthmān ibn Abī l-ʿĀṣ said: "A hard-earned

dirham spent on a worthy cause is better than ten thousand dirhams taken from a vast fortune and spent on a whim." By encouraging one another to act hospitably and exhorting one another to self-sacrifice, the Bedouin ensured that goodness was not perverted from its true course[67] and did not peter out and die. Arṭāh ibn Suhayyah said:

My guest can have whatever I place before him
 apart from my wives—they are off-limits.

Ibn Abī Zinād reported that ʿAbd al-Malik ibn Marwān said: "How I wish that, of all the Arabs, ʿUrwah ibn al-Ward had sired me![68] For ʿUrwah said:

I share the broth in my pot,
 but you keep the pot for yourself.
Do you, all fat and soft, scoff at me, because you see
 I've wasted away by doing right by others?
I divide my body among many,
 and I am left with clear, cold water."

ʿUrwah means that he divided up his food among his guests; it is as if he had divided up his body because the meat that was supposed to feed him was actually feeding others. He drank water during the winter and in times of drought because he gave away all the milk he had. So pause over this poem and over the noble meanings it conveys. Another poet said to a woman:

When you prepare food, find someone else
 to share it with me because I refuse to eat on my own.
Relative or stranger, no matter.
 Otherwise I fear for my reputation.
How can a man enjoy his meal when his neighbor's
 stomach is empty, his poverty and misery obvious?[69]

1.9.2 Here no doubt my opponent will say that I seem to have forgotten about Muzarrid and Ḥumayd al-Arqaṭ and how they lampooned their guests. How, he will ask, does this talk of generosity compare with their repulsive dishes—the snakes, lizards, jerboas, and bloodied fur they ate and the camels' stomach juices and blood they drank? How does it compare with their eating camel flesh, partially roasted and raw, veins, neck muscles, table scraps and all, during a game of *maysir*? Nothing seemed to fill those Arabs with disgust or loathing—not even carrion or food eaten by dogs! Our opponent will go on to boast about the superior food of the Easterners, of their sweets and table manners, about how they eat in the Easterner style, with forks[70] and knives!

Let's consider these two poets who lampooned their guests by describing them as stuffing their faces with their food. Ḥumayd was poor and in dire straits, but when a guest came to stay with him, he had no choice but to give him what little he had or at least share it. As a consequence, he would spend the night starved and the next morning wake up hungry, seething with rage at his plight. A poet in such straitened circumstances will inevitably reach the end of his tether and seek to console himself by talking about how his guest stuffs his face and by describing how he eats and talks. He may have been the one who said about a guest: 1.9.3

His hands grab whatever his fingers can reach,
and his pharynx sends it down his esophagus.
As he settles down to receive his food, he says:
"Tell me about what al-Ḥajjāj is doing to the people."
I reply: "This is not why you've come to pass the night with us.
So eat and while you eat, shut up about the news!"
Not even Saḥbān Wā'il could match
the eloquence or knowledge of his table-talk.[71]

This poet also described his guests as follows:

They spent the night crowded round a basket filled with choice dates,
fingernails dug in like knives.

Next morning, the date stones were piled high where they
had slept:
poor men don't throw the stones away.[72]

What he meant was that some guests actually eat the stones and the dates, this being an indication of how miserably poor they are.

1.9.4 Muzarrid, for his part, was simply a ravenous glutton, and gluttony generally goes hand in hand with stinginess. It was he who said:

I mixed a pound of date stones with two pounds of wheat,
adding a pound of butter to float on top,
Then I said to my stomach: "Rejoice today!" For now
it can safely enjoy what I usually keep hidden.
This is the cure for hunger,
today my empty stomach will be full.[73]

Al-Ḥuṭay'ah said:

I got a hunting dog ready for my guests
along with a cudgel from an *arzan*[74] tree,
And my excuses: lies, a vexed face,
and complaints about how hard times are.[75]

It does not get much worse than that. But every group has its good and bad people. The world was set up to work that way, and so it is that men have gone about their lives. The good would not be recognized if not for the bad. You can only judge on the basis of the most prevalent circumstances, and on how someone appears to behave. Three or four poets cannot cancel out the magnanimity of thousands of other men, nor nullify all their good deeds.

1.9.5 There's Ka'b ibn Māmah, who died of thirst because he gave his companion al-Namarī his share of water. And there's Ḥātim, from the tribe of Ṭayyi', who divided up his property ten times over. On one journey, he met a man taken prisoner by the tribe of 'Anazah. The prisoner sought his help, but Ḥātim had nothing to give him, so he purchased him from the people of 'Anazah, released him, and then took his place, in chains, until he could pay his ransom. Any boast the Ṭayyiʾ tribe, which holds sway over the two mountains in Najd, may make derives from the Nizār clan, which serves the Ṭayyiʾ as a model of good breeding and fine comportment.

From after the coming of Islam, there is also ʿAdī, who split his wealth with the poet Ibn Dārah, and Maʿn, of whom it was said: "Talk about Maʿn? You might as well talk of the sea!"[76] When someone asked him for a beast to ride, he called to his slave: "Give him a steed, a workhorse, a mule, a donkey, a camel, and a slave woman." Then, he said to the petitioner: "If I could think of anything else you could ride, I'd give you that too."

Nahīk ibn Mālik ibn Muʿāwiyah sold his camels and set off for Minā with the proceeds but gave his money away instead.[77] The people said he was insane, but he said:

> I am not crazy, no. I am generous.
> Wheat was scarce. I gave away what I had.[78]

This is a vast topic about which one can speak at great length, but a more extensive analysis would divert our book from its proper subject. Our goal, rather, is to use a few examples simply to hint at what is treated comprehensively in my book, *Choice Narratives*.[79]

To come to those who attack the Arabs for their repulsive dishes, 1.9.6
such as bloodied fur and snakes, and for their repulsive drinks, such as the stomach juices and blood of camels, such things are only consumed by those who live in barren lands and deserts as a last resort in times of famine and exceptional hardship. A poet has said:

> In a year of drought, what is forbidden is allowed.[80]

He means that during such years they eat carrion. As al-Rāʿī said:

> Heading for the light of a fire where people roasted leather straps.
> Guests can still receive hospitality, while the hosts eat roast leather.[81]

Eating such foods is only shameful if the Arabs freely choose to eat them in times of ease. Some of the Easterners choose to eat flies when they do not need to, or crayfish when chickens are available. All people experience hard times. Anyone without meat will eat jerboas and lizards, and anyone without water will drink camels' blood and stomach juices. Al-Aṣmaʿī said: "Ḥuraythah's camels were taken in a raid, so he rode one of the sacred camels.[82] Someone asked him: 'Is that an unlawful mount you're riding?' and he replied: 'A man rides an unlawful mount if he doesn't have a lawful one.'" A poet has said:

> Oh for a pair of sandals made of hyena hide!
> A man with sore feet and no shoes will wear any kind of shoe.[83]

1.9.7 The following line of poetry confirms that wealthy Arabs did things differently from indigent and destitute ones:

> We do not use crow meat for provisions,
> nor crayfish from the waters of the Barīṣ.[84]

Here the poet refuses crow meat and shames another group for eating it. Another poet said to his wife:

> May I drink camel's blood if I do not find another wife to keep you company,
> a woman with long, dangling earrings[85] and a pleasant scent!

If he thought that drinking camel's blood was praiseworthy, he would not have included it in his oath. Just as when someone says, "May I commit idolatry if I fail to do such-and-such a thing!" Another poet has said:

> Even on an empty stomach, we are disgusted
> by bone marrow and bare tail-stumps.[86]

He means that no matter how hungry he is, he prefers to eat his bread with animal fat rather than dates.

1.9.8 An Arab was once offered locusts by a host.[87] Disgusted, he declaimed:

God damn a tent that black night
drew me to, when all slept.
I saw an old man sitting in the courtyard.
He was an ass, though he could talk.
He brought me a pouch full of locust larvae,
but I had never had a meal of locust larvae.
So I said to him: "Take your pouch and get lost!
Would a Muslim ever try such a thing, you bastard?"

People in the grip of poverty will always eat neck tendons, veins, and raw meat, go without fine foods, and have poor table manners. Persons of wealth and rank, on the other hand, are familiar with delicacies and know how to enjoy them with the best manners. Consider the following special dishes:[88] **1.9.9**

Maḍīrah: Its very name is the byword of the Arabs' discernment. It is cooked with *māḍir*, sour, sharp-tasting milk, from which its name is derived.

Harīsah:[89] So called because it is mortared, *tuhras*, that is, pounded finely. The instrument used for pounding is called a mortar, *mihrās*.

Washīqah: The common people call it *ʿashīqah*. It is called *washīqah* because it is cut into slices, *tūshaq*, meaning cut finely.

ʿAṣīdah: So called because it is turned, *tuʿṣad*, when made; that is, it is twisted. When you twist something you turn it. Thus, when someone moves his neck he is said to turn it, to be *ʿāṣid*. Muzarrid was referring to *ʿaṣīdah* when he said:

I mixed a pound of date stones with two pounds of wheat,
adding a pound of butter to float on top.

Umayyah ibn Abī l-Ṣalt said about ʿAbd Allāh ibn Judʿān:

One man drums up guests walking through Mecca,
another stands atop his house, inviting others
To great wooden porringers
laden with the finest wheat mixed with honey.[90]

He is describing *fālūdh*.

1.9.10 Of all peoples the Arabs are the best at describing food, and the subtlest in how they refer to it. Abū Ḥātim informed me, citing al-Aṣmaʿī, who cited Abū Ṭufaylah, who said he heard a Bedouin elder say: "We were the guests of a man whose wheat was like sparrows' beaks and whose dates were as soft as the neck of a monitor lizard, a delight to chew." We also learned that al-Aṣmaʿī quoted a desert Arab, who said: "Our dates are a sumptuous feast—flat-nosed, a delight to chew, with stones like birds' tongues. When you put one of our dates in your mouth, you feel its sweetness in the tips of your toes." I cite ʿAbd al-Raḥmān, who cites his paternal uncle citing an elder from Medina, who said: "Someone once brought me a broth that looked like it was infused with red clay. All I could see was a bit of liver floating in it. I dipped my hand in and found a lump of meat. I pulled on it, and it stretched. I looked like I was playing a ney."

The Arabs' many cooked dishes include *ghassāniyyah*, which, like *ḥaysah*, *rabīkah*, *khazīrah*, and *lafītah*, is unfamiliar to non-experts. I therefore omit it, limiting myself to familiar dishes. The Arabs are used to saying: "The most delicious cuts of meat are those that take refuge." What they mean is that the best bits are those next to the bone, so called because they seem to have taken refuge there. They also used to say: "When you eat, invoke God's name and keep close." By "keeping close" they meant eating whatever is in front of you.

The Arabs found brains unpalatable and believed it was gluttonous to extract them. A poet once mocked someone by saying:

> He's not embarrassed to take marrow from skulls.[91]

There are also some Arab tribes who detest sheep rump, calling it a dish made from the anus.

An Arab said:

> It is better to die than visit a miser
> who scrutinizes his guest's fingers.[92]

The Arabs are also praised for eating very little. Aʿshā Bāhilah recited the following line: 1.9.11

A strip of grilled liver satisfies him,
flood water is all he needs.

They decry voraciousness, ravenousness, and slothfulness, and mock stingy food-grabbers by saying: "What, do you shuffle the arrows but not join the game?"[93] What they mean is that this person would not share a thing with his companions but still ate two of their dates. The basic sense of "not joining the game" is a person who does not join his tribe on the march. A *rajaz* poet said:

Don't get me started about her husband!
A deceitful swindler who weeps when hungry,
Who does not supply his people with firewood or give them drink,
Who does not look for their camels when they stray.
He eats dates, stones and all,
And shows his privates by the fire.
He is like a sack packed with straw!

Al-Aḥnaf said: "Do not talk about women and food at our gatherings, for I dislike it when someone goes on about his stomach and his privates all the time. It is proper for a man to forgo food when he craves it." One of the Arabs' sayings is: "Eat little, and you'll sleep better." Another saying is: "Gluttony got the better of my intelligence."

On the day when the two arbiters reached their decision, ʿAmr ibn al-ʿĀṣ advised Muʿāwiyah:[94] "Give them more food, for, by God, when people have full stomachs, they become less discerning. A man's resolve is not effective if he has slept with a full stomach." There are many more such sayings for anyone who wants to track them down. How then could the Arabs' knowledge of food and how to enjoy it in a refined manner not be as we have described?

Regarding the criticism that the Arabs do not cook meat thoroughly,[95] I know this to be true in one situation only—when they 1.9.12

are on campaign. Indeed, they praise themselves for doing so in such situations because it shows how ready they are to act on their decisions. As al-Shammākh said:

> Many's the disheveled man, his shirt shredded by travel,
> who pulls his meat off the fire with a stick before it's done![96]

And al-Kumayt said:

> I hastened to a stomach heated with stones,
> as the fat spluttered but was still white.[97]

At drinking sessions, young princes and others would rush to snatch and devour the meat before it had been thoroughly cooked. A desert Arab who had slaughtered his camel during a drinking session declaimed:[98]

> Give me another drink! Life in this world is but another drink!
> Quit blaming and finding fault with me.
> Snatch the barely browned meat from your pots.
> Quench my thirst—and God keep the camels away![99]

1.9.13 Regarding the accusation that they eat the bits of food that fall from the table, all this does is to show a high regard for food and recognition of what a blessing it is! It is simply a form of expressing gratitude to the One who gave it, whereas it would be disrespectful and insulting to toss scraps onto the rubbish heap, depriving the Giver of what His gift merits. When someone gives you a gift and you cherish and respect it, he will naturally give you more. But if you undervalue it and treat it with contempt, it is only natural that he will stop giving. The greatest blessing God bestows on His creatures is knowledge of Him. Next comes food, since it maintains a person's spirit and keeps him alive. Thus, those who cherish food respect God's blessing and deserve more of it, whereas those who mistreat it belittle it and deserve His displeasure.

Yazīd ibn ʿAmr informed us that Ayyūb ibn Sulaymān cited Muḥammad ibn Ziyād, who cited Maymūn ibn Mihrān, who heard

Ibn 'Abbās say: "'Honor bread, for God put the heavens and the earth to work for it.' As far as I know the Prophet is the only one to have said this." Therefore the Prophet (God bless and cherish him!) commands and encourages us to eat whatever falls from the table. It is simply astounding for people who follow Islam and whose prophet is Muḥammad (God bless and cherish him) to criticize, discredit, and oppose Muḥammad's very commands and prohibitions. The relevant reports have been transmitted without interruption, yet these people dismiss them because they fail to understand the reasoning behind them. One wonders why they bother, as contempt confers no benefit and acceptance would do them no harm.

As for the boast that the Easterners eat with knives and forks, it 1.9.14
is obvious that using cutlery spoils food and reduces the pleasure of eating it. Apart from those obstinate liars who say the opposite of what they know in their hearts, everyone else knows that the best foods are those you touch with your hand. The palm of your hand was created for this very purpose—for picking up food. It is foolish and strange to think that hands are unclean when they have been properly washed. It makes more sense to view saliva, phlegm, and mucus—which you need in order to swallow food easily—as unclean, rather than hands. Cooks and bakers touch food with their hands, but people don't think this is unclean and are perfectly comfortable with it.

Some say the Arabs are not a courageous people. On the question 1.10.1
of valor, the pre-Islamic Arabs were more mindful of their honor than any other nation, more protective of their womenfolk, more difficult to control, and quicker to take offense at any threat to their pride.[100] They would mount night raids on the marches of Persia, forcing her kings to make pledges and sue for peace. The Easterners boast of the Persian cavalry and their regional governors. I do genuinely agree that they were courageous and intrepid, but a distinction has to be made between them and the Arabs: the Easterners were wealthier, equipped with better weapons, had better

forts, and were more united. They waged war under the leadership and guidance of a potentate.[101] Such circumstances would bolster any fighter's stamina, fortify his constitution, intensify his resolve, and give him the confidence to stand his ground. The Arabs, on the other hand, fought in scattered bands, with no overarching social structure, in a state of disorder, and with no unity. Most of them would battle on foot with a blunt sword or a very basic spear. Even their horsemen would ride into battle on Arabian horses without saddles, and if any of them actually had a saddle, it would be threadbare and have no stirrups. The Easterners tended to fight with bows and arrows; the Arabs with swords and spears. Still, men with swords and spears are typically more committed, tend to be routed less frequently, and show more evidence of endurance in battle.

1.10.2 Arab heroes during the pre-Islamic era included such champions as ʿUtaybah ibn al-Ḥārith ibn Shihāb, "the Hunter of Horsemen"; Bisṭām ibn Qays; Bujayr and ʿIfāq, the sons of Abū Malīl; ʿĀmir ibn al-Ṭufayl and ʿAmr ibn Wudd. After the advent of Islam, they included men such as al-Zubayr, ʿAlī, and Ṭalḥah, and the Allies ʿAbd Allāh ibn Khāzim al-Sulamī and ʿAbbād ibn al-Ḥuṣayn. Someone said: "I never imagined that a single man could face a thousand horsemen until I saw ʿAbbād at the night-raid on Kabul."[102] Fighters like Qaṭarī ibn al-Fujāʾah, Shabīb al-Ḥarūrī, and many more were as numerous as grains of sand. If you study the stories about them you will discover that each and every one of them was braver than any elite Persian warrior.

1.10.3 Only the Arabs fought on foot. Abū ʿUbaydah reports: "Al-Muntashir ibn Wahb al-Bāhilī, Sulayk ibn ʿUmayr al-Saʿdī, and Awfā ibn Maṭar al-Māzinī are the most famous Arab foot-soldiers. They could chase a gazelle and catch it by the horns. In springtime, they would fill a pierced ostrich egg with water and bury it. And then, in summertime when it was not the raiding season, they would continue their raids. They had a better sense of direction than a sandgrouse and could locate where to dig for water, which they would drink up." I heard Abū Ḥātim report that he heard al-Aṣmaʿī say:

"Sulayk could run so fast that if an arrow fell from his quiver while he was running it would bury itself in the ground. When he prayed, he would ask: 'O God! Protect me from failure. But fear—I have no fear.'"[103]

I have read in the books of the Easterners that Bahrām Gūr lived in the desert under the protection of an Arab king. Bahrām learned that his father was dead and that the Persians had decided to crown someone else as their king. So he traveled with the Arabs to the plains of Iraq, where he billeted his army, laid his claim to the throne, and fought the Persians. In the end they acknowledged his claim and made him king. The Arabs also defeated the Easterners at the Battle of Dhū Qār when Khosrow sent a military expedition against the Shaybān and the Shaybān routed his troops. The account of how God subsequently united the Arabs under their leader to fight the Persians and how He guided and governed them is so famous that it requires no elaboration here. Yet the story of Khosrow Parviz is an indication of how proud, hard, disdainful, and fanatically zealous the Persians were during the pre-Islamic era. Parviz was notorious for his ferocity in war, and would show his enemies no mercy. He asked al-Nuʿmān ibn Mundhir for the hand of one of his daughters in marriage, but al-Nuʿmān, who did not wish it, refused and fled. Khosrow Parviz took him prisoner, however, and killed him. 1.10.4

The Quraysh have always had custodianship of God's ancient Sacred House, which He defended by sending flocks of birds against the invaders.[104] To this day the Quraysh remain its guardians and custodians. They are responsible for its management, and are charged with upholding its rites and ceremonies. They were called the "people of God" and said to be "under God's protection" because they dwelled in the Sacred Precinct of Mecca and lived next to His House. They kept alive what was left of the original monotheism that they had inherited from Ishmael (God bless and cherish him), including circumcision, ritual ablution, pilgrimage to the Sacred House and the performance of rites there, and the rules governing divorce and the manumission of slaves, as well as the prohibition of 1.10.5

unlawful marriage to close kin, those who were nursed by the same woman, or those related through marriage. When an Arab named Ḥājib ibn Zurārah was sent as an envoy to Khosrow, and saw how the Easterners married their sisters and daughters, he foolishly decided that he should emulate them and join their religion. He married his own daughter but subsequently regretted it, saying:

God curse your religion, invented by an uncircumcised man!
It makes sisters and daughters legally permissible!
I snared my family in abomination,
and put on a collar of shame.
Permanent disgrace hangs around my neck;
the censure will live on after my death.
A young woman—mounted by her father.
Such a virtuous young girl! Such an evil old man!

1.10.6 Another remnant of the original monotheism the Quraysh kept alive was their belief in the two recording angels. One of our companions reported to us that he heard the poetry critic ʿAbd al-Raḥmān ibn Khālid say: "Al-Ḥasan ibn Jahwar, a member of al-Manṣūr's household, provided one of the descendants of Sulaymān ibn ʿAlī ibn ʿAbd Allāh ibn al-ʿAbbās ibn ʿAbd al-Muṭṭalib with a document that belonged to ʿAbd al-Muṭṭalib ibn Hāshim, written in his own hand. This individual was surprised to observe that ʿAbd al-Muṭṭalib's handwriting was like a woman's. This was what the document said: 'In Your name, O Lord. This is a record of the obligation of So-and-So al-Ḥimyārī, of the people of Zawl in Sanaa, to ʿAbd al-Muṭṭalib ibn Hāshim, of the people of Mecca. He owes one thousand dirhams of good silver weighed out precisely. When ʿAbd al-Muṭṭalib calls it in, he will pay him. God and His two angels are its witnesses.'" Likewise in a poem of al-Aʿshā we find:

Do not reckon me ungrateful for your favor.
O God's witness, bear witness to my witness![105]

The phrase "to my witness" means "God's witness, the angel, is witness to what my tongue says."

Other remnants include rules from pre-Islamic times that God confirmed through Islam. It is quite likely that the remnants of the religion of Ishmael (God bless and cherish him) included the rules that the bloodwite due for a slain man is one hundred camels; that the gender of a hermaphrodite is to be determined by the manner of urination; and that a man and woman must separate after the man's third declaration of divorce rather than after his first or second such declaration.

This is how the Arabs were before Islam, to say nothing of their 1.10.7
many strengths in learning and knowledge, which we will later set forth fully, God willing.[106]

God subsequently brought Islam, and from the Arabs elevated the 1.11.1
Prophet (God bless and cherish him), chief of all prophets, seal of the messengers, abrogator of all earlier revealed laws, and the most virtuous of men. God caused the Arabs to multiply, put an end to dissension among them, supported them with His angels, and strengthened them with His power. He established them in the land and enabled them to tread upon other nations' necks. He endowed them with the caliphate, with succession to prophethood, and then with the imamate—an eternal, inherited imamate, singular and impossible to replicate, that will continue until the Messiah (God bless and cherish him) comes and prays behind the Imam.

It was then, when there were no Easterners present, that God 1.11.2
addressed the Arabs, saying: «You are indeed the best community that has ever been brought forth for mankind.»[107] To them belongs the excellence to which He refers. Other communities acquire excellence after the Arabs. As for his words to the Children of Israel, «It is He who has exalted you above all peoples,»[108] that is a general statement by which something particular was intended, as is the case when He quotes Abraham declaring, «I am the first of the

submitters»[109] and when He quotes Moses saying, «I am the first of the believers,»[110] even though the prophets before them had also been believers and submitters. He means simply that Moses was the first of his era. The same is true of His statement «I favored you above all other people»:[111] He means above all those who lived in the era of those He addressed.

1.11.3 God's words to the Quraysh «Are they better than the people of Tubbaʿ and those who came before them?»[112] do not prove that the people of Yemen are more reputable than the Quraysh, nor even that they are comparable. The people of the Quraysh are descendants of Abraham (God bless and cherish him) and are included among the offspring whom God «chose» . . . «above all His creatures.»[113] Yemen, meanwhile, has had no prophetic forebearer since Noah. In this verse, God is actually addressing the polytheists among the Quraysh, reminding them of the ancient peoples He destroyed for rebelling against Him and threatening to strike them down in turn. Thus He asks: «Are they better» than all the people including Tubbaʿ and other powerful kings and their armies whom «We destroyed»[114] for their faults? The term "better" may be understood in various senses. For example, it is said, "Of the two horsemen, he is the better," meaning he is the more capable. Likewise, "Of the two woods, this is the better," meaning it is the harder of the two. As God said, the Quraysh were few in number, but then He multiplied them;[115] they were considered weak, but then He gave them of his strength; and they were afraid that hostile kings would take control of them, but He sheltered them in His Sacred Precinct.[116] He thus alludes to the firm foundation He laid for them and to His plan to strengthen them, grant them authority, make His light manifest to them, and subject other nations and kingdoms to their rule. God has decreed that the Quraysh are superior to all His creation by making them our rulers and awarding the caliphate exclusively to them. What proper and devout Muslim, who abides by the requirements of his religion, would deny the Quraysh precedence or put others on a par with them? Leadership signifies precedence. The

Messenger of God said: "Our leaders come from the Quraysh." This statement is unequivocal and no exegete can circumvent it.

Wakīʿ cites al-Aʿmash, who cited Jābir, who reported, "The Messenger of God (God bless and cherish him) said: 'People follow the example of the Quraysh, whether it is good or bad.' The Messenger of God (God bless and cherish him) also said: 'The Quraysh are a people who show patience and faithfulness. On the Day of Resurrection God will smite all who curse them.' And he (God bless him) said: 'Learn from the Quraysh; do not teach them. Place the Quraysh ahead of you; do not put them behind you.'" Al-Zuhrī cites Ṭalḥah ibn ʿAbd Allāh ibn ʿAwf, who cites ʿAbd al-Raḥmān ibn al-Azhar, who cites Jubayr ibn Muṭʿim, who reports that the Messenger of God (God bless and cherish him) said: "A Qurayshī has the power of two non-Qurayshīs." When al-Zuhrī was asked, "What did he mean by 'power'?" he replied, "Excellent judgment." It has also been said: "The Quraysh are the scribes, the reckoners, and the salt of this community. What one of their men of learning knows would cover the earth." [117] The Messenger of God (God bless him) said: "No one should take up arms for anyone but a member of the Banū Hāshim." I heard from Yazīd ibn ʿAmr, citing Naṣr ibn Khālid al-Ḍabbī, who cited ʿAbd Allāh ibn ʿAlī ibn Waththāb al-Madanī, who cited Muṭarrif ibn Abī Khuwaylid al-Hudhalī, who reported that the Messenger of God (God bless and cherish him) heard a man saying: 1.11.4

> My genealogy is that I am a man of Ḥimyar.
> My fathers come neither from Rabīʿah nor Muḍar.

The Messenger of God responded: "That debases you and makes you further from God and His Messenger."

The Messenger of God (God bless and cherish him) said: "Salmān! Do not hate me and thereby forsake your religion," to which Salmān said, "Messenger of God! How could I hate you when God has guided me through you?" The Prophet responded, "Do not hate the Arabs and thereby hate me." The Messenger of God (God bless and cherish him) also said: "Anyone who deceives the Arabs will not be 1.11.5

included in my intercession and will not earn my love." And he (God bless and cherish him) said: "When people disagree, the truth lies with Muḍar." Abū Nuʿaym cites al-Thawrī, who cited Yazīd ibn Abī Ziyād, who cited ʿAbd Allāh ibn al-Ḥārith, who cited al-Muṭṭalib ibn Abī Wadāʿah, who reported that the Messenger of God (God bless and cherish him) said: "God created His creatures and placed me among the best of them. He divided them and placed me within the best division. He created tribes and placed me within the best one. He created families and placed me within the best one. I therefore have the best family of all and am myself the best among you."

1.12.1 After the Arabs in nobility come the people of Khurasan. They are the ones who proclaimed the Abbasid mission and supported the Abbasid revolution. For most of the Sasanian period, they were unconquered and paid tribute and tax to no one. The Easterner kings had settled Balkh before the period of the "petty kings." From there they moved to Babylonia.[118] Afterward, Ardashīr Bābak settled Fārs, which became the seat of the Sasanian kingdom while Khurasan became the seat of the Hephthalite kings. It was the Hephthalites who killed Peroz, son of Yazdagird, son of Bahrām, the king of Fārs. This happened when Peroz raided the territory of the Hephthalites, who tricked him into following a route where travelers died of thirst. They then marched against him, taking him and most of his companions prisoners. He pleaded with them to treat him and his fellow prisoners kindly, and swore a pledge in God's name that he would not raid them or cross their borders again. In the presence of his regional governors and cavalry, he set a stone marker between the two lands and called on God as his witness that he would observe it as a boundary. So the Hephthalites set him free. But when Peroz returned to his kingdom, he was seized by indignation and fury over what had befallen him, and resumed his raids in spite of his oaths and his contravention of the terms by which he had secured his safety. He even removed the stone marker he had erected and had it carried in front of him so that he could claim that since he had not passed the stone, he had not crossed the boundary. All the while the Hephthalites implored him in God's name to recall his promises to them and the terms under which he had received protection. Undeterred, Peroz repudiated his oath, so they attacked, killing him along with his guards and his warriors, plundering his property and seizing his dependents, who remained captives until they were manumitted and released. A great while later the Hephthalites also killed Peroz's son, Khosrow. This story appears in the royal biographies written by the Persians themselves.[119] If the people involved were willing to concede to their enemies a story as damning as this, just imagine all the awful things they are not telling you.

Among the messages that passed back and forth between Peroz and the Hephthalite king, they quote one that I would like to include here in order to demonstrate Hephthalite wisdom, resolve, and grasp of tactics. When the two parties met and assumed battle formation, Ikhshinwāz, the Hephthalite king, sent the following message to Peroz: 1.12.2

> Pride has led you to this, I know. We did trick you, but you had come to visit something worse on us. We did not start this by committing some offense. We acted only to protect ourselves and our women. And yet you and your men have repaid us badly: you have broken the treaty and the pledge by which you bound yourself. You should feel more shame and remorse over this than over how we have treated you. You were prisoners and we freed you. You were on the brink of death and we dealt with you mercifully. We could have shed your blood but chose to spare you. We did not compel you to accept the conditions that you proposed. Rather, it was you who wanted them and you who sought them from us. 1.12.3
>
> Think on this and decide for yourself which would bring greatest shame and disrepute. Imagine yourself to be a man who goes on a quest, which is not fated to succeed. He 1.12.4

follows a path, but achieves nothing he set out to achieve. His enemy captures him when he is in a state of exhaustion, and his companions in dire straits. His enemy treats him benevolently and sets him and his companions free on the basis of conditions he himself stipulates and terms of surrender he himself offers. He suffers his ill fate bravely, however galling it might be, for he thinks of himself as a man of his word. Is this worse than the alternative, wherein you make a lying pledge, break your word, and destroy your reputation? I suspect that your confidence in the size of your army and your belief in the quality of their equipment are what buttress your obstinacy. Remember, however, that the majority of your forces are here against their will. They know you have made them complicit in an injustice by commanding them to join you in defying God. Their hearts are not in this fight, so they have no incentive to give you good counsel. Consider what someone who goes to war under these circumstances has to gain. What could he possibly achieve by inflicting harm on his enemy when he knows that if he is victorious, he wins with shame, and if he is killed, he faces the fires of hell? Let me also remind you that you named God as your guarantor. Did I not display great kindness to you and your men when you had given yourselves up for lost? I urge you to choose the wiser course, which will bring you good fortune. Abide by the treaty and emulate your ancestors, who always kept their promises, cheerfully or otherwise, and by doing so secured a good reputation. Remember, too, that you cannot be certain of victory over us, because we seek to defeat you just as you seek to defeat us. In us you have provoked an enemy who may well be granted victory. So take my advice: as God is my witness, none of your comrades will make you a better offer. Do not let the fact that it comes from me blind you to its benefits. Men of good judgment understand that sound advice is sound even when it comes from an enemy, just as suffering is no less painful when inflicted by friends.

But if you conceitedly decide to put your trust in the size 1.12.5
of your army and number of your comrades, then we put our trust in God, knowing ourselves blameless, for we have upheld our part of the oath you swore by Him. You should know that I do not make this appeal because I fear battle or because my troops are few in number. Rather, through you I want to improve the virtuous appeal of my arguments and thereby better deserve God's gift of victory.[120] If peace and security cannot be had, I am ready to go to war.

Undeterred, Peroz stuck obstinately to his argument about the 1.12.6
stone that he had carried in front of him. This prompted Ikhshinwāz to say: "Don't be misled! You fool no one but yourself by carrying that stone in front of you. If people were to make treaties according to your precedent—saying one thing, while intending to do the opposite—then it would be impossible for anyone to be tricked[121] by an assurance of safety or to place trust in a treaty. No one would ever do so. Rather, treaties are based on transparency and on the good intentions of the parties involved." Then Ikhshinwāz pulled out the document Peroz had written and raised it on a spear so that Peroz's soldiers could see it. The soldiers realized the extent of his deceit and injustice, abandoned him, rebelled, and fought among themselves. Before long his army was routed, with all but a few of his soldiers killed or imprisoned. Among the dead was Peroz himself. Afterward Ikhshinwāz said: "How true are these sayings: 'What is predetermined cannot be withstood. Nothing ruins good judgment like passion or obstinacy. Nothing is more futile than giving advice to someone not prepared to receive it or not strong enough to bear whatever unpleasantness it entails. Nothing produces a swifter punishment or a worse outcome than injustice or deceit. There is nothing more shameful than to be monumentally weak because you are full of pride.'"

1.12.7 When Anushirvan came to power, he married into the family of the Khāqān and sought his assistance against the Hephthalites. The Khāqān did indeed help Anushirvan to exact his revenge by killing the Hephthalite king and his household. However, Anushirvan's need to seek aid from the King of the Turks only reveals his weakness . . .

1.12.8 Such, then, is the story of the people of Khurasan before Islam. Then God sent Islam. By the grace of God and His special mercy to them, of all the nations, it was they who embraced it first, and they did so with passionate enthusiasm, flocking to accept it of their own will and surrendering their cities without a fight. Because there was no bloodshed or any need to take captives, the people of Khurasan paid a light land tax and suffered little.

1.12.9 When God saw *how the sinners had laid waste to the land*,[122] their misappropriation of revenue from the conquests, their addiction to music and entertainment, and their disregard for the obligations attached to the authority He had granted them, He sent soldiers from Khurasan against them, mustering them from all over the province as if they were the scattered clouds of autumn. He clothed them in dread, and snatched any mercy from their hearts. They were like a dark night advancing, dressed in black, sporting long hair, shunning the touch of women. They stripped power from the noblest Umayyad king—the Umayyad best served by scribe and vizier, the one who could boast the greatest resolve and judgment, and the best military equipment and soldiery—and handed it over instead to the Abbasids.

1.12.10 Here are the words of Muḥammad ibn ʿAlī ibn ʿAbd Allāh ibn al-ʿAbbās to the Abbasid propagandists when he laid out his plans to send them to the garrison towns: "In Kufa, the Party of ʿAlī and his descendants; in Basra and its fields, the supporters of ʿUthmān, who profess restraint and say: 'Better to be killed by your fellow Muslim than to be guilty of killing him.' The Jazirah contains the apostate Ḥarūrīs, as well as uncouth Bedouin peasants and Muslims who behave like Christians. The people of Syria recognize only the family of Abū Sufyān, and profess allegiance only to the Marwānids. Their animosity is deep-rooted, their savagery extreme. Mecca and Medina profess loyalty to Abū Bakr and ʿUmar (God have mercy on them).[123] Go, therefore, to the people of Khurasan. There you will find many recruits: men of obvious hardiness, sincere men with open hearts unriven by heresies, men who are not divided into sects and who have not been corrupted. They will be formidable soldiers: well-trained bodies, powerful shoulders and necks, well-groomed hair and beards. They will spread terror with their booming voices, their terrible shouts. I see good omens in the East—where the lamp of creation rises and illumines the earth."

When God's will had come to pass regarding the Umayyads and Abbasids, the people of Khurasan and their successors lived as excellent steadfast subjects of the empire. They were exceptionally faithful, peacable, and obedient, adoring their rulers and treating their subject population fairly, providing them with an example of good conduct and intervening to prevent them from engaging in unseemly actions. Then God's decree came to pass and the Rightly Guided Caliphs decided to replace them and to give their administrative responsibilities to others . . . 1.12.11

Khurasan *is blessed with fertile* soil, sweet fruit, and *excellent* craftsmanship; with tall and handsome residents who carry themselves well, dressed in protective armor and clothing of high quality; and also with men of great experience. Therefore anything that originates in Khurasan is the best of its kind in the world . . . *There is no one* braver, with a tougher constitution or better able to withstand personal suffering than a *Khurasanian* Turk, nor anyone less likely to cause dissension or to be obsequious. It is through them that God has protected Muslims from their enemies, as the hadith says: "Leave the Turks alone so long as they leave you alone." And there is a hadith about Khurasan that seems to set it above every other land, except for the Sacred Precincts of Mecca and Medina and the Holy Land. Aḥmad ibn al-Khalīl reported to me that he heard Muḥammad ibn al-Khaṣīb ibn Ḥamzah cite Sulaymān ibn 1.12.12

Buraydah, citing Aws ibn ʿAbd Allāh ibn Buraydah, who quoted the Prophet (God bless and keep him) as saying:[124] "Buraydah! When I am gone, missions will be dispatched. When your turn comes, join the mission to the East, the mission to Khurasan, the mission sent to a place called Merv. When you arrive, stay in the town itself, for Dhū l-Qarnayn built it and prayed there. Its rivers flow with blessings, and there is an angel stationed at every gate, with a sword unsheathed to defend the people from evil until the Day of Resurrection."[125] Buraydah duly went to Merv and perished there, God show him mercy!

1.12.13 Whenever anyone wants to attack the Khurasanians, he accuses them of short-sighted parsimony. He slanders them, expressing sentiments similar to those of Ibn Thumāmah, who said: "In every country the rooster feeds his young from his beak, except in Merv, where roosters steal grain from the beaks of chickens."[126] This is a blatant lie, as anyone can see! Only a brazen-faced slanderer who could not care less about his own reputation would say something like this. The rooster of Merv is no different from any other rooster in the world, nor are the people of Khurasan any more miserly than anyone else—miserliness is after all simply a bad quality, and people with bad qualities are many times more numerous than people with *good qualities* . . . Among them there is no *shortage of* wise sages and brave men, *nor of* fools, cowards, misers . . . On this basis our world was founded, and through it the decree of our kind and knowing God operates.

1.12.14 The people of Iraq may base their opinion of the people of Khurasan on the Khurasanians they encounter on the hajj. In any given year, most of the people who perform the hajj are village folk and riffraff from rural districts. Petty-mindedness and poor manners are typical of this class of people. But Khurasan has produced exceptionally generous men who cannot in any way be rivaled, such as the Barmakids. I know of no one, free or slave, who—having obtained the power that they did—gave gifts as lavishly, offered patronage as generously, or filled coffers as much as they did. It is widely known that Khālid ibn Barmak built a palace for every single one of his brothers according to their rank, and that he set up an endowment for their children to support them in perpetuity. His brothers' children were all born to female slaves whom Khālid had personally given to them. And there is also Qaḥṭabah, and his descendants . . .[127] ʿAbd Allāh ibn al-Mubārak distributed his property to his brothers and let them enjoy the profits first. He would wear a robe worth a third of a dinar but sometimes give the keeper of the baths or his cupper a whole dinar.

By contrast, consider a nation that began mightily but ended in obliv- 1.13.1
ion, namely the Persians, whose military might in ancient times was unassailable and wealth unimaginable. They ruled supreme, acknowledged by kings in all provinces and regions, all of whom *sought* to make peace. The Arabs used to call them "free men" and "sons of free men" because it was they who took captives and employed servants but were never themselves taken captive or employed as servants. But then God sent Islam, and the Persian fire died, its ashes scattered to the wind. The Persians were completely torn to pieces and they lost their unity and their nerve.[128] Hardly any notables survived the coming of Islam, with the exception of Ibn al-Muqaffaʿ, al-Faḍl ibn Sahl, and his brother al-Ḥasan . . .

If someone objected, "Persia can be defended *by the statement of* 1.13.2
the Prophet (God *bless him*), 'If faith were hung from the Pleiades, the Persians would be able to reach it.'" We reply that this hadith refers to their eagerness to accept God's religion and their adherence to the customary practice of the Prophet (God bless and keep him). But the statement is tantamount to your saying, "If you were in the most remote part of the country, I would still visit you," where you mean, "I would endure hardships to reach you." . . . The words of Almighty God cannot be contradicted or overturned. If we diligently seek confirmation of this statement among the people of Persia, we find no evidence at all, be it at the beginning of Islam or more recently. As I have already noted, in the beginning the Persians were

the implacable enemies of the Muslims and fought against them until they were conquered, defeated ... and torn to pieces. There is no *gainsaying* those who are in such a situation. Furthermore, as far as I am aware, very few Persians acquired exceptional religious knowledge, whether in Hadith or jurisprudence, or for their exertions in acts of worship ... Among the people of Khurasan, *on the other hand, are those who accepted* Islam willingly and voluntarily ... right from the beginning and they have been the most committed and intensely devoted to God's religion among latter-day Muslims. They have among them accomplished and famous scholars of Hadith, scholars at the forefront of jurisprudence, and paragons of pious worship and devotion. In general, man's desire for virtue, knowledge, and culture tends to wane and decline, but among the Khurasanians it increases and is constantly renewed. Anyone *who considers the merits of the* collectors of hadiths will find this *to be true*, since anywhere you look you find at least one, *two*, or more Khurasanians among the scholars of Hadith. The remainder hail from the other provinces.

1.13.3 If someone were to object, "The Messenger of God (God bless him) attributed this virtue to the Persians, so how can you now apply it to the Khurasanians?" we would reply that for the Arabs, Persia and Khurasan were one and the same thing because they share a border and also a common language, namely Persian. The Arabs therefore refer to both peoples as "Persians." Similarly, according to those who do not use Arabic properly, the speakers of Arabic *include* the people of Yemen and the Hijaz ... *but also* they would judge *bordering land* as if *it* were *Arab*. The point I am making is supported by something Abū Bakr (God have mercy on him) *said* in a sermon in which he discussed death: "Which of your territories is 'Kharisah'? God will soon make you rulers of the whole territory, to its very farthest reaches."[129] Is it not obvious that this word "Kharisah" refers to Khurasan, given that the name "Khurasan" itself was so little-used and that when the Arabs referred to the East collectively they simply said "Persia"? Further proof for my argument is furnished by a hadith ʿUmar ibn Jīlān reported to me: "The whole world measures twenty-four thousand *farsakh*s in total. The kingdom of the Blacks is twelve thousand *farsakh*s, the kingdom of Byzantium eight thousand, the kingdom of Persia three thousand, and the land of the Arabs one thousand *farsakh*s." The Prophet mentioned Persia but did not mention Khurasan because Persia is larger than Khurasan and because by Persia he meant the entirety of the East. In similar fashion, he mentioned Byzantium but not the other countries on its borders because by Byzantium he meant all of them . . .

Someone reported, "I[130] heard the Prophet (God bless him) say, '*In the future they will impose* religion on you just as you imposed religion on them in the beginning.'"[131] If we look for corroboration of this among the Easterners, we find it in the people of Khurasan because it was they who went to war with the Arabs and the people of Syria. Outraged at what the Umayyads had done to the religion of God and at how they lived their lives, the Khurasanians stripped them of power and transferred the seat of power from Syria to Iraq. 1.13.4

Yazīd ibn Abī Ziyād relates, citing Ibrāhīm, who cited ʿAlqamah, who cited ʿAbd Allāh ibn Masʿūd, who reported that the Prophet (God bless him) said: "When I am gone, the People of My House[132] will suffer trials and exile until a people bearing black banners comes from the East. They will demand what is right, but will not be given it. So they will fight and be victorious. They will be given what they seek, but will only accept it when they can give the world to a man of my House. Then he will fill the world with justice, just as our enemies[133] filled it with injustice. If any of you are alive then, join them, even if you have to crawl through snow." I read in the Gospels, "*And I say to you, many* a people from the East *and West shall come and sit with Abraham, Isaac, and Jacob* in the Kingdom of Heaven" and "*but the children of the kingdom shall be cast out into darkness and* that there will be weeping and gnashing of teeth . . ."[134]

Our comments about Persia become even clearer when we remember that the Prophet (God bless him) sent Ḥanīs ibn ʿAbd Allāh ibn Ḥudhāfah al-Sahmī to Khosrow with a letter that opened 1.13.5

with the Prophet's name. When Khosrow read it, he tore it up in a rage and sent a clump of earth back to the Prophet. The Prophet (God bless him) said: "Just as he tore up my letter, so too his kingdom will be torn asunder; because he has sent me a clod of earth, you will wrest his lands from him." How can we celebrate the steadfastness in Islam of a people whom the Prophet described would be torn asunder? And in fact, no one can deny that the Persians have effectively disappeared.

1.13.6 Today the Persians are servile and obsequious, putting up with much injustice, suffering terrible humiliation, and paying more land tax than anyone. A group of Persian elders told me that they have never, ever known justice, and that even the reforms of ʿUmar ibn ʿAbd al-ʿAzīz,[135] while encompassing all lands, did not help them, since the governor that ʿUmar sent them died en route . . .[136] God showered blessings on the people of the Sawād and gave them nobility . . . and might through the Arabs. He improved their lot greatly—only a half-wit or a malicious ingrate would deny it. The Arabs conquered the Sawād by force. In cases involving conquest by force, the leader has a choice between killing and enslaving his opponents, between ransoming and freeing them. The Arabs made the best choice: they set their opponents free, spared their blood, and let them retain their property, bringing them under the protection of the Abbasid caliph and the Khurasanians in his retinue. The caliph appointed people from the Sawād to be his scribes, viziers, and companions, selecting them to preside over his affairs and making them his confidants. In this respect they fared better than those who had given up their lives and wealth to pave the way for the caliph. These people appointed by the caliph are famous, but there is no need to name or list in detail any of those who are unknown or forgotten. We would only antagonize the people of the Sawād, even though they are peaceable, and we would encourage them to emulate those who currently attack the Arabs. . . .[137]

1.14.1 I have heard that one of the Easterners *cites as evidence* the words of Almighty God: «Mankind! We have created you from a male and female, and made you into peoples and tribes, so that you might come to know each other. The noblest of you in God's sight is the most pious.»[138] And he offered the following explanation: "The term 'peoples' refers to the Easterners, and the term 'tribes' refers to the Arabs. God mentioned the 'peoples' first, and what is first is better than what is last."

I have seen the Proponents of Equality cite this verse as proof for their case, but I never thought an intelligent person would use it as a basis to claim superiority or to settle differences. The interpretation is mistaken on two counts. First, a thing may be mentioned first but this does not mean that it has priority in merit. Almighty God said: «Company of jinn and mankind!»[139] In this verse He put the jinn before mankind, though mankind is superior to the jinn. God also said: «Not the smallest particle on the earth or in heaven is hidden from your Lord.»[140] In this verse He put the earth first, though heaven is superior to it. There are many instances like this. We just need to look for them. Second, the Easterners have no more right to be called a "people" than the Arabs. Any group that grows in size and spreads throughout the lands turns into numerous "peoples." Ibn al-Kalbī quoted his father as saying: "A people is bigger than a tribe, and then come subtribes, clans, subclans, extended kin, and immediate kin.". . .[141] The Easterners can be referred to as "peoples" for the simple fact that the number of peoples who descended from them is more numerous than those who descended from the Arabs. These distinct groups came, accordingly, to be known as "peoples." 1.14.2

The Proponents of Equality include a group whose members have reached pious but mistaken conclusions. They cite the statement of Almighty God «The noblest of you in God's sight is the most pious»[142] as well as the statement of the Prophet (God bless and keep him) "God has taken away from you the arrogance of the Age of Ignorance with its boastful pride in ancestors. Now, there are only pious believers or unfortunate sinners." They also cite his statements "All the Children of Adam weigh equally in the scales;[143] superiority is based on piety alone" and "People are indistinguishable, 1.14.3

like the teeth of a comb" as well as "People are like a hundred unsaddled camels: you cannot tell them apart."

1.14.4 In fact, this group bases its judgment on the superficial meaning of these words but does not go into enough depth. They do not compare these statements with other ones in order to develop a proper understanding. If all people were equal, then no one would actually be superior to anyone else in this world—only in the world to come. This world would contain neither nobleman nor commoner, and no one *would be* superior or inferior. What then would be the meaning of the statement of the Prophet (God bless and keep him), "Respect the nobleman whoever he may be"? Or the meaning of his remark when some visitors identified their chief to him as Jadd ibn Qays, in spite of his stinginess, and he said: "Is there a disease worse than stinginess?" Similarly, the Prophet once described Qays ibn ʿĀṣim as "the chief of the nomads." And then he said: "The most auspicious of men will come through that pass" just before Jarīr ibn ʿAbd Allāh came through it. In the same vein, he once advised us: "Disregard the errors of prominent men."

The Arabs have a saying: "People flourish so long as they are dissimilar, but when they are all equal they quarrel." What they mean is that people prosper so long as there are noblemen and elites. When no one is distinguished, they quarrel. On this topic, a poet has said:

> They're all equal, like the teeth of a donkey:
> the white-haired man is no better than the callow youth![144]

1.14.5 Muṭarrif said: "There are three kinds of people: humans, half-humans, and those who are barely human-like."[145] It's said: "Four qualities make the slave a master: manners, self-restraint, truthfulness, and loyalty."

ʿUmar ibn al-Khaṭṭāb once saw a crowd following a man arrested on suspicion of a crime and exclaimed, "Now there's a bad lot: people who only show up when there's trouble."

1.14.6 No one who studies human behavior and capabilities will find two men equal in physical constitution, character, or action—how could they be when an individual's limbs and joints are not actually equal? One part is superior to the other. The head, for example, is superior to the rest of the body because it contains the intellect and the five senses. The heart is superior to the other internal organs because it contains knowledge and understanding. Wise men have a saying: . . .[146] They compare the heart to a king. Similarly, the right hand is superior to the left, and the thumb to the little finger. As you know, people wear silk on their head, cotton on their body, and leather on their feet. It would make no sense to change this and wear cotton on your head or silk on your body or feet. . . .[147]

A man called on ʿIsā ibn Mūsā when Ibn Shubrumah was present. ʿIsā ibn Mūsā asked Ibn Shubrumah: "Do you know this man?" Ibn Shubrumah replied: "Yes, indeed, he is a man with a household, stature, and standing." But in fact Ibn Shubrumah did not know him at all. What he meant by "a household" was simply the house where he lived; by "stature," simply that he had an upper body; and by "standing," the feet on which he walked.[148] Similarly, one says "heads" and, for inferior people, the "the lowly," based on a comparison with the lower parts of a camel, that is, its legs.

To provide the proper interpretation of the hadiths cited earlier:[149] the Prophet (God bless him) was sent at a time when mankind was preoccupied with tribal factionalism and clan partisanship. Favor was shown to men who could boast of past noble deeds and withheld from those reviled for past ignoble deeds. Blood payment would be assessed according to the worth of a man's family, which meant that a sum for one man might amount to what would ordinarily be paid for two; or a sum ordinarily paid for two men might be paid for just one, or many men might be killed in reprisal for a single man's death. The two parties might disagree but reach an agreement that . . .[150] I cite al-Sijistānī, who cited al-Aṣmaʿī, who had it from . . . ibn Ḥayyān, who cited Hishām ibn ʿUqbah, the brother of Dhū l-Rummah . . . who said: "I saw[151] al-Aḥnaf visit the leaders of a people engaged in a blood feud. When they had spoken, he said: 'Go ahead, decide among yourselves.' They said: 'Two blood 1.14.7

payments are due.' Al-Aḥnaf said: 'Agreed.' But, when they had quieted down, he said: 'But be careful what you wish for. Let me tell you something. God (blessed and exalted) imposed one blood payment, and indeed, the Arabs exchange one blood payment among themselves. Today you are the ones seeking restitution, but what if tomorrow you are the ones who must make restitution, and your opponent is only satisfied with the course of action you insisted on for yourselves? Think it over.' 'God has told us to ask for one payment only,' they answered. Relieved, al-Aḥnaf praised God, got up and rode off." (The narrator added: "I saw at that moment his cloak rise up over his shirt, and his shirt rise up over his waist-wrap.")[152]

The Messenger of God (God bless him) taught them that when it comes to religion and its rules, no one is superior to anyone else by reason of nobility, power, or clan might. The Prophet said: "Every memorable achievement from the pre-Islamic era now lies at my feet. The one who takes a life will lose his life; the one who steals will lose his hand; the one who engages in illicit sex will receive divinely mandated punishment; and the one who gouges out another's eye will have his own gouged out. . . .[153] We depend on God for our reward . . . and ask his pardon."

1.14.8 Consider the following words of the Prophet (God bless him): "It follows that if you are wealthy, you will be reputable; if you have a good character, you will display proper conduct; and if you fear God, you will have right religion." And also the statement of ʿUmar ibn al-Khaṭṭāb: "Wealth is a man's good repute, religion his nobility, and proper conduct his character." Good repute, as I have already informed you, comes from the accomplishments of one's forefathers. Now, a man's ancestors might lack nobility, but he himself may be wealthy, so he can do good deeds and observe his religious obligations. His name will be on everyone's tongue, as they sing his praises in gratitude. In this case, wealth stands in for repute, and he becomes reputable, because good deeds are what he intends. As the poet said:

Wealth makes a fool of reputable folk
and elevates a man not born a chief.[154]

Al-Riyāshī declaimed:

He was irate, knowing that wealth granted him
what religion and moral character did not.[155]

... The most magnanimous man is the one who ... says "God grant me praise and glory, but let it be praise for what I do and glory for what I give." A man might be rich, and treated with respect even if he has not given away any of his wealth. People might come to him even though he does not visit them. This is why someone said: "I wish I had So-and-So's gold to put to no use." Al-Hudhalī said: 1.14.9

I see great companies of men, showered with praise,
sated, their faces bloated and ugly,
While men of little means lie prostrate before them,
lacking even watered-down milk to drink.[156]

From another poet, we have this line:

They are a people who revere you when you come into money.
Money makes anyone look good.[157]

A man might be a great sinner, and in grave error, but all will be forgiven because of his prosperity. In a similar vein, it is said: "Wealth is a forgiving lord." Along the same lines, you have: "Proper conduct is what constitutes a man's character because proper conduct is the avoidance of repulsive or evil actions." Muʿāwiyah said to ʿAmr ibn al-ʿĀṣ: "What is the most pleasant thing?" ʿAmr said: "Order the young men of Quraysh to stand up." When they did, he said: "Making others neglect proper conduct ..."[158] They are grateful for it and go out of their way to make excuses for it, dissuading others from speaking ill of it. Let us suppose that he is someone with bad morals. In this case, they accuse him of crimes that he has not committed, invent lies about him, and use anything against 1.14.10

him. Here, too, conduct constitutes a man's character, because it replaces it, just as wealth replaces good repute.

1.15.1 Among the Arabs, there is a group whose own bigotry matches the Bigots' immoderation, as they claim that they are the lords and masters of the Easterners simply because God gave them the Prophet (God bless and keep him) as their guide and freed their necks from the chains of unbelief and from the torments of Hell. These Arabs develop this into an analogy between the bondage caused by unbelief and the bondage caused by captivity. But this analogy will only apply to the Arabs in the case of peoples whom they were obliged either to enslave or to kill but whom they graciously allowed to live. In other words, it is an analogy based on bondage through ownership. In the case, however, of those who were happy to enter Islam and were quick to obey, the only favor and patronage relationship that obtain are those due to Almighty God, since it was He who gave them guidance, and, after God, to the Messenger of God (God bless him) . . .[159] We cannot think of any Companion of God's Messenger (God bless him) who said: "I am a client of the Prophet (God bless him)." Salmān would say, "I am Salmān, the son of Islam," not "the client of the Prophet (God bless him)." Abū Bakrah did say, "I am the client of God's Emissary (God bless and keep him)," because when the Prophet (God bless him) besieged the people of al-Ṭā'if, he said: "Any slave who comes to me shall be free." Subsequently Abū Bakrah lowered himself over the wall with a pulley and was freed. Zayd ibn Akhzam informed me, citing Salm ibn Qutaybah, who cited Abū l-Minhāl, who said . . . he heard . . . ʿAbd al-ʿAzīz ibn Abī Bakrah quote his father, Abū Bakrah, as saying: "When the Prophet (God bless him) besieged al-Ṭā'if, I let myself down with a pulley. He—that is, the Prophet (God bless him)—asked: 'How did you manage to escape?' I answered: 'I let myself down with a pulley.' He replied: 'Then you shall be known as the man of the pulley.'"[160] A slave freed by a group belongs to them and becomes one of them, according to a rule given by the Messenger of God (God bless and keep him).

Al-ʿUtbī cited his father, citing Abū Khālid, who quoted his father as saying: "My dear son! I leave to you as my legacy what your lord bequeathed to me. I was a slave to ʿAmr ibn ʿUtbah, who made me go to school to learn to write. When I began doing well there and had acquired an education *he called out to me* 'Abū Yazid!' I turned to my right *and he said,* '*You are now a client!* I am talking about you,' he said. 'We are kinsmen *and we call* our clients by their names. Not so long ago you belonged to me, but now you're one of us. It's by God's law, not by some accident of birth, that you become a person's kin. Look: if a man has an illegitimate daughter, he doesn't count her children as his descendants, does he? So if a man's son counts as his son because God's law says so, a client counts as his kinsman because the Prophet said so. God's law has blessed you, so guard that blessing by thanking Him for it!'" 1.15.2

What a good comparison ʿAmr ibn ʿUtbah makes—that the relationship of a manumitter to his client takes precedence over any relationship to him as a cherished slave! Clients are obliged to aid and defend a manumitter, and to show him preference with gifts and charity over neighbors or wayfarers—even though clients lack the parity of birth required for a marital relationship and are not alike in nobility, because parity entails equality and proportionality. A man who receives a favor is not equal to a man who grants one, a benefactor is not equal to the person who receives the benefaction, and the upper hand is not equal to the *lower hand, so* to take a wife from among his freed slaves *disobeys the ruling of God's Emissary* (God bless and keep him) and contradicts the spirit of parity . . . Were it possible for him to marry into them, they would inherit from him, whereas he would not inherit from them, and likewise they could act as his agent for marriage contracts, but he could not act as theirs. Nothing could make a marriage contract more suspect than these two circumstances, because God (glorious and mighty) has legislated against him . . . He is not worthy to marry her, and because God has legislated against him inheriting from her, it is only appropriate that he not have sexual intercourse with her or become 1.15.3

related by marriage to those who receive his benefaction. Marriage is one of the two types of genealogical relations. God (mighty and glorious) said: «It is He who has created human beings from water, and He has granted them the ties of blood as well as those of marriage. Your Lord is all-powerful.»[161] The phrase "genealogical relations" is used for blood relationships, whereas the phrase "ties of marriage" refers to marriage relationships.

1.16.1 This is the end of the first part. All praise is due to God, the Lord of the Universe. God bless His Messenger, Muḥammad, and his pure progeny. The second part follows.

Book Two: The Excellence of Arab Learning

In the name of God,
the Merciful and Compassionate

We have spoken about nobility in terms that God would not regard as improper since we have kept within the extent of our knowledge and the limits of our ability. Those who desire God and search for the truth find our method is salutary and effective. But those who exceed their bounds, transgress their limits, wrong their opponents, and make inappropriate claims simply cheat themselves, overreach their intelligence, and anger their Lord. But God does not permit their obfuscation to affect either the truth itself or its advocates: the signs of the truth are never effaced, nor is its fire ever extinguished. Falsehood leads to poverty, oblivion, and insignificance, especially since our book has broken the seal, lifted the veil, shown the truth, and discarded the dross. If anyone has an allegation to make, let him present it, or if he has a case, let him adduce it cogently: we will examine his claims and respond if he is wrong, or concede if he is right. In any event, we do not claim exhaustive coverage of a subject just for the sake of asserting full mastery over it, nor do we claim to be unerringly apposite in everything we say. Rather, we rely on hope; our intention is sincere and the truth is our goal. God always bestows protection and success on good intentions and honesty. 2.1.1

We will now discuss the Arabs' stake in different areas of knowledge and the wise sayings in their poetry and rhymed prose. We will not provide exhaustive coverage of any one subject, nor will we go into comprehensive detail, as our goal in this book is to raise awareness of, and offer evidence for, the Arabs' knowledge, and to rebut the arguments of those who call the Arabs boorish and stupid. 2.1.2

2.1.3 There are two kinds of knowledge. One is Islamic, a product of the Muslim religion and the Arabic language. It includes jurisprudence, grammar, and the study of poetic themes. These fields are particular to the Arabs. Non-Arabs can master them only by learning and parroting; the Arabs alone possess the brilliance and glory of having developed them. The other is age-old knowledge common to all peoples. God has granted the Arabs a share of every field of which I am aware, and in some they alone came to possess unrivaled knowledge.

Horse Husbandry

Horse husbandry is one of the areas in which the Arabs developed unique knowledge. One finds that the Greeks, Persians, Indians, and Romans possess only a smattering of this art, barely worthy of note or consideration. The Arabs, for their part, have familiar vernacular names for each particular part of the horse, from the tip of the forelock to the tail, from the withers to the pastern. With innate perspicacity, the Arabs know the horse's qualities and characteristics and can discern those horses that meet the highest standard and those that fall short. They can also tell a purebred charger from a half-breed grade,[162] whether bareback, wearing a cover, or galloping. They can tell from its gallop, too, whether a horse has been trained under a special regime or not.[163] 2.2.1

Al-Sijistānī informed me, citing Abū ʿUbaydah Maʿmar ibn al-Muthannā, who had the Arabs as his authority, that they discern the pedigree of a horse from the thinness of its lips and its muzzle; from the width of its nostrils; from the lack of flesh beneath its eyes and the protrusion of the bones on each side of its face; from the slenderness of its loins and of the hair that sticks up above its ears; from the slenderness of its poll and crest; from the softness of its hair; from the fineness of the hair around its knees, fetlocks, and hooves; or from the suppleness of the hair on its forelock and at the base of its mane, which is, in fact, the clearest sign. 2.2.2

2.2.3 The Arabs would say: "A horse has become a truly fine steed if it is spirited and if it has a broad nose, long neck, robust withers where the saddle is fitted, a sturdy underbelly, long jaws, imposing forearms, taut veins in its legs, bulging joints, and strong and hard hooves."

2.2.4 The Arabs would say: "When a horse's nose is broad and does not *allow through much*[164] breath, then it is not strong . . ."[165]

And they would say: "Every trait desirable in a mare is desirable in a stallion too, with the exceptions that mares tend to stand for long periods, they seldom lie prone on their bellies, and their palates are lean." As the Arabs used to say: "A stallion likes to sleep; a mare stands tranquilly without stirring to eat."

2.2.5 An Arab said that the finest horse is one you would call "bolting" when you face it from the front, "blazing" when you face it from the back, and "bellowing" when you face it from the side.[166] And he said that the most serviceable nag is the one that is led by his eyes and whose whip is the bridle.

Uqayṣir[167] said that the finest horse is the one you describe as "rearing back" when you face it from the front, "lying on its chest" when you face it from behind, "level" when you face it from the side, "pounding the earth" when it walks, and "scattering pebbles" when it gallops. In this vein, a poet once said:

Seen from the front,
it's as if he's a hawk held back, though it's seen its prey;
Seen from the back,
he's driven by a stomping leg with popping tendon;
And from the side,
he's like a charger—you'd say he's a wolf prowling the thicket.[168]

2.2.6 Isḥāq ibn Rāhawayh informed us that when the fighting had come to an end, ʿAmr ibn al-ʿĀṣ composed the following verses:[169]

War broke out, so I readied for it
a high-shouldered, broad-flanked steed.

Of colossal chest, bulging a-midsection,
when you drive it to gallop
It flies into full speed.
When the cavalry slackens, it hastens.

Ibn al-Aʿrābī said that a tribesman of the Asad was asked about purebred horses and sluggish grades. He said: "The purebred war-horse is strapping like an onager, taut as a leather strap. When it runs, it streaks into the charge; when it's tethered, it stretches out across the ground;[170] and when it draws itself up, it looms tall. For its part, the sluggish grade does not have prominent haunches; it has a thick muzzle and a coarse neck, and it needs loud exhorting in a race. When you cut it loose, it says 'rein me in'; while when you rein it in, it says 'set me loose.'" 2.2.7

Muslim ibn ʿAmr advised one of his cousins who was buying a horse for him: "Consider all the qualities you find desirable in a dog and look for them in a horse." 2.2.8

I was told by ʿAbd al-Raḥmān, who cited al-Aṣmaʿī on the authority of Abū ʿAmr ibn al-ʿAlāʾ, who said that ʿUmar ibn al-Khaṭṭāb—God show him mercy—was not sure whether certain horses were purebred or grade. So he summoned Salmān ibn Rabīʿah al-Bāhilī, who brought a basin of water (or a shield with water in it). It was placed on the ground and the horses were led to the water one by one. The ones that turned the tips of their hooves to drink were declared half-breeds, whereas those that drank without turning their hooves he confirmed to be true Arabians. This is because the necks of grade horses are a little short, so they cannot drink water directly without bending their hooves, whereas purebred horses have long necks. 2.2.9

Abū Ḥātim recited a poem that he had heard from Abū ʿUbaydah to me. Abū ʿUbaydah had told Abū Ḥātim: "I do not know the poet's name and its prosody is imperfect," but Abū Ḥātim informed me that the poem was by ʿAbd al-Ghaffār al-Khuzāʿī:[171] 2.2.10

He frightened the wild oryx with a smooth-cheeked,
broad-breasted, full-chested steed,
With imposing "five longs," compact "four shorts,"[172]
and ample "six-broads": towering legs, solid and firm.
Its "sevens" chiseled and "nines" stripped:[173]
it is truly a sight to behold.
Its "nine clothed parts" are fully formed;
its chest and nostrils expansive.
Its "ten longs" are far apart, its "ten shorts" close together.
The "five talls" tower high.[174]
We nourish it with pure milk, even before our sons.
It has plentiful fodder imported from town.[175]
We water it—by morning or by night—
with the milk of she-camels,[176]
Till in winter it's plump:
they say we starve ourselves for it.
A sturdy physique, an expansive chest, built for speed,
a wide-paced gallop when raced.
With brawny legs and muscular build,
a taut barrel and croup.
Its "fives" sleek, its "fours" strapping,
bulky where the saddle sits, but with fine-haired fetlock.

2.2.11 The above poem summarizes for you the physiognomy of horses. I have explicated the meanings of this poem in my book about the constitution of horses. What the Arabs have said about horses is plentiful. Should you wish to learn more, you will find it, God willing, fully detailed in my aforementioned book or in my book about the education of secretaries.[177]

Stars

Another science about which the Arabs possess unique knowledge is the study of the appearances of stars, their names, their seasonal timing, their ascent and descent, the means to navigate by them . . .[178] 2.3.1

> She leaned toward him in longing, and he was encircled
> just as the night stars circumambulate the pole.[179]

(This is because the stars revolve around the pole.)

Kuthayyir said: 2.3.2

> Forget Suʿdā! Suʿdā only approaches al-Nawā
> at the conjunction of the Pleiades, and then sets.

Kuthayyir meant that the Pleiades coincides with the new moon on only one night each year, and then sets. Likewise, he could only meet Suʿdā once in the year. Only the people most knowledgeable about astral appearances and the keenest surveyors of the stars could know this.[180]

Another poet[181] said: 2.3.3

> When the moon and the Pleiades conjoin
> on the moon's fifth night, then winter has passed.

The Pleiades coincides with the moon on the fifth night of the month twice a year, once when the cold season and the fruitful season are over, and a second time when the hot weather has passed. As another poet said:

When the moon and the Pleiades conjoin
on the fifth night, then summertime's over.

2.3.4 Al-Akhṭal composed the verse:

When Capella and the Pleiades rise
animals conceal themselves[182] between Pisces and
Scorpionis.[183]

Capella and the Pleiades rise together during the most intensely hot part of the year. When these two constellations rise at dawn, then Pisces will rise at night. Hence the poet is saying that when the heat becomes intense, we travel at night.

2.3.5 Ḥātim once said:

Many's the woman who briskly censured me by night
once the Pleiades's Capella had inclined and set.

Ḥātim conjoined Capella with the Pleiades because it rises when they do—Capella is not part of the constellation of the Pleiades.[184]

2.3.6 Al-Akhṭal once mentioned the Sulaym, saying:

They shall not claim a lineage to Farrāṣ
until the moon appears with Ursa Minor.

Ursa Minor is the star by which the direction of prayer is determined. It is not within one of the moon's mansions since it lies behind Ursa Minor near the pole, and hence the moon can never link with it.

2.3.7 Regarding traveling by the stars, Dhū l-Rummah once said:

So I said: Take the light of Ursa Minor's stars on the right
and the plunge of al-Nasr on your left.

2.3.8 Another poet[185] composed the following verse about the stars and omens:

Today travel by Scorpionis
it's equally a good or a bad omen for you.

He meant: Travel at the time of the descent of the Heart of Scorpio, which is a bad omen.

Al-Aswad ibn Yaʿfur said: 2.3.9

You were born under Ḥādī l-Najm, driving its consort along,[186]
and under the Heart, the flaming Scorpio.

Ḥādī l-Najm refers to Aldebaran, which is also a bad omen.

Another poet said: 2.3.10

On the morning he set out for the king, seeking bounty,
he chanced upon a star that was like Aldebaran.[187]

And another said: 2.3.11

Saʿd came at the appointed time, evil in tow,
His armies mustered by his heat.

The poet meant the star Saʿd of the Tents, and by "the armies," he meant insects and vermin. The star rises just before the warm weather begins,[188] and the vermin that have been in hiding come out and scatter, sensing the onset of spring. This is why it is called "Saʿd of the Tents."[189]

As further evidence of their abundant knowledge, the Arabs also have rhyming sayings about stars, such as "When Canopus is ascending, the night starts chilling, floods are threatening, and young camels are starving; with the rise of the Pleiades, shun meat and beware of disease."[190] (The Pleiades rises on the night of May 13.)[191] 2.3.12

The Arabs are also the most skilled at identifying clouds correctly and discerning which are rain-bearing and which not. They say: "Show me a wispy streaky cloud, and I'll show you a rain cloud" and "If you see a sky like the belly of a white she-ass that means abundant rain." 2.3.13

After Muʿaqqir al-Bāriqī went blind, he once asked his daughter, "My dear little girl, describe the clouds to me." She replied, "I see a great black one, pregnant like the camel's amniotic sac, with tendrils reaching to the ground and moving very limply." He then said, "My dear little girl, carry me to a place where the *quflah* tree grows." That tree only grows in uplands safe from the floods.

There is a prophetic hadith that goes "If a cloud forms from the sea and then heads north, there will be a torrential downpour like an abundant spring."[192] And the Arabs say: "When clouds bring rain from the direction of Mecca, the Arabs call this 'Rain from the Source.'" They say "the Source" is a byword for the direction of Mecca from the perspective of Iraq. "The Source" is also a term for rain that continues for days.

2.3.14 Of all people, the Arabs are also the most knowledgeable about the winds. They know the sources from which winds blow, which clouds are rain-bearing and which ones are barren. They know about the varieties of lightning—those that signal rain and those that do not. Sometimes the Arabs used lightning bolts alone to guide their migrations, not sending out any scouts, so confident were they in their knowledge. They would also praise rain that came on the last night of the month, and in the last part of that night.

2.3.15 Al-Riyāshī informed me: "I asked a Bedouin about the following verse of al-Rāʿī:

> The star announcing rain came on the last night of the month;
> the best stars appear on the last night.

"And the Bedouin explained: 'One year we had rain on the penultimate day of the month, and the land turned to expansive pasture.'" (Al-Riyāshī cites al-Aṣmaʿī's explanation: "He built a house and expanded it," where a similar word is used to mean "expanded.")

2.3.16 The Arabs also praised rain that fell on the first night of the month. Al-Kumayt said:

Storm clouds bedecked with flashing lightning
on the first morn of the new moon.

The only thing they praised about the end of the month was rain. Jirān al-ʿAwd[193] composed the line: 2.3.17

They brought her to me a night before month's end;
that whole month was a waning moon.

. . . In the Holy Qur'an, God says that He released «a howling wind against them on the day of disaster.»[194] The Arabs took a red sky and red and yellow clouds as signs of a drought. The poet Umayyah described this: 2.3.18

Woe to my people
when the rain dries up and everything turns blood red,
And the sun rises turbaned in cloud,
rainless wisps of clouds like dyer's woad.

The Arabs knew they could be sure of rain if they saw the type of lightning known as "double-flash"—lighting with a consecutive double flash. Ṣakhr al-Ghayy said: 2.3.19

After the dispersal, from Shammāʾ's direction
all night I imagined I saw lightning flashing twain.

The Arabs could infer from the slow movement of a cloud that it held much water. ʿAdī ibn Zayd once said: 2.3.20

A bank of drooping rain clouds after the stillness of night
urged by the north wind like a broken-legged camel.

The north wind drives the cloud along, but it moves slowly because it is so weighed down with water, and thus travels like a camel with a broken leg.

The Arabs thought that a white or reddish-white cloud would not bring rain. Describing clouds, the poet al-Nābighah said: 2.3.21

Red-hued clouds hit the side of Mount al-Tīn
one after another with only scant, cold drizzle.[195]

2.3.22 ... A man recovered and returned to his people. They began asking him about his recovery, but he would not tell them. So they approached ʿAbd Allāh ibn Masʿūd, and he sent for the man and told him: "Inform them, as there is no obligation of silence upon you."[196]

Somatomancy

The Arabs' expertise also includes somatomancy (divining using the human form) and anthroposcopy (divining by physical appearance). Many mistakenly believe that the Arabs have no proficiency in these fields, though they actually have the greatest share of it. A poet said,[197] 2.4.1

Don't ask a man about his character,
the evidence is in his face.

Another poet said, describing the Messenger of God (God bless and keep him): 2.4.2

Even without clear proofs of prophethood,
the first glance would tell you immediately.

Al-Kumayt described Mukhallad ibn Yazīd ibn al-Muhallab as follows: 2.4.3

When you were but an infant,
eyes and ears focused on you.
In the cradle they saw in you
penetrating intellect.

Bukayr ibn al-Akhnas saw al-Muhallab when he was a boy and said: 2.4.4

Take my word for it! He'll lead their chiefs,
and will be of peerless brilliance.

And it was as he predicted.

2.4.5 A man once looked at Muʿāwiyah when he was young and said: "I think this child will lead his clan," and Hind replied, "If that's all he'll ever lead, then may he perish!" [198]

On the authority of al-Aṣmaʿī, who cites Jamīʿ, who had it from Abū Ghāḍir (an aged Bedouin, and one of the matrilineal descendants of al-Zibriqān ibn Badr), ʿAbd al-Raḥmān said: "Al-Zibriqān used to say that among his young boys the one he hated the most was the 'little pigeon-breasted male' who looked as if he was peering out of his hole, and when asked 'Where is your father?' would reply: 'With you.'" [199]

A Bedouin was asked, "How can you tell which of your children will become leaders?" and he replied, "We have no doubt that the one with a pure white mien and a long foreskin, who's bulky about the waist and a little foolish, will lead."

A Bedouin was once asked, "Which child is most likely to be a leader?" and he replied, "The one who is foolish and has a long neck and wide jaws—count on him to be the next leader."

Muʿāwiyah said: "There are three signs of leadership: baldness, an ample belly, and avoidance of envy."

Al-Riyāshī recited the following poem to me:

Saʿīd the noble Saʿīd—
Is bald, and exalted by his bald ancestors.

2.4.6 Al-Sijistānī heard al-Aṣmaʿī report that Mūsā ibn Saʿīd al-Jumaḥī heard Abū Muṣʿab al-Zubayrī report as follows: ʿUthmān ibn Muḥammad ibn Ibrāhīm ibn Ḥāṭib al-Jumaḥī, an esteemed and learned man, told me: "A Qurayshī youth came to me asking for advice about a woman he was marrying. I asked him: 'Brother, is her lineage short or long?' He looked as if he did not understand, so I said, 'Son, I can tell from people's eyes if they have understood or not: if they have understood, the eyes contract, if not, they bulge, and if they are somewhere in between, then their eyes are tranquil'" (that is, still).

Physiognomancy

Physiognomancy is another field of the Arabs' knowledge. I do not know whether they are unique in this discipline, or if other peoples know it as well. It is similar to somatomancy in that it involves discerning patterns and understanding signs in children and relatives. 2.5.1

Physiognomancers come from the Mudlij. Al-Aṣmaʿī informs us that two men brought a dispute to ʿUmar about a boy they both claimed as theirs. ʿUmar questioned the mother, who said, "One of them had intercourse with me, and then I bled. Then the other had intercourse with me." So ʿUmar summoned two physiognomancers and put the question to one of them, who asked, "Shall I pronounce in public, or in private?" "Privately," responded ʿUmar. When the physiognomancer reported that they both shared in the child, ʿUmar beat him to the ground. Then he asked the second physiognomancer, who gave the same response. So ʿUmar said, "I didn't think that this could be the case, though I do know that several dogs can copulate with a bitch and she can give each of them a pup of their own." 2.5.2

Abū Ḥātim reported to me that he heard al-Aṣmaʿī report that a man of the Abū Masrūḥ heard ʿAwsajah ibn Mughīth the Physiognomancer say, "Our dates were being stolen, but we identified the thieves' tracks; they rode donkeys, but we discerned the marks of their hands in the date trees." "Marks" means "traces." 2.5.3

Abū Ḥātim reported to me that he heard al-Aṣmaʿī report that a man of the Abū Masrūḥ heard Ibn Abī Ṭarafah al-Hudhalī say: 2.5.4

"Two physiognomancers saw a camel's tracks when they were leaving ʿArafah a day or two after the pilgrims. One said that it was a she-camel, the other that it was male. They followed it, and sometimes made out complete hoofprints, and at other times its gait. When they eventually entered one of the mountain passes at Minā, they found the camel. They inspected it, and lo and behold, it was a hermaphrodite!"

2.5.5 The lore about physiognomancers also tells of one who was said to have been able to differentiate between the tracks of female and male ants on stony ground.

2.5.6 Al-Aʿshā said:

Look at my palm and its secrets:
can your threats do me any harm?

2.5.7 They would say that a narrow palm was a sign of miserliness, as al-Akhṭal said:

They hung one of the Calumniator's[200] tiny hands:
killing him was no big thing for them.

Ibn al-Aʿrābī said that they accused the "Calumniator" of miserliness. The smallness of the palm of his hand indicated that.

2.5.8 Surāqah ibn Mālik ibn Juʿshum al-Mudlajī was a physiognomancer who, on account of his expertise in following footprints, was sent by the Quraysh to track the Messenger of God (God bless and keep him) and Abū Bakr as they escaped on their Emigration to Medina.

Mujazzaz was another physiognomancer. Muḥammad ibn ʿUbayd reported to me that Abū ʿUyaynah heard al-Zuhrī report that ʿUrwah said: ʿĀʾishah said that Mujazzaz was given an audience with the Messenger of God (God bless and keep him). He saw Zayd ibn Ḥārithah and Usāmah asleep on a mat. They had covered their faces, but their feet were showing, and Mujazzaz said: "These feet are related!" This pleased the Messenger of God (God bless him).[201]

Augury, Lithomancy, Geomancy, and Soothsaying

The Arab sciences of the pre-Islamic era also included augury, geomancy, lithomancy, and soothsaying. 2.6.1

Augury is divination from birds by interpreting their names, the places they alight, their flight patterns, and the sounds they make.

A poet has said:[202] 2.6.2

> Two birds sang of Salmā's departure
> on the branches of the desert poplar and moringa.
> Moringa means dear Salmā's gone,
> desert poplar means she's departed, and is no longer close.

They would divine absence from the desert poplar, and departure from the moringa.[203]

Al-Kumayt said to the Judhām when they left for Yemen: 2.6.3

> Your name is a sign of your departure
> should an augur read the birds.

Al-Kumayt is referring to their name, Judhām, from which separation can be divined.[204] From the crow they divined absence, and they would call it "the necessitator" because they thought that crows signaled inevitable departure.[205]

Most augurs were members of the Asad. Abū Ḥātim informed me that al-Aṣmaʿī heard Saʿd ibn Naṣr report that a band of jinn were once discussing the augury practiced by the Asad. Wanting 2.6.4

to see it for themselves, the jinn visited the Asad and claimed, "One of our she-camels has gone missing, might you send an augur with us?" "Go with them!" the Asad told one of their youngsters. A jinn sat the boy on the back of his camel, and they set out. When they came across an eagle that had a broken wing, the boy broke out in goosebumps and started to cry. "What's wrong with you?" the jinn asked. "It broke one wing and raised the other," the boy replied. "I swear truly by God! You're not human and you're not looking for she-camels."

Geomancy

2.6.5 Geomancy is divination from lines drawn in the sand. Abū Ḥātim informed me that Abū Zayd al-Anṣārī said that he drew two lines in the sand and named the two lines "Sons of ʿIyān." And when he performed geomancy he would say, "Sons of ʿIyān, show the truth, and quickly!" Al-Rāʿī once described a gaming arrow:[206]

> A lucky arrow, worn yellow, when its owner goes out to play
> the Sons of ʿIyān come back with the fresh grilled meat.

The poet means that the owner of the arrow knows that when he plays with it, he will certainly come out as the winner and get the grilled meat. Hence the man's departure with this lucky arrow in hand is itself a sign that the grilled meat is coming.

Ḥalīs the Geomancer was one such diviner. Al-Thawrī is said to have posed some questions to him and others, and Ḥalīs told him everything that he knew. Al-Thawrī said: "This made it easy for me to understand the hadith narrated by Abū Hurayrah from the Prophet (God bless him): 'One of the Prophets practiced geomancy.'" Ibn ʿAbbās said that the phrase «or some vestige of divine knowledge» in the Qur'an[207] refers to geomancy.

Lithomancy

2.6.6 Lithomancy is divination by scattering stones on the ground and interpreting the pattern of their falling, grouping, and dispersal, and the various shapes they make. Lithomancy (*ṭarq*) is akin to what the barley sower used to do: he was called a *ṭāriq* because whenever he would scatter barley, he would hit the earth with it—the word *ṭarq* means "hitting." For example, one can say, "I hit the wool" if one beats it with a carding stick. The stick of an upholsterer is called a *miṭrāq*, and the bar of the blacksmith is called a *miṭraqah*. The poet said:[208]

> I swear that the women who hit the ground with pebbles
> and augur from birds know not what God will do.

Soothsaying

I reason that soothsayers have jinn as companions. Yazīd ibn ʿAmr informed me, citing Muḥammad ibn Ṣāliḥ al-Ḍabbī, citing al-Qāsim ibn ʿUrwah, citing ʿĪsā ibn Yazīd ibn Bakr al-Laythī, that soothsaying was once mentioned in the presence of the Messenger of God (God bless him), and Zabbān al-ʿAdawī said, "I swear, Messenger of God, that I have seen it yield some wondrous things." 2.6.7

"What were they?"

"My mother Unaysah gave birth to five boys, and I was the eldest. Once, I went on a journey and left them together, and when I returned, I saw that they had rambled off to the south and descended the mountain. I followed their tracks until I came across a man of the Nahd. Then a young girl of his appeared leading her sheep. She was just over five hands tall, and had a large leather milking pail around her neck. When the man saw her, he said, 'Greetings, my dear little girl, be well and safe!'

"She said, 'I was as you say, and the same for you, may you always be under a good rain cloud where plants glisten with dew.'

"He said, 'Tell me, my dear, how did you fare after we left, and how did we fare after you left?'

"And she said, 'I pastured my flock and they ate their fill; I watered them and they were quenched. As for you, well, your guest's wife gave birth to a son she named ʿIṣām, and four young men with a split-snouted she-camel have stopped among you. They napped in the morning, and as noontime shone upon them, they set off to water the camels in a little vale.[209] They will arrive in the dark, sip from its water, return worn out, and they will all die.' Then she tossed down her milk pail, clapped her hands and said: 'The game's ruined: this'—meaning me—'is their brother, by the Lord of the Kaaba!'

"The man asked: 'Do you see any hope for them?'

"'Yes, if he leaves in the late afternoon, and reaches them by sundown as they go to water before the wind puffs and the wormwood spreads its perfume, the water will be good and the return safe.'

"I took off. When I thought my camel was slowing, I drove her on at a frantic pace. When I found them they had already drunk, and were all dead."

The Messenger of God (God bless him) marveled at this.

2.6.8 These are ancient sciences from the pre-Islamic era. Demons would eavesdrop on God and reveal knowledge to their human masters, but God put a stop to this with Islam: the skies were guarded by the stars. These sciences do not unlock the secrets of the unseen known exclusively to God. We should accordingly reject them, just as we reject the astromancers' claim to know what is fated by studying the stars.

Oratory

Of all peoples, the Arabs are the most eloquent extempore orators: they have the most mellifluous tongues, they are models of clarity of expression, and they speak with the most pithy concision when required. 2.7.1

When the people of Merv withheld water from Abū Ghassān and poured it out in the desert, Abū Ghassān wrote to them: "To the assholes of Merv: Provide me water tonight, or my cavalry will be on you at daybreak." They supplied them with water before the first third of the night. Abū l-Haydhām said: 2.7.2

> Seek protection in candor, not bluster.

Abū Ḥātim informed me that he heard al-Aṣmaʿī report that Khalaf al-Aḥmar said: "I saw a man of the Yarbūʿ walking along, quarrelling with two Bedouins of the Asad. He was weak from sickness, so I expressed my sympathy to him for the rudeness of their company, but he shook with rage, saying 'By God, you're selling me short!' 2.7.3

> I am famous, I rise to the top.
> When I remove my turban, you know who I am.

"He pointed his finger at his eyes, and the two Bedouins recoiled in fright, conceding him his right."

2.7.4 When Qutaybah ibn Muslim learned that the Caliph Sulaymān intended to sack him from the governorship of Khurasan and replace him with Yazīd ibn al-Muhallab, Qutaybah wrote three letters, entrusting them to a messenger with the following instructions: "Give the first letter to the caliph. If he hands it to Yazīd, give him the second one. If the caliph curses me when he reads it, give him the third." When the messenger arrived, he presented the first letter. It said: "Commander of the Faithful, I have endured many hardships"—which he listed—"in the service of your father and brother."[210] The caliph handed the letter to Yazīd, so the messenger gave him the second letter. It said: "Commander of the Faithful, how can you trust the son of Daḥamah with your secrets? His own father didn't even trust him with the mothers of his children!" The caliph then cursed Qutaybah, so the messenger presented the third letter. It said: "From Qutaybah ibn Muslim to Sulaymān ibn ʿAbd al-Malik: I greet the one who follows the right path. I guarantee you a tether so strong no sprightly colt can break it." Upon reading this, Sulaymān exclaimed: "I've been too hasty about Qutaybah! Renew his governorship over Khurasan."

2.7.5 Mālik ibn Dīnār said: I know no one more persuasive than al-Ḥajjāj. If he were to ascend the pulpit and describe how beneficent he had been to the Iraqis and how treacherous and wicked they had been to him, I would think he was telling the truth and they were lying!

2.7.6 Al-Ḥajjāj assailed Khālid ibn Yazīd one day and censured him in the presence of ʿAmr ibn ʿUtbah, who felt compelled to intervene: "Khālid has matched those who came before him and surpassed those who will come after him. He has mastered the glory of old, and his renown will not be outstripped." Al-Ḥajjāj apologized, "Ibn ʿUtbah, we beg your pardon! But this is how we hoped you would respond when we upbraided Khālid. Since you are the master of equanimity,[211] our intention was deliberately to provoke your mercy. We know how much you love to be equanimous, and therefore we make trouble in order to give you a chance to do what you love!"

When Muʿāwiyah demanded allegiance be pledged to his son Yazīd and people began standing to make speeches, Muʿāwiyah asked ʿAmr ibn Saʿīd to join them. ʿAmr stood, praised and lauded God, and then said, "Yazīd ibn Muʿāwiyah is the hope you seek; of a long reign you can be sure. He will show you great mercy, if you ask for it. His judgment will guide you, if you request it. If you are in need, he will give generously and provide. He is a sturdy steed. When raced, he wins. When contested, his nobility prevails. When challenged, he triumphs. He is the scion of the Commander of the Faithful. He will never be bested." "Well spoken, Abū Umayyah!" Muʿāwiyah declared, "Sit down." 2.7.7

One of the caliphs once said to a retainer,[212] "I have a task for you," to which he replied, "Commander of the Faithful, in me, God has provided you with a heart sworn to give you counsel, a hand outstretched in fealty, and a sharpened sword against your enemies. Command me as you will." 2.7.8

Al-Maʾmūn said to al-ʿAttābī, "I heard you had died and I was dispirited. Then I heard you had arrived and I was delighted." "Commander of the Faithful," responded al-ʿAttābī, "There is neither salvation nor comfort without you. If these words were parceled out among all the people on earth, they would provide for them all very generously." The caliph then asked, "What gift do you wish?" and al-ʿAttābī replied, "Your hand is more bounteous than my tongue." 2.7.9

When al-Hudhayl ibn Zufar was given an audience with Yazīd ibn al-Muhallab to petition about requisitions imposed upon him, he said, "You are too mighty for us to seek help against you, and when you dispense justice you are yet more just yourself. It would not be surprising if you acted; no, it would be surprising if you did not act." 2.7.10

A man petitioned Asad ibn ʿAbd Allāh, who made excuses for being unable to help him. Then the man said, "To be honest I didn't need any help." "Why then did you ask me?" he inquired, and the man replied, "When I realized that you favor people whom you've helped get through hardship, I decided to try feigning hardship myself in order to gain your friendship." 2.7.11

Poetry

2.8.1 Poetry is the Arabs'. No other nation has ever equalled the Arabs' meters, prosodies, and rhyme schemes, nor the Arabs' descriptions of love, encampments, traces of bygone settlements, mountains, desert sands, wastelands, night journeys, or the stars. The Easterners' poems and songs were in unstructured speech and prose. Some did subsequently hear the Arabs' poems and grasped their meters and prosody, which they then tried to contrive in Persian in imitation of the Arabic.

Poetry is the source of the Arabs' learning, the basis of their wisdom, the archive of their history, the repository of their battle lore. It is the wall built to protect the memory of their glories, the moat that safeguards their laurels. It is the truthful witness on the day of crisis, the irrefutable proof in disputes. He who has no decisive proof to support his claims of nobility, or his claims about his ancestors' glory and praiseworthy deeds, will find that his efforts are in vain, even if his glorious deeds are famous. Their memory will be effaced over time even if they are momentous. But he who has his merits committed to rhyming verse and bound in meter, and gives them renown through a choice verse, a memorable maxim, or a subtle notion will immortalize them for all time. He will secure them against disavowal, and protect them from the plots of enemies. He will repel the jealous eye. Even if his glories are modest, they will forever be evident for all to see and recollect, akin to the line of al-Khuraymī:

His reasoned words about you
stand in men's hearts like cavalry massed in rank.

Another poet said:[213] 2.8.2

Rhymes and deeds resemble a necklace
perfected by a unique stone:
His deeds are like scattered gems—
when arranged as poetry, they become an adorning necklace.
Thus the ancient Arabs
would call him a limited lord:[214]
They thought that all glory would disappear,
except what is bound and preserved in robust verse.

He also said: 2.8.3

There is nothing like beneficence:
it seems an expense, but it's actually profit!
Without poetry, glory's heights
are an unmarked, uncharted wasteland.
It is words that travel by night, so by day
signs of brilliance shine on men's faces.
Even a frivolous line is deemed wisdom,
its verdicts, even if unfair, are final.
Were it not for the paths marked out by poetry,
men chasing glory's heights would not know how to obtain them.

In the past, some Arab tribes were esteemed for their riches, their numbers, their generosity, or their strength. For example, the Ḥanīfah ibn Lujaym included 2.8.4

Hawdhah al-Ḥanafī, "Lord of the Crown," whom the poet al-Aʿshā described as follows:

Seeing Hawdhah drives the unabashed to prostration.

That is, "there is no shame" in prostrating to him. (His father and paternal uncles were known as "the Seas.")[215]

Najdah al-Ḥarūrī, based in al-Yamāmah, who, in the aftermath of Yazīd ibn Muʿāwiyah's death, gained control over al-Baḥrayn. When he performed the hajj, he and his companions prayed in one area, Ibn al-Zubayr prayed in another, and Muḥammad ibn al-Ḥanafiyyah (eternal peace be his) prayed in a third.[216]

Nāfiʿ ibn al-Azraq, leader of the Azraqī Kharijites.

ʿUmayr ibn Salmā, one of the three "Arab Dependables." He killed his own brother, Qurayn, to honor a guarantee of protection—a story we related earlier.[217]

ʿUbayd ibn Thaʿlabah ibn Yarbūʿ, who was called the "Lord of Ḥajr"—Ḥajr is the principal city of al-Yamāmah. He was the one who demarcated Ḥajr's boundaries with his spear and settled the Ḥanīfah there after he had expelled the remnants of the Ṭasm and Jadīs.

Qatādah ibn Maslamah ibn ʿUbayd, the leader who took a fourth part of the spoils from forty different raids in the pre-Islamic era.

The Ḥanīfah had other notables of similar substance, resolution, and valor, but despite this, most people count these tribesmen as minor figures. This is because glory can only be ensured through praise, praise can only be secured through meritorious deeds, and deeds are only evident when recounted. The Ḥanīfah had no poets, hence their glorious past is now known only among experts. Nobility and leadership become celebrated only with recognition by the common masses.

2.8.5 And then there is the ʿIjl ibn Lujaym, who are the kin-brothers of the Ḥanīfah. They are not counted among the nobility of the pre-Islamic era—with the exceptions of Abū Ḥajjār Abjar ibn Jābir, and ʿUtaybah ibn al-Nahhās. In the Islamic period, their honor is traceable only to Idrīs and his son ʿĪsā, who settled around Isfahan. But they had poets, including Abū l-Najm, al-Aghlab al-Rājiz, and al-ʿUdayl ibn al-Farkh, who said:

We hold feasts at our gravesite in the winter.
We hold steadfast under glinting, quivering swords.

He merely means that one of their men provided for the charitable distribution of food at his grave. The poet commemorated the act by glorifying it in verse, and turned it into a specific point of pride and an immortal badge of honor.

This is to say nothing of how God loosened the tongues of the poets in praise of the sons of Idrīs, commemorating their good deeds and giving significance to the insignificant among them. Take the verses of Ibn Jabalah: 2.8.6

> Abū Dulaf is the whole world
> on campaign and at home.
> Where Abū Dulaf leads,
> the world follows in his footsteps.

Or a similar poem by an Azdī tribesman: 2.8.7

> He resembles the thunder when it claps
> He is like the lightning when it flashes;
> Like Death when it advances into battle
> Borne by striding cavalry.
> Glory moves when he moves, stops when he halts.
> Behold the pinnacle of nobility,
> Glory's utmost and its true summit:
> Does anyone besides Abū Dulaf
> Have the power and mettle to attain it?

Because there are so many examples of such poems, the masses rank the ʿIjl above the Ḥanīfah.

Through poetry, God enabled groups to be exalted before and after Islam. He graced those groups with panegyrists who circulated praise poems throughout the land, making them famous in all corners of the earth, and gaining them renown in the Easterners' regions too. Their accounts were then recorded in books, their tales taught in study circles, and God conferred the glory of their worthy deeds on their descendants and kin. The descendants who nurtured 2.8.8

their deeds—preserving and cultivating them with laudable behavior, noble manners, and their own virtue—built upon the foundations their forebearers laid, reaped the fruits of what they had planted, and, through their own personal merits, graced the honor bequeathed them by their ancestors. And even those who did not attain this still have the merits of their ancestors' preeminence and virtue, notwithstanding their own decline—people will not hesitate to continue to treat them with reverence, exalt their standing, defer to them, and forgive them some of their faults.

For this and similar reasons, the ancients were fervent about a good reputation. They expended their lifeblood and choicest wealth on it. They were averse to a life of ease, calm, and comfort, preferring the hardships of travel, the endurance of midday heat, night journeys, contests with rivals, and combats with heroes.

2.8.9 The Tamīm said to Salāmah ibn Jandal, "Glorify us with your poetry!" and he responded, "Do something I can describe! The finest statement is one corroborated by worthy action. That will spread the farthest, last the longest, and give a man the rank of glory."

ʿAmr ibn Maʿdīkarib's verse is similar to Salāmah's words:

> If my people's spears could incite me to speak, I would—
> but their spears have slit my tongue.

He means that they did not use their spears on the day of battle such that he could sing their glories. They fled in failure, thus slitting his tongue as a young camel's tongue is slit when it is time to be weaned to prevent it suckling.

God, mighty and glorious, quoted the words of the chosen companion of God (eternal peace be his), «Give me a reputation for truth among later generations,»[218] and He said to His Prophet (God bless him), «It is certainly a reminder to you and your people, and you will be called to account.»[219] He means "the Qur'an is a source of honor for you and the Quraysh, since it was revealed to you, and you are from the Quraysh, and so the Quraysh shall be asked about their gratitude for it."

Among those given an exalted status by God through poetry is the family of Sinān from the Nushbah ibn Ghayẓ ibn Murrah ibn ʿAwf ibn Saʿd ibn Dhubyān. They were noble and powerful, which God made manifest by gracing them with the fine poetry of Zuhayr. For example, Zuhayr once said: 2.8.10

You will trace their line to Sinān, their father,
good stock, begetting good offspring.
If any people could rise above the sun in nobility, they would,
eminent in ancestry and glory.
Furies when angry, humane when at ease.
noble and magnanimous when praised,[220]
Envied for their blessings,
may God never make them less enviable!

Another example is Zuhayr's verses about Harim ibn Sinān: 2.8.11

The miser is blamed wherever he is,
but Harim is generous, even in hard times.
He is the generous one, granting gifts freely;
even if asked inappropriately, he'll still give.

He means that even if someone made an impossible request, Harim would not rebuff him. The word "inappropriately" means "placing something in the wrong place"; hence he who asks for something that cannot be had, or that is beyond all reach, acts "wrongly" in his petition. Zuhayr was the master of this theme. No one can match him except Kuthayyir when he said:

I saw Ibn Laylā[221] wipe out his capital to meet
varied petitions, from rich and poor.
If he had it, his hands dispensed it,
if the request was outrageous, he countenanced it and gave.

2.8.12 This is also like Zuhayr's poem:

Enough! Turn to praising Harim!
The best of men, lord of townsfolk.[222]
By God, the Dhubyān's nobles learned
in the year when the camels were kept in their pens,[223]
What a fine encounter he pitched for the hungry,
with fine aromas of roast meat and splendid wine.[224]
How good a protector you are,
how capable a bearer of others' burdens.
A just protector, safeguarding his charge,
you can trust the feelings he hides in his heart.
The man who lights his hearth in welcome is praised,
in dire times, none curse his cooking pots.
Meet him in private,
you'll find him wise, generous, and kind,
His every act is for praise,
patiently enduring burdens, joyfully earning a good name.

Some transmitters added a verse of al-Musayyab ibn ʿAlas into this poem:

If you were something other than human,
you would be the shining light of the full moon.

People will be attracted to poetry that is well constructed with choice words, good rhymes, and subtle themes. These poems combine all such attributes.

2.8.13 One poetry transmitter was once given an audience with al-Rashīd, who asked him to recite this ode. The caliph found it beautiful and said, "By God, those who could produce poetry like this are gone!" and the transmitter responded, "By God, those who deserve to be described in such a way are gone!" The caliph had him expelled, and people thought him an idiot.

2.8.14 Dhū l-Ruqaybah was another who achieved an exalted status through poetry. Al-Musayyab ibn ʿAlas said:

I have experienced men and their deeds,
but Mālik Dhū l-Ruqaybah has precedence.
His hands leave legacies by destroying his wealth,
his gifts are of transcendent bounty.

The proverb "build legacies by destroying your wealth" derives from this poem.

2.8.15 The Badr are another group granted exalted status through poetry. Ḥātim al-Ṭā'ī described them thus:

If you disapprove of our ways,
then go settle with the Badr!
They slash with swords in the bridle,
they thrust lances on galloping steeds.
I sought their protection in distress,
in dire straits, an excellent tribe.
Steadfast with rusty swords in battle's din,
they keep poverty at bay.
They served me their sweet water,
they didn't leave me to suffer their well's black mud.
They invited me to their assemblies,
and never looked at me askance.

The Badr were verseless: they never composed any poetry themselves, but those grateful to them proclaimed their virtues, and the praise-poets ensured that the Badr did not need to enumerate their own merits themselves.

2.8.16 One of the remarkable things about poetry is that it is an exception when it comes to the usual effects of self-praise and self-eulogizing, which even if truthful, always backfire and detract from their speaker. Self-praise is permitted in poetry because the Arabs wanted to immortalize their stories and enumerate their battles. They could not achieve this without recording it, and poetry was their only type of record since they were unlettered. When someone wants to inform you about something he did which you need to know, but which you could not know unless he told you himself, then there is nothing distasteful in his telling you, even if it entails self-praise. This is the reason why the prophets praised themselves, while still remaining humble before God and adhering to His moral strictures. In this manner, Joseph (God's blessings be upon him) said: «Put me in charge of the storehouses of the land; I will be a good custodian.»[225] And the Prophet of God (God bless him) said: "I am the chief of the sons of Adam, no boast!" This is also the case when one says, "I fasted," or "I prayed," or "I gave charity," or "I paid the alms-tax." One says these things because one wants other Muslims to emulate and follow one's example.

2.8.17 Another group given an exalted status through poetry was the Anf al-Nāqah, the "Sons of the Camel Snout": ʿĀmir and ʿAlqamah, sons of Hawdhah ibn Shammās, and Baghīḍ ibn ʿĀmir. Al-Ḥuṭayʾah shifted his protection to Baghīḍ from al-Zibriqān ibn Badr and said:

> What was Baghīḍ's offense? He saw a man
> living in need atop wild crags,
> Whom others wearied of providing for:
> their dogs would snarl and maul him with gnashing fangs.

The Camel Snout's original name was Ḥanẓalah ibn Qurayʿ ibn Kaʿb.[226] He acquired the name "Camel Snout" because he once ate the head of a camel, and "snout" is the forepart of a thing. His sons did not like their ancestry being associated with this name and considered it an insult until al-Ḥuṭayʾah said:

> These people are the head, the others tails;
> who can equate a camel's snout with its tail?

And after that, they only wanted to be associated with the "Camel Snout." In this way God increased their fame and renown, redirecting their name's meaning in the way He did.

2.8.18 Just as God conferred exalted status through praise poetry, He similarly derided groups both before and during Islam through lampoon poetry. He impaired their merits and detracted from their virtues, and they became known among the general populace by the stigma of lampoon, and even specialists grew suspicious of their merits. The only thing most people know about the Numayr's genealogy is the verse of Jarīr:

> You are from the Numayr: look down in shame!
> You do not measure up to the Kaʿb or Kilāb.

This verse became an indelible disgrace for them, a proverbial source of shame for supporters, and a favorite insult for attackers. Thus a poet[227] said about another people:

> My lampoon will debase you even more,
> just as the lampoon debased the Numayr.

Another said:

> Numayr is threatening to kill me!
> But did they ever kill the one who lampooned them?

A Bedouin woman once passed by a group of the Numayr, and 2.8.19
they looked her up and down. So she said: "Numayr! By God, do you never learn! Neither from God's words, «Tell the male believers to lower their gaze,»[228] nor from the poet's words:

> You are from the Numayr: look down in shame!
> You do not measure up to the Kaʿb or Kilāb."

The men were embarrassed and hung their heads in shame.

A man from the Numayr was once traveling on a mule in the com- 2.8.20
pany of ʿUmar ibn Hubayrah al-Fazārī, and ʿUmar said to him: "Cast *down*, away from your mule!" The Numayrī replied: "Certainly not, it's *trussed up*!" Ibn Hubayrah was referring to Jarīr's line:

> You are from the Numayr: look *down* in shame!

The Numayrī was referring to the verse of another poet:

Mind your young she-camel if you've left her alone with a Fazārī,
truss up her vulva with thongs!

2.8.21 And so the masses are unaware that the Numayr were one of the Burning Ember Arab tribes. Muʿāwiyah, father of al-Rāʿī, who before Islam was called "the Boss" because of his leadership skills, and Khulayf ibn ʿAbd Allāh ibn al-Ḥārith, who dispersed the Bāhilah and the Ghanī, were members of the Numayr. In Islam, Hammām ibn Qabīṣah, whom Yazīd ibn Muʿāwiyah dispatched against Ibn al-Zubayr, was a member, as was ʿAbd al-Raḥmān ibn Abān the Orator, who commanded the frontier of Fārs. It was about the latter that the poet said:

The people are one flank, the emir the other.
They are the two wings: you are the center.

2.8.22 The ʿAjlān ibn ʿAbd Allāh ibn Kaʿb ibn Rabīʿah ibn ʿĀmir ibn Ṣaʿṣaʿah was another group humiliated by lampoon poetry. Al-Najāshī said about them:

When God brings wrath on the iniquitous and vile,
may he strike the ʿAjlān, the band of Ibn Muqbil.
A tiny tribe who cannot even betray their guarantee of protection,[229]
nor inflict even a peppercorn's wrong on people.
They come to the waterhole only in the evening,
when the drovers have left all the wells.
Hunting dogs refuse to eat their flesh,
though they eat the flesh of the Kaʿb ibn ʿAwf and Nahshal.
They are only called "al-ʿAjlān," the Quick, for the saying:
"Take the pail and start milking, slave: be quick about it!"[230]

This poem had precisely the desired effect on the ʿAjlān. Because they understood the wickedness of al-Najāshī's crime against them and their descendants, the ʿAjlān appealed to ʿUmar ibn al-Khaṭṭāb for assistance. He brought in Ḥassān ibn Thābit, and threatened to cut out al-Najāshī's tongue if he ever lampooned them again. You will, God willing, find the full story in my book of poets.[231]

The ʿAjlān lacked any nobility to speak of. Honor was vested in their cousins, Qushayr ibn Kaʿb, whose members included Mālik Dhū l-Ruqaybah. At the Battle of Jabalah, he captured Ḥājib ibn Zurārah, who ransomed himself for one thousand camels. Another member of Qushayr was Hubayrah ibn ʿĀmir, who captured al-Mutajarridah, al-Nuʿmān's wife, and married her.

The tribes of the Ghanī and Bāhilah were also humiliated by lampoon poetry. The poet Zayd al-Khayl once said: 2.8.23

The disappointment of those who raid the Ghanī,
Bāhilah ibn Aʿṣur, and the beasts!
Booty comes to those who raid the Qushayr,
or who take prisoners from the Kilāb.

These verses have two possible interpretations, one of which plummets from the pinnacle to the nadir: If someone launches a raid which goes wrong and proves abortive, he can regroup and attack the Ghanī and Bāhilah and be sure of success, because they cannot defend themselves from attackers. The poet equates them with "beasts," that is, camels, since camels cannot defend themselves from any raiders. The second meaning is that anyone who captures a member of the Bāhilah or Ghanī will be disappointed at the meager ransom offered: worthwhile spoils can only be had by capturing members of the Qushayr or Kilāb.

Abū ʿUbaydah notes that a man once said to the Prophet of God (God bless and keep him) "Will our blood be given equal compensation, Prophet of God?" (that is, in the case of requital by blood payment), and the Prophet responded, "Yes." The man repeated the question once or twice, and the Prophet replied: "Yes, even if you kill a man from the Bāhilah, I would kill you!" If this were true, it is a catastrophic remark, a shame for all time, but I have no doubt whatsoever that the story is fabricated, because the Prophet (God bless and keep him) was most fearful of and knowledgeable about 2.8.24

God, and was too careful with his words to let one slip that could become an enduring disgrace or shame on even a single Muslim, let alone a whole tribe upon which God had bestowed much goodness, nobility, and knowledge through people such as the following:

Abū Amāmah al-Bāhilī, Companion of the Prophet of God (God bless and keep him).

Al-Mustawrid ibn Qudāmah, who testified to the genealogy of Ziyād.

Ḥabbān ibn Zayd: who, when Abū Mūsā l-Ashʿarī said to him, "The Bāhilah were sheep. You've turned them into men!"[232] responded, "Shall I tell you about a people more disgraceful than the Bāhilah? The ʿAkk and those Ashʿarīs who mixed with them." Abū Mūsā then said: "O ho! You insult your emir!"

Ḥātim ibn al-Nuʿmān: chief of the Aʿṣur and conqueror of Herat.

Ḥātim's son, ʿAbd al-ʿAzīz . . . of the Bāhilah: who led the war against the Qays when they were fighting the Taghlib.

Al-Muntashir ibn Wahb: one of the great Arab foot-raiders,[233] whose story we have already related and about whom the poet Aʿshā Bāhilah said:

> Since you must follow the path you're fated,
> go, Muntashir! May God not keep you from His grace.
> People were never secure from him: day or night,
> he may come raiding from anywhere; if he does not attack,
> they wait in apprehension.
> Never limping from weariness or discomfort in his legs,
> he always leads from the front, following tracks in
> wastelands.
> Never hanging back in wait for food in the pot to be ready,
> hunger never grips his ribs.
> A strip of grilled liver satisfies him,
> a small cup of water is enough.

Muslim ibn ʿAmr ibn Ḥaṣīn al-Bāhilī and his son *Qutaybah ibn Muslim*, master of Khurasan, and his son *Salm ibn Qutaybah*: with them, the nobility of the Bāhilah reaches its climax. Muslim ibn ʿAmr was the closest confidant of Yazīd ibn Muʿāwiyah. His agnomen was Abū Ṣāliḥ. A poet once described him as follows:

> If Quraysh should end its reign,
> then the caliphate will vest in the Bāhilah.
> To Abū Ṣāliḥ, the master of al-Ḥarūn,
> that would not be just practice.

Al-Ḥarūn, "the restive," was his horse.

And if the Bāhilah could count only two of their clients, namely ʿAbd al-Malik ibn Ḥamīd (Abū Jaʿfar al-Manṣūr's minister and chancellor) and Jabalah ibn ʿAbd al-Raḥmān (governor of Isfahan and Kerman), that would be sufficient!

Lampoons also made infamous the Ḥabiṭāt, or "Puffy Tummies," of the Tamīm. The name traces back to their father, al-Ḥārith ibn ʿAmr ibn Tamīm, who was called al-Ḥabiṭ, ("Puffy Tummy") because his stomach became swollen from something he ate: the word *ḥabiṭ* means bloating of the stomach. Ziyād al-Aʿjam said: 2.8.25

> I found donkeys to be the worst of mounts,
> just as the Ḥabiṭāt are the worst of the Tamīm.

But how can they be the worst of the Tamīm? Their members include Abū ʿAttāb Hasakah ibn ʿAttāb, Abū Jahḍam ʿAbbād ibn Ḥuṣayn, the knight of the tribe, and his son al-Miswar, chief of the Tamīm, about whom the *rajaz* poet said:

> Miswar ibn ʿAbbād, you're made for the times
> When swords are unsheathed from their scabbards.

ʿAbbād was once asked, "When is the best time to face an enemy?" and he responded, "When it's not yet my time to die."

The only lampoon poems that can inflict humiliation are those which the general populace can easily recite and comprehend. 2.8.26

Saʿīd ibn Muslim said: Some boys attended a poetry competition between Abū Nukhaylah and al-ʿAjjāj. Someone got up to shoo them away, but al-ʿAjjāj said, "Let them stay: they'll learn the verses and disseminate them."

I heard al-Sijistānī report that al-Aṣmaʿī said: Only clear poems will circulate. The best poems are those which a person hears and thinks he could do as well himself, but he'd be more likely to let a dog rip his nose off than compose a line like it!

2.8.27 Well-rehearsed lampoons include the line of Jarīr:[234]

These people: when their dogs bark at guests,
they say to their mother, piss on the fire!

While the following verse by another poet is not so famous:

The Dārim take the Manāf up the anus,
just as the Barājim take the Ẓulaym up the anus.

Al-Ḥutay'ah said to al-Zibriqān:

Leave noble traits aside: don't go searching for them.
Sit down! Enveloped in robes, you look good at dinner.

Al-Ṭirimmāḥ said:

With keener sense than sandgrouse, the Tamīm know the paths to shame;
if they ever sought the ways to glory, they'd be lost.

2.8.28 I would have expected certain other verses to have been catchier than this one, but for whatever reason they never caught on. For example, take al-Ṭirimmāḥ's poem:

If a tick, riding the back of an ant, were to charge
against two-thirds of the Tamīm, the Tamīm would run away.
If a flea were skinned and a waterskin made out of it,
the Tamīm would drink from it, and drink again.
If the Tamīm one day mustered their forces
against a tethered ant, it would stand and fight them.

If a spider built a web over them on a wet day,
it would shield them all.

Or take this poem of his:

May he find no glory, if, on horseback
to raid the Tamīm, he seeks anyone else's aid.
If it were the Tamīm's time to draw water, but they heard
the Azd were at the pool of the Messenger, they would keep back.
Even if God revealed that He would punish them
if they did not fight the Azd, they would still stay away.
Time can efface all ignoble lineages,
except Ḍabbah's vile pedigree, which can never change.[235]

Or al-Ṭirimmāḥ's description of the Asad:

If any of His creation could stay hidden from the All Merciful
it would be the Asad.
A people whose elders settled in the abode of humiliation—
like the place where tent pegs choose to live.

Sometimes equally clear lampoon poems, though biting and painful, still fail to circulate, as with the verse 2.8.29

A land, far removed from friends,
where an ʿAnazī insulted me, and I did not speak.

I do not know how to explain this, other than to count it as a vicissitude of fortune. Luck and misfortune play on everything, even poetry and epistolography. How many solidly written pieces are confined to books, while we hear so many silly sayings that become ingrained in our hearts!

The Jarm were another group humiliated by vicious lampooning. Ḥumayd ibn Thawr dispatched two men to a woman he was wooing, telling them: 2.8.30

If you pass through the land of the ʿĀmir
and the tribes Nahd and Khathʿam,
Say: "We are two strangers from the Jarm ibn Rayyān"—
in the heat they refused us even a cupping glass of water.

He was instructing them to claim that they were from the Jarm since no Arabs feared raids from them, and everyone held them of no account. In those days, this was the height of weakness and worthlessness.

Similarly, another poet said:

The Rūmān did no good,
the Rūmān did no ill,
The Rūmān were created last
after everyone else.

2.8.31 Another example of worthlessness:

Riḍwān dodges his guest,
Didn't my warnings reach him?
You need only know that people know
how plentiful your wealth is,
But your meat has no taste: like an unweaned camel's flesh,
you have neither sweet, nor sour.
You resemble the first milk in an udder,
that scatters when the teats are squeezed.
When people hasten, you don't come to them,
as if you were sired by donkeys.
Guests and night travelers know
that all you provide is hollow hunger.

There are so many more examples of this. If we pursued the topic, the book would become long, and our goal is not to report meritorious deeds and vices but, rather, to demonstrate the tremendous power of poetry and its great ability to extol some groups and humiliate others.

When a boy with the ability to compose poetry or compose *rajaz* while leading a camel or while drawing water from a well turned up among an Arab tribe, his family would be delighted and his clan would rejoice. They would promote and exalt him, nominating him to defend them and uphold their dignity, and relatives and neighbors would come to them for help. Al-Aʿshā said to his people: 2.8.32

> I defend your honor, and I lend you
> a tongue as sharp as al-Khafājī's shears.

Jarīr said: 2.8.33

> Was I not a fire that burned your enemy?
> A refuge in which you sought sanctuary?
> Did I not deal you goodness with my right hand,
> and snatch ill from you with my left?
> Do not fear that I shall hide when calamity strikes;
> rather, fear Death, who will deprive you of me.

Al-Riyāshī informed me that he heard al-Aṣmaʿī report that he heard Juwayriyah ibn Asmāʾ say to Musāwir ibn Hind: "Why do you compose poetry?" and Musāwir said, "Because poetry pours my drink, finds my food, and fulfills my needs. If you can give me all this, I'll stop!" 2.8.34

ʿUmar ibn al-Khaṭṭāb said: "Poetry is the potent speech of the Arabs. It abates anger, it extinguishes the flame of war, it feeds the tribe and gives gifts to the petitioner." He also said: "What a good gift is poetry for a noble man: verses will serve him in his need, win over the generous, and force ingrates to surrender." 2.8.35

When people need subtle words to achieve their desires, to slip from the clutches of ill-will, to praise, boast, rebuke, revile, urge, or endure matters patiently, and much else besides, prose cannot match the great effectiveness of poetry. 2.8.36

Al-Riyāshī writes: Khulayd ibn ʿAynayn appeared before Ziyād's administrator over one of the districts of Fārs and requested money, 2.8.37

but the administrator gave him nothing and said: "You pride yourself on your poetry, so go away and say whatever you want!" Khulayd responded: "When I'm through with you, you'll wish I'd only lampooned you." And he said:

Taym[236] has sacks of coins,
if you shake the sacks, they call for Ziyād.
They call out in longing to him,
but their throats are throttled by bag ties.

When the poem reached the ears of Ziyād, he said: "Ho, my sacks of money! I'll rescue you from Taym!" and he sent an order against Taym for the seizure of one hundred thousand dirhams. Even if this poet was as persuasive an orator as Saḥbān Wāʾil or as exhaustive as the peacemakers when they address the tribes, if he had complained of the administrator's dishonesty in prose, his speech would not have been as effective as this couplet, and he would have been just another complainant.

2.8.38 God often makes poetry beneficial in battle, where it can be used to steady the ranks.

ʿAbd al-Malik said to his sons' teacher: "Instruct them in poetry so that they will become illustrious and brave."

And Muʿāwiyah said: "The following verse of Ibn al-Iṭnābah al-Khazrajī encouraged me in my conflict against Ibn Abī Ṭālib (eternal peace be his):

When my soul agitates and swells in panic
I say: 'Be still, act laudably, relax!'"

2.8.39 In the same vein, Qaṭarī ibn al-Fujāʾah said:

When warring heroes panic my soul,
I say: "Shame on you—will you not pay heed?
Should you beg for one day beyond your allotted time,
your wish would be in vain."

Nahshal ibn Ḥarrī said: 2.8.40

We endured many battles when men seemed to stand and burn
from war's embers, though there was no fire;
Steadfast until the flames subsided:
relief from war's hateful days comes only from endurance.

Another poet said: 2.8.41

My companion cried when he saw Death loom over us,
tears that poured like a heavy rain from black clouds,
But I told him: "Stop your crying eyes,
tomorrow heralds honor for those who endure.
Retreat does not delay fate's pressing moment,
attack will not hasten what fate has postponed."
So we returned to a state where there's no grief,
and he plunged into battle's foggy chaos.

Al-Sijistānī informed me that al-Aṣmaʿī reported as follows: ʿĀṣim ibn al-Ḥadathān was an old man of the Arabs, head of the Kharijites in Basra. Messengers would regularly arrive from the Jazīrah to consult him about points of contention. Al-Farazdaq walked past once and said to ʿĀṣim's son: "Abū Firās, recite a poem!" and he recited: 2.8.42

When battle looms, those men are grandees,
they long persevere when sword blades intertwine.
They weave through the thick of the deadly fray,
deeming mortal lives nothing before God.
They march under your command into thickets of spears,
bolting eagerly toward charging lances.

Then al-Farazdaq said: "Watch out! Keep this poem secret! Don't let the weavers hear it, or they'll attack us with their looms!"[237]

Al-Riyāshī informed me, citing ʿUbayd ibn ʿAqīl, who cited Jarīr ibn Ḥāzim and Muḥammad ibn Sīrīn, who both said: Ḥassān ibn Thābit, 2.8.43

ʿAbd Allāh ibn Rawāḥah, and Kaʿb ibn Mālik were the poets of the Muslims. Kaʿb ibn Mālik filled the non-Muslims with fear of battle, ʿAbd Allāh upbraided them for their unbelief, and Ḥassān attacked them through their genealogy. Ibn Sīrīn also said: "I was informed that the Daws only accepted Islam out of fear of Kaʿb and his line:

> We settled the blood scores in Tihāmah and Khaybar,
> then sheathed our swords.
> We let our swords choose: if they could speak
> their sharp points would say: 'Daws or Thaqīf!'

"Upon hearing these verses, the Daws said: 'Run off and save yourselves! Don't let what befell the Thaqīf happen to you!'"

Ibn Sirīn added: ʿAmr ibn al-ʿĀṣ, ʿAbd Allāh ibn al-Zibʿarī, and Abū Sufyān ibn Ḥarb were the poets of the polytheists.

2.8.44 Abū l-Yaqẓān reported that al-Ḥārith ibn ʿAwf, leader of the Murrah, and the man who settled the blood feud between ʿAbs and Dhubyān, lived into the Islamic period and accepted Islam. The Prophet of God (God bless him) sent one of the Allies with al-Ḥārith, under his protection, to spread the word of Islam, but he was killed by one of the Thaʿlabah. When news reached the Prophet (God bless him), he told Ḥassān: "Compose poetry about this," and Ḥassān said:

> Ḥārith! Who among you betrays a covenant to protect his charge?
> Muḥammad does not betray his covenants.
> The security of a Murrī, when you entrust him,
> is like glass: once broken, it cannot be mended.
> If you have betrayed it—then betrayal is your custom.
> Betrayal grows in the roots of the ficus.[238]

Al-Ḥārith sent an apology and dispatched some camels as indemnity. The Prophet (God bless him) accepted them and paid them to the man's heirs.

Pause and consider this story. Reflect on how the Prophet of God (God bless him) said "Compose poetry about this." He did so because he (God bless him) knew poetry's power over the heart, and its subtle ways into it. He knew how poetry excites, wounds, chastens, and shames, and that indemnity could be the only possible reply.

The Prophet of God (God bless and keep him) also used to give gifts to poets. A poet once praised him, and the Prophet said: "Silence this poet's tongue!" Upon which, they gave him a gift.

The Prophet bestowed a mantle on Kaʿb ibn Zuhayr when he said, 2.8.45

> I am told the Prophet of God threatened me,
> but pardon can be sought from the Prophet of God.

Muʿāwiyah bought the mantle from Kaʿb for twenty thousand dirhams,[239] and it remains in caliphal hands to this day.

Al-Ziyādī informed me that he heard ʿAbd al-Wārith ibn Saʿīd cite 2.8.46
Muḥammad ibn Juḥādah, who heard Muḥammad ibn ʿAlī say: "A man praised God and His Prophet. The Prophet of God (God bless him) gave him a robe for praising God, but nothing for praising him."

Khallād al-Arqaṭ said: Giving gifts to poets is part of filial piety.

A poet praised Ibn Shihāb, and he paid him, saying "Protecting oneself against evil is part of aspiring to good!"

The Prophet of God (God bless him) said to Ḥassān: "Defend your people! And ask Abū Bakr about the Quraysh's vices." (Of the Quraysh, Abū Bakr was the most knowledgeable about the tribe.) He also told Ḥassān: "By God, your poetry wounds them more than an arrow fired in the black of night." The Prophet (God bless him) also said to Ḥassān: "Lampoon them! Gabriel is with you!"

The Arabs used to ask for poetry to be recited, for it is a vast store of 2.8.47
noble tales and uncommon wisdom.

Ibn ʿAbbās would say: "Poetry is the summa of Arab knowledge. It is their archive, so study it. And you must learn the poetry of the Hijaz, since it is the poetry from before Islam, and it has been exonerated."[240]

Muslim ibn Bashshār said: After hearing Saʿīd ibn al-Musayyib chanting poetry, I asked him, "You recite poetry?" to which he said,

"Don't they recite it among you too?" "No," I replied. He then said, "Then you follow a non-Arabic piety," adding that the Prophet of God (God bless him) said: "Non-Arabic piety is the worst form of piety." [241]

The Prophet (God bless him) said: "There is indeed wisdom in poetry."

2.8.48 The following is from Shuʿayb ibn Wāqid, who had it from Ṣāliḥ ibn al-Ṣaqr, who in turn had it from ʿAbd Allāh ibn Zuhayr: ʿAlāʾ ibn al-Ḥadramī came to the Prophet of God (God bless him) and the Prophet asked, "Can you recite any of the Qurʾan?" He recited the Surah ʿAbasa, and then added something of his own, as follows: "He is the one who, from the pregnant, brings forth a living thing, moving between the ribs and innards." "Stop!" the Prophet (God bless him) exclaimed, "The surah is fine the way it is!" Then the Prophet asked him, "Do you know any poetry?" and he recited the following:

Greet those who harbor spite—it beguiles them.
  Your pleasant greeting mends sandals.
If they incite hatred, be virtuous, show kindness.
  If they refuse to speak, don't ask.
It is what you hear that hurts you,
  what they say behind your back was never said.

The Prophet (God bless and keep him) exclaimed: "There is indeed wisdom in poetry, and magic in eloquence."

2.8.49 The Easterners are enamored with the sayings of Buzurgmihr and Anushirvan, and other kings and priests, and they boast about the wisdom and pithy sayings ascribed to them. But they would find exactly the same thing, or indeed even better material in the poetry of the Arabs and the words of Arab sages such as Aktham ibn Ṣayfī l-Tamīmī, Abū Hajjār Abjar ibn Jābir al-ʿIjlī, ʿĀmir ibn al-Ẓarib al-ʿAdwānī, and others, if they only looked. I will mention a little to draw attention to the Arabs' share in this—even if only cursorily—and with that, God willing, end this book.

Wisdom Poetry

Ibn ʿAbbās said: These are the words of a prophet— 2.9.1

Time will show you what you did not know,
unexpected guests will bring you tidings.

One of the Easterners' wise sayings goes: "When a rarity is obtained, it loses its charm." 2.9.2

In this, or a similar vein, a poet once said:[242]

When she withholds, my affection mounts—
man loves most what is denied.

They say: "The obtainable is dreary and dull"; and "Man yearns for what he does not have."

The supporters of analogical reasoning[243] say: "What you see is proof of the unseen." A poet has similarly said: 2.9.3

She wagged her finger and said:
what you've seen will make up for what you haven't.

The *Easterner*[244] sages say: "May the maker of the rule be content to be judged by it." This is similar to what Abū Dhu'ayb[245] had said: 2.9.4

Never regret a trail you blazed,
the one who strikes a path first enjoys its fruit.

The sages say: "Nature prevails." A poet had said as much:[246] 2.9.5

What one contrives against his nature,
will be abandoned as character prevails.

Another poet has said:[247]

All return to their essence,
though they may affect different traits for a time.

And in another poet's words:

To your own way only be true,
feigning will cede to the real you.

2.9.6 The Easterner sages also say: "Eagerness dispossesses." And ʿAdī ibn Zayd has said:

The man slow to act can achieve his lot:
good luck can strike where effort fails.

2.9.7 Buzurgmihr was once asked, "Is there anyone without fault?" "No," he responded, "the man without a fault would be immortal." In this vein, Abū Mūsā Shahawāt has said:

The only fault we can see
for people to find in you is that you are mortal.
You're the best of all things—if only you could live forever—
though permanence is not for mankind.

2.9.8 The Easterners say: "Too much patience breeds impotence." And al-Nābighah al-Jaʿdī has said:

There is no good in forbearance
without outbursts of indignation to keep its purity unspoiled.

The verse was recited to the Prophet (God bless him), and he said: "May God keep your teeth safe!" And he lived a century without losing a tooth.

2.9.9 The sages say: "Those who share your hardships most deserve to share your good fortune." A poet has said:[248]

Those who most deserve to share your happiness
are those who comfort you in adversity.

It is written in a book: "A tree felled by an ax may regrow, flesh cut by a sword can heal, but wounds inflicted by the tongue never mend." Imru' al-Qays said: 2.9.10

The tongue is as injurious as the hand.

And Ṭarafah said:

The arrogance of a quarrelsome man
is parried by a bone-revealing gash
Either from your swordblade, or your tongue—
resolute words are like the deepest slash.

Similarly there is the verse:[249]

Words pierce where the needle cannot.

The sages said: "Where goodness fails, evil saves the day." And al-Find al-Zimmānī has said: 2.9.11

There is deliverance in malice,
when beneficence cannot save you.

They say: "Haste is bound to slip." And al-Qaṭāmī said: 2.9.12

People pander to the successful;
the loser's mother is bereft.
The deliberate often attain;
the hasty often slip.

An Indian book has this saying: "One sign of a friend is that he is a friend to his friend's friend, and an enemy to his friend's enemy." In this vein, a poet has said:[250] 2.9.13

You love my enemy, then allege we're friends—
you're shameless!

My brother does not just show his love in plain view:
in absence my brother holds true.

2.9.14 The sages say: "Silence is assent." And a poet has said:[251]

Hilāl! Why didn't you control your fool?
A fool unrestrained will be heeded.

2.9.15 A poet also said:

I've seen men sleep soundly on their travels,
then be carried away in the night, unawares.

2.9.16 Jurists and judges are of the view that legal rights are determinable in three ways: by oath, by judicial proceeding, or by documentary proof. Zuhayr had already listed all three in this verse:

Rights are settled by three things—
oath, judgment, or proof.

The verse was recited to ʿUmar ibn al-Khaṭṭāb (God show him mercy), and he marveled at Zuhayr's grasp of how rights are established. A verse of ʿAbdah ibn al-Ṭabīb was also recited to ʿUmar:

Life is but scarcity, anxiety, and hope.

And ʿUmar began repeating it, lauding how well it set things forth.

2.9.17 God says: «God will not call you to account for your meaningless oaths, but He will call you to account for the oaths which you swear in earnest.»[252] Likewise a poet said:[253]

You're only accountable for words
intended in solemn earnest.

2.9.18 The Easterners said: "If your best trait is not reason, your worst traits will be your death." A poet had said in the same vein:

A tongue ruled by passion sets
a lion loose into your house.

A certain Indian book contains this saying: "The poor are always reviled for the same trait for which the rich are praised. If a poor man is brave, he will be called rash; if grave, he will be called apathetic; if eloquent, a babbler; and if solemn, dumb." Likewise a poet has said:[254] 2.9.19

A poor man among his people will praise wealth,
even if his line is illustrious on both sides.
Those who give are beneficent, though some are misers,
and regard his polite silence as incapacity.
Poverty mars a man's intellect,
even if he's the strongest and most ingenious of all.

The wisdom of the poets includes the following: 2.9.20

Try to conform to an idiot,
and you'll become a reckless fool too.
Engage in boorishness with boors once,
and they'll reap your dignity as spoils.
Don't trade on a fool's honor—treat him kindly,
with forbearance; if he exhausts you, cut him loose.
Handle the fool with forbearance and passion,
be between enmity and peace with him.
He'll plead with you at times, fear you at others,
in the meantime, be wary.
If there's no recourse but fury,
call in boors against him: that is decisive action!

Kuthayyir said: 2.9.21

Those who do not turn a blind eye to their friends,
overlooking some faults, will die full of scorn.
Those who pursue their companion's every slip,
will find flaws, and find themselves ever companionless.

Ibn al-Aʿrābī cited the following: 2.9.22

I overlook some faults in a friend:
lest I live companionless.

2.9.23 Al-Nābighah was the first to express this sentiment:

The faultless should not be your only friends.
Are there any flawless men?

2.9.24 Suwayd ibn al-Ṣāmit said:

How many you call a friend! Would that you knew
his words in secret—his calumnies do you ill.
His words, like honey to your face,
in secret slash at the throat.
But the eyes reveal what he conceals,
hatred veiled in a sideward glance.
For as long as you pare me, feather me well!
but the best comrades fletch and do not pare.[255]

2.9.25 A man from Ghaṭafān said:

If you don't keep your companion
despite some blemish, you'll be critiquing often.
I keep a foul man as precaution
against the enmity of a carping meddler.
I fear the dogs of strangers
if no kinsmen's dogs answer their bark!

2.9.26 Al-Nuʿmān ibn Bashīr said:

I gift to those who do not ask,
I deal inequity to the obdurate comrade.
And when he crosses me,
there's no separating us in the fray.
Don't think your comrade is one who shares in your good fortune,
your real comrade is one who shares in your loss.

If a relation appeals to kinship to curry favor,
    yet cheats and dismisses you, he is not your kin.
The kinsman is someone who is distressed by your pain,
    and who levels his bow at your foe.

Ka'b ibn Zuhayr said: 2.9.27

Without confronting dread, desires are not achieved.
    A foot set in place by God cannot be moved.[256]
Shun fury, eschew sin,
    lest you harm the wise, or succumb to the uncouth.

And another poet said: 2.9.28

When you see what you fear, you're terrified.
    but the unseen from which God protects us is greater.

Iyās ibn Qatādah said: 2.9.29

Our hands mete out punishment, our judgment is forbearing,
    we are rebuked for acts, not speech.

And another said:

I am a man, I defend my sanctum
By forbearance and by leaving wickedness to the wicked.
Forbearance is a better defense than a tyrannical hand.

Likewise, al-Aḥnaf said: "I found forbearance a better ally than soldiers."

And Imru' al-Qays said: 2.9.30

None boast against you like a vaunting weakling
    and there's nothing worse than losing to a loser.

Suwayd said: 2.9.31

When the matter appears uncertain,
when the wise can see its convolutions,
When the time comes to defend what is right,
I relinquish a life of comfort for what is more proper.

2.9.32 And Zuhayr said:

You're shielded from obscenity, but
between you and goodness, there's no barrier.

2.9.33 Ḥassān ibn Thābit (or his son) said:

Happy is the man who takes to bed and rises secure
but for the misdeeds he inflicted upon himself.

2.9.34 Al-Farazdaq said:

The Bakr ibn Wāʾil have cut their ties with me,
I never thought their love for me would cease.
When slights affront me, they think little of them;
one drop can cause the vessel to overflow.

2.9.35 Kuthayyir describes women and his way of managing them as follows:

When I came, they esteemed my visits,
they held me in awe, and never frowned.
They were wary of the old jealousy
they knew so well, so they never mocked, and only smiled.
You see them giving only a backward glance
or turning a wrist.
Silent, they speak only in response,
replying to what he had asked.
If they said something that pleased him,
he concealed his delight, and presented a severe mien.

2.9.36 Al-Qaṭāmī said:

Disobeying once those who care for you
 will prompt you to heed them more.
The best matter is the one before you,
 not the one you wish to pursue.
So it is, and yet I see people
 racing to temptation's call.
You'll see them mock those they deem weak,
 yet shirk those who wield the sword well.

Wisdom in the Prose and Rhyming Aphorisms of the Arabs

2.10.1 Aktham ibn Ṣayfī said: "Live apart, and you will come together in love."

ʿUmar ibn al-Khaṭṭāb wrote to Abū Mūsā: "Order relatives to visit each other, but to not live next to each other." When a Bedouin was asked: "What do you have to say about cousins?" he replied: "They're your enemies and your enemy's enemies."

2.10.2 Muʿāwiyah said: "Extravagance indicates ill-gotten wealth."

2.10.3 ʿAmr ibn al-ʿĀṣ said: "The wise man is not someone who can discern good from evil, but rather someone who can tell the better of two evils." Ziyād said: "The wise man is not someone who uses his ingenuity to escape trouble, but rather someone who uses it to evade trouble."

2.10.4 Aktham ibn Ṣayfī said to a group who wanted to wage war on another group: "Refrain from disagreeing with your leaders—know that much shouting is a sign of failure. Man inevitably falls short. Be patient—the most resolute side is the steadfast one.[257] Haste often leads to delay. Face battle. Use the cloak of night: it lessens the risk of disaster. Those who disagree will be scattered."

2.10.5 Abjar ibn Jābir said to his son when they arrived at a settlement: "Make many friends, never worry about enemies. And be wary of making speeches: they are an enterprise full of mishaps." And

Aktham said: "Being a recluse helps your rivals, while free-spending garners bad companions."

A Bedouin said: "God recompenses what people have consumed; time consumes what they have gathered. How often does the search for life lead to death?[258] Life is exposure to death." Abū Bakr (God show him mercy) once said to Khālid ibn al-Walīd: "Be intent on death, and you will grant yourself life." 2.10.6

The Arabs also say: Bear hardship, and deliverance will be near. Privation is the absence of reason. Generosity is swift spending. Staying true to ties maintains friendship. If gratitude is difficult, don't underestimate ingratitude. Sloth and incompetence breed poverty. Awkward silence gathers more praise than faltering speech.[259] Too much advice begets suspicion. The walls have ears. Feeling safe prompts circumspection. Who dares, wins. Exertion, not drudgery. A leader is the first to act—be him. Many words are more cutting than blows. Don't pee on a hill, and don't share a secret with a maidservant. To avoid death, look before it's too late. A lesson learned is not money wasted. When you take care of your wealth, you preserve the two things dearest to you.[260] He who knows the land will master it, he who doesn't will be mastered by it. Only friends will carry your saddle. True friends admonish. Showing the way to goodness is as good as doing it. Poverty is the son of disgrace. The freeman is free, even in hardship; the slave is a slave even in comfort. Swift censure is not justice. Begging is the last resort. The forbearing will suffer the boor. Those who travel on level ground do not slip. Fraternize with the high-minded, no one else. One hand strikes, the other nurses.[261] Just hearing about evil suffices. Note the exit before entering. Tracing a man's lineage via his mother is shameful enough. The overeager provides the worst help. No sin is punished quicker than rebellion. Be quick to help, not just to say yes. Resignation helps patience.[262] If you have no hope of getting something, you can do without it. Delay spoils a good deed. Gaining the upper hand dispels a grudge. Patience occasions 2.10.7

victory. Caution is useless against fate. Facing death is better than turning away from it. Hearts are captured with words. The best thing to keep safe is what's hidden. To lose loved ones is to live in exile. Duck, and danger will miss you. The man who won't refuse your request is the man most worthy of your gift. Unison is a fortress. Poverty at home is exile, wealth abroad is home. Evil begins in little things. Many rains begin as drizzle. Virtue is a trickle, vice a torrent—which resembles the poet's verse:

You can milk vice aplenty,
virtue only trickles from the udder.

2.10.8 Eschewing sin is easier than repenting. The animosity of a wise man is better than the friendship of a fool. Concern about another's lot is a tribulation. Who overcomes desire extinguishes it. Who overcomes craving has come of age. To love evil is to be vanquished by it.[263] A man is defined by his two smallest possessions.[264] The best possession protects you, the worst is that which you protect. Disdain things and they will be denied you.[265] All that is going to come is at hand. Success begins with perseverance. To keep the contents, fasten the lid. Redressing silence is easier than retracting hasty speech. Guarding your own property is far better than coveting another's. Oppressing the weak is the worst oppression. Procrastination breeds loss. Be gentle, and you will lead; seek knowledge, and it will grow. If you are going to regret what you've lost, you might as well regret what you never had. Affection breeds suspicion. Impede evil, else you may speed its onset. Protecting women is a sign of nobility. A traitor truly deserves to be shown no trust. The slip of the pious man is the most serious slip. Lies are the ugliest sickness. Modest living makes a little grow.[266] Thrift averts destitution. A modest life will not cause poverty. There's no good in a pleasure that is followed by regret. Joking breeds hatred. New ruler, new age. Know your companion before taking to the road, and know the neighbor before buying the house.[267] Goodness should be a habit, wickedness is for an occasion. Truth is luminous, falsehood murky.

These are the sciences of the Arabs, and we have only availed ourselves of some of the evidence at our disposal. All this knowledge belongs to them and them alone. No one contests them for it, nor does any people claim that the Arabs took any of it from them. But everything the Persians know, they learned from other peoples—they walked in the footsteps of other nations. 2.10.9

When we inquire about the forefathers of medicine, we will be led to Hippocrates and Galen; when we inquire about the origins of astronomy and computation, we will be led to Euclid and the *Almagest*; when we inquire about the realm of logic, we will be led to the book of Aristotle; when we inquire about musicology, we will be led to the *Book of Music*. All these works were written by the Romans and the Greeks. The Persians have no more of a share in them than any other beneficiary who profits from them. The Romans developed agronomy; the Indians have chess, *Kalīlah and Dimnah*, and computation using the nine sigla, and they possess ancient, accurate medical knowledge derived from discoveries quite different from those of the Greeks. The Persians themselves admit this in their *Book of Kings*, where they record that when Shapur grew old and his vision dulled and his powers faded, he complained to his subjects that he was too weak to rule and ordered them to find someone proficient to replace him. But this was too much for them to bear, and they rejected his suggestion outright. They asked his permission to find him a doctor, and he agreed. They sent a messenger with great gifts to the king of India, asking him to send the best doctor he had. The doctor tended to Shapur until the king recovered his strength, his skin regained its color, his sight returned, and he could ride on the hunt and cavort with women. Shapur repaid the doctor with great munificence, and asked him to 2.10.10

choose the part of the kingdom where he would most like to settle. The doctor chose Susa, settled there, and the people of Susa thereby inherited his medical knowledge. They also say that a Roman prisoner was settled in Susa, and that the Persians learned medicine from him too. Thus the people of Susa became the doctors of the Persians. These accounts must be true since we find a combination of Indian and Roman elements in the *Medical Compendium* composed in Susa. Some of the Bigots argue, on the other hand, that when Alexander invaded Persia, killed and captured its inhabitants, and laid waste, he transported their scientific books to Greece, had them translated into Greek and burned the originals—thus Persian knowledge became Greek.[268] But we can rebut this by saying: "The first account is corroborated by your very own books, whereas the second account is a claim about the actions of a different people, so you need corroboration from the Romans to prove it."

[Colophon]

So ends the *Book of the Arabs and Their Sciences*, and praise be to God, Lord of the Worlds. And peace be upon our noble Prophet Muḥammad and his blessed family. God is sufficient for me! How excellent a guardian. Hibat Allāh, Abū l- Futūḥ ibn Yūsuf ibn Khamartāsh finished the copy of this book for himself in Rabiʿ al-Awwal 589 (March 1193). He holds my soul in His hand, I am thankful to Him, I pray for His chosen messenger, His special prophet, and for his blessed progeny. God forgives those who ask for forgiveness from Him, and for all Muslims. **2.11.1**

Amen!

Notes

1 For "the zealotry of the pre-Islamic era" (*ḥamiyyat al-jāhiliyyah*), see Q Fatḥ 48:26.

2 Q Zukhruf 43:32.

3 The translation here is tentative.

4 The Qur'an often refers to scriptural revelation given to previous prophets or messengers as *kitāb* (pl. *kutub*, as here), "book, scripture" and consequently to Jews, Christians, and a group called the Sabians as *ahl al-kitāb*, generally translated as "People of the Book."

5 The origin of this quotation is unknown and cannot be traced in biblical writings. It does appear in a rarely reported *ḥadīth qudsī* (hadith reporting words spoken by God); see, e.g., Ibn Abī Ḥātim, *Tafsīr*, 3:978.

6 See also Ibn Qutaybah, *ʿUyūn al-akhbār*, 2:9.

7 Q Tawbah 9:32.

8 Abū Tammām, *Dīwān*, 1:402.

9 The Arabic expression *taḥrīf* is Qur'anic, referring to the polemical charge that Jews and Christians, as recipients of God's divine word, distorted their respective scriptures. Ibn Qutaybah thus uses a loaded term: his opponents distort traditions meant to convey the Arabs' virtues, just as Jews and Christians distorted their scriptures.

10 Ṭurayḥ ibn Ismāʿīl al-Thaqafī, *Dīwān*, 75.

11 In *ʿUyūn al-akhbār*, 2:17, Ibn Qutaybah attributes this statement to Buzurgmihr, the vizier to the Sasanian king Anushirvan (r. AD 531–79).

12 Also cited in Ibn Qutaybah, *ʿUyūn al-akhbār*, 2:19, without attribution.

13 Also cited in Ibn Qutaybah, *ʿUyūn al-akhbār*, 2:14, without attribution.

14 His father was said to have been Jewish. Ibn Qutaybah may be referring to this or to another aspect of his parentage.

15 Ibn Qutaybah refers to a story whereby Ḥājib gave his bow as a pledge to Khosrow Parviz in exchange for permission to pasture his clan's flocks in Sasanian territory.

16 The tribe of the aforementioned Wakīʿ, who killed Qutaybah ibn Muslim.

17 For the context, see Abū ʿUbaydah, *Naqāʾiḍ Jarīr wa-l-Farazdaq*, 349–71, esp. 349, line 43, and 371, line 45.

18 As further evidence of the importance of the bow among the Arabs, Ibn Qutaybah notes here that the bow was sufficient guarantee for Sayyār's promise of a thousand camels, and that, on delivery of the camels, the bow was returned.

19 This poem is widely attributed to the pre-Islamic poet Qurād ibn Ḥanash al-Ṣāridī from the tribe of Ghaṭafān. See, e.g., Abū l-Faraj al-Iṣfahānī, *Al-Aghānī*, 11:111.

20 Ibn Qutaybah here refers to the legendary rivalry between two pre-Islamic poets, ʿĀmir ibn al-Ṭufayl and ʿAlqamah ibn ʿUlāthah, and an anecdote about their contemporaries' fears of judging between them. See Abū l-Faraj al-Iṣfahānī, *Al-Aghānī*, 16:283ff.

21 See Jirān al-ʿAwd al-Numayrī, *Dīwān*, 18.

22 The lines probably should be attributed to Qays ibn ʿĀṣim, a pre-Islamic poet whose life extended into the early period of Islam; see Ḥātim al-Ṭāʾī, *Dīwān*, 312. These attributes, meager though they may seem, were cited in praise of the woman's lineage.

23 By this formula, ʿĀmir meant that all of the power of the legendary ancestor, Maʿadd, had passed down to the tribal unit, Bahdalah. Among Maʿadd's clans, Bahdalah is the most distinguished in descent and the most powerful.

24 Al-Farazdaq, *Dīwān*, 2:177.

25 Q Ṣād 38:32.

26 The point is that only something Solomon truly loved could distract him from prayer.

27 For this sense of *ayyām*, see esp. Q Ibrāhīm 14:5; see also ʿAmr ibn Kulthūm's "Muʿallaqah" in Ibn al-Anbārī, *Sharḥ al-Qaṣāʾid al-sabʿah al-ṭiwāl*, 388–89.20; and al-Jāḥiẓ, *Rasāʾil*, 2:187.

28 Ṭufayl, *Dīwān*, 35.

29 Al-Asʿar ibn Ḥumrān al-Juʿfī, in *Al-Aṣmaʿiyyāt*, 140–43.

30 This hadith appears in several different versions in the canonical hadith collections. E.g., Mālik ibn Anas, *Al-Muwaṭṭaʾ*, 349, no. 1016.

31 See the chapter on horse husbandry in Book Two, §§2.2.1–2.2.11.

32 This might be a reference to the Achaemenid ceremonial capital at Persepolis or to the necropolis of Naqsh-e Rostam, both in the south-western Iranian province of Fārs.

33 She means family members in whose presence she would not have to wear modest dress.

34 Ninth-century texts are often exercised by whether the comparison of two elements was appropriate; it was a central feature of debate culture that comparisons be well founded and apposite.

35 According to the concept of "abrogation," the Qurʾan was revealed throughout the Prophet's lifetime, with some later Qurʾanic verses replacing earlier ones. Muslim scholars also referred to the abrogation of Judaism and Christianity by Islam. See n. 43 below.

36 The point of the proverb, which engages in word play, is to highlight the tenuous association.

37 Ibn ʿAbd Rabbih, *Al-ʿIqd al-farīd*, 3:408–10, draws from §§1.6.1–1.6.3, 1.7.1–1.7.2, and 1.14.3–1.14.6.

38 Cf. Abū Nuwās, *Dīwān*, 3:324.

39 In classical usage the term has more vulgar connotations than Ibn Qutaybah lets on here; it can refer to the alleged smell and uncleanliness of uncircumcised peoples. See Ibn Manẓūr, *Lisān al-ʿArab*, s.v. *l-kh-n*, 13:383.

40 The story of Jacob tricking his father and so securing the blessing intended for his brother was widely known by Muslims. For the biblical story, see Genesis 27.

41 Q Hūd 11:42.

42 The Arabic term, *ṣaqālib*, was applied to light-skinned northern peoples of all sorts.

43 In the fields of Qur'anic commentary and Islamic law, the concept of abrogation (*nāsikh/mansūkh*) allowed the harmonization of apparent contradictions in legal rulings. Ibn Qutaybah's use of the term suggests the religious basis of the Persians' eclipse.

44 In the period immediately preceding Islam, a Sasanian expedition to Yemen succeeded in establishing a Persian presence in the territory.

45 Q Āl ʿImrān 3:33.

46 Q Āl ʿImrān 3:34.

47 Deuteronomy 18:18.

48 Cf. al-Masʿūdī, *Murūj*, sections 664 and 741.

49 I.e., after Yaʿrub ibn Qaḥṭān.

50 Yielding *ʿArab* and *ʿArabiyyah* (the Arabic language).

51 Al-ʿAjjāj, *Dīwān*, 138. In each case, the root letters of the tribal name are used to create a fifth-form verb.

52 This idea is common in the exegetical tradition on Q Baqarah 2:30.

53 Q Aʿrāf 7:58.

54 The translation of this line is conjectural. The verses are also quoted with slight differences anonymously in Ibn Qutaybah, *ʿUyūn al-akhbār*, 4:44.

55 Also reported in al-Mufaḍḍal al-Ḍabbī, *Al-Mufaḍḍaliyyāt*, 2:57.

56 Ibn Qutaybah, *Al-Shiʿr wa-l-shuʿarāʾ*, 2:666.

57 For this and the following three poems by al-Ḥuṭayʾah, see, respectively, *Dīwān*, 277, 276, 282, 329.

58 This type of toilet (*kiryās*) was located on the upper floors of a building, making use of gravity for the disposal of its contents. See Ibn Manẓūr, *Lisān al-ʿArab*, s.v. *k-r-s*, 6:194–95.

59 See also Ibn Qutaybah, *ʿUyūn al-akhbār*, 3:222.

60 Q Shams 91:9–10.

61 Al-ʿAbbās ibn Mirdās al-Sulamī; see Ibn Qutaybah, *ʿUyūn al-akhbār*, 2:7; and al-Jāḥiẓ, *Ḥayawān*, 6:463.

62 See Ibn Ḥabīb, *Al-Muḥabbar*, 352.

63 The poet is Hilāl ibn Muʿāwiyah al-Ṭāʾī; see Ibn Abī l-Ḥadīd, *Sharḥ Nahj al-balāghah*, 3:275.

64 See Ibn Qutaybah, *ʿUyūn al-akhbār*, 1:287.

65 Miskīn al-Dārimī, *Dīwān*, 45.

66 Al-Ḥuṭayʾah, *Dīwān*, 140–41.

67 By "goodness" here, Ibn Qutaybah seems to refer to God's plans for the Arabs.

68 For the verse, see ʿUrwah, *Dīwān*, 30–31.

69 The poet is Qays ibn ʿĀṣim. These verses are also attributed to Ḥātim al-Ṭāʾī. See Ḥātim al-Ṭāʾī, *Dīwān*, 312.

70 *Al-bārajīn*, possibly from the Persian *bar chīndan*, "gather, collect"; see Khāliṣ, ed., 68n8.

71 The poem is widely attributed to Ḥumayd; see Ibn Qutaybah, *ʿUyūn al-akhbār*, 3:242–43. The point of the poem is that the longer the guest spoke, the more he ate, which imposed great hardship on his host, and that his topics of conversation were trumped up to allow him to eat more food. Not even the eloquence and learning of Saḥbān Wāʾil could prevent him from talking.

72 This poem is also widely attributed to Ḥumayd. See, e.g., Ibn Qutaybah, *ʿUyūn al-akhbār*, 3:243.

73 See Ibn Qutaybah, *ʿUyūn al-akhbār*, 3:204.

74 A hard kind of tree from which walking sticks were made.

75 The attribution of these verses to al-Ḥuṭayʾah is contested. Wabr ibn Muʿāwiyah al-Asadī is identified as the poet by Hārūn in his edition of al-Jāḥiẓ's *Kitāb al-Bayān wa-l-Tabyīn*, 3:79; and by al-Jubūrī in his edition of Ibn Qutaybah's *Gharīb al-Ḥadīth*, 1:440–41.

76 See al-Maydānī, *Majmuʿ al-amthāl*, 1:368.

77 It would seem that Nahīk raised money to pay for a sacrificial animal as part of the hajj rituals but decided instead to part with his money.

78 See Ibn Qutaybah, *ʿUyūn al-akhbār*, 1:339.

79 Ibn Qutaybah, *ʿUyūn al-akhbār*.

80 The poet is al-Farazdaq; see al-Marzūqī, *Al-Azminah wa-l-amkinah*, 489.

81 See al-Rāʿī, *Dīwān*, 2.

82 This type of camel, termed *baḥīrah,* was a female with slit ears that was allowed to roam freely and was not put to work.

83 The second line is a common proverb.

84 Waʿlah al-Jarmī, as in *Gharīb al-Ḥadīth,* 1:239; and al-Jāḥiẓ, *Ḥayawān,* 2:317.

85 A set expression indicating she has a long, beautiful neck.

86 The Cairo manuscript begins here at f. 15a. The verse is included in Khalīl ibn Aḥmad, *Kitāb al-ʿAyn,* 1:234, under the lemma *ʿ-j-f,* where it is also unattributed.

87 This anecdote also features in Ibn Qutaybah's *ʿUyūn al-akhbār,* 3:211, where he reports that the Arab man visited a Bedouin.

88 What follows is an etymological discussion linking names for the Arabs' foods to the care given to their preparation. Ibn Qutaybah makes much of the Arabic roots of words.

89 As fate would have it, Ibn Qutaybah reportedly died from heartburn induced by eating *harīsah* (though there are contradictory reports on the manner of his death); al-Khaṭīb al-Baghdādī, *Taʾrīkh Baghdād,* 10:170.

90 Umayyah ibn Abī l-Ṣalt, *Dīwān,* 381.

91 Qays ibn ʿAmr ibn Mālik al-Najāshī; see Ibn Qutaybah, *Al-Maʿānī l-kabīr,* 1:487.

92 Qays ibn Sāʿid; see Ḥātim al-Ṭāʾī, *Dīwān,* 312, where this verse is part of a poem that also contains the verses quoted at §1.5.6 and §1.9.1 (the final three verses quoted there). The poet of these other verses is identified as Qays ibn ʿĀṣim.

93 Meaning the game of *maysir.*

94 When the first generation of Muslims broke into bloody conflict over leadership of the community, one side was led by ʿAlī ibn Abī Ṭālib, who appointed Abū Mūsā l-Ashʿarī as his representative in negotiations at Ṣiffīn, while the other side was led by Muʿāwiyah, who appointed ʿAmr as his representative. These are the "two arbiters."

95 In §1.9.2 above.

96 Al-Shammākh, *Dīwān,* 80.

97 Al-Kumayt, *Shiʿr,* 1:199.

98 In Ibn Qutaybah's *ʿUyūn al-akhbār*, 3:213, these verses are preceded by the following statement: "A man from Salūl passed by some youths who were drinking. He joined in, drank, and then set upon his camel, and killed it." The poet is al-ʿUjayr al-Salūlī; see al-ʿAskarī, *Dīwān al-Maʿānī*, 1:315.

99 The poet would seem to mean that if he continues to drink, he will slaughter his herd in an act of generosity.

100 Presumably the criticism was reported in an earlier part of the treatise that has not survived, or was leveled by an opponent, possibly in a work Ibn Qutaybah is refuting.

101 The Arabic here is *sulṭān*, a word which was originally an abstract noun meaning "power, authority," but which by the fourth/tenth century often passed to the meaning "holder of power, authority." Ibn Qutaybah's use of the term here seems an early instance of the second sense. Kramers and Bosworth, "Ṣulṭān."

102 In his *Al-Maʿārif* (414), Ibn Qutaybah attributes the quotation to the Prophet's grandson al-Ḥasan.

103 This is a pun on the Arabic proverb "Anxiety brings failure." Ibn Manẓūr, *Lisān al-ʿArab*, s.v. *kh-y-b*, 1:368.

104 The phrase "flocks of birds" (*al-ṭayr al-abābīl*) is a reference to Q Fīl 105:3, traditionally interpreted as referring to an episode in the campaign against the Kaaba by Abrahah.

105 Al-Aʿshā was a pre-Islamic poet. By citing the verses, Ibn Qutaybah is seeking to demonstrate the pre-Islamic Arabs' belief in God and His angels. Al-Aʿshā, *Dīwān*, 193.

106 This seems to be a reference to Part Two.

107 Q Āl ʿImrān 3:110. This verse is more often interpreted as referring to Muslims as the best *ummah*, not Arabs.

108 Q Aʿrāf 7:140.

109 Q Anʿām 6:163. The Arabic term here is *muslimīn*, which is used in the generic sense of someone in a state of submission to God, and which invokes the idea of Islam as the religion of every prophet before Muḥammad.

110 Q Aʿrāf 7:143.

111 Q Baqarah 2:47.

112 Q Dukhān 44:37.

113 Q Āl ʿImrān 3:33.

114 Q Dukhān 44:37.

115 An allusion to Q Aʿrāf 7:86: «Remember when you were few in number and He multiplied you.»

116 I.e., the Sacred Precinct (*ḥaram*) of Mecca.

117 Ibn Qutaybah attributes this saying to al-Aṣmaʿī in *Gharīb al-Ḥadīth*, 364.

118 Ibn Qutaybah refers here first to the Parthians and then to the Arsacid Empire, which ruled Iran from about 250 BC to about AD 226.

119 Ibn Qutaybah may be referring here to the *Khudāy-nāmag*, the now-lost Sasanian-era chronicle which was translated multiple times into Arabic.

120 Our reliance on Kurd ʿAlī's edition ends here.

121 The text seems corrupted here, as surely the meaning must be the opposite, that it would be impossible for anyone to place trust in an assurance of safety or a treaty.

122 Italics indicate our conjectural reconstruction of the text.

123 That is, not to the Abbasid family. Muḥammad ibn ʿAlī's speech reflects the diversity of views once held on the legitimacy of the early caliphs, before a consensus arose among Sunni Muslims on the legitimacy of the first four rulers of the Muslim community after Muhammad's death: Abū Bakr, ʿUmar, ʿUthmān, and ʿAlī. See Crone, *Medieval Islamic Political Thought*.

124 This list of authorities would appear to contain errors; see Ibn al-Jawzī, *Virtues*, chapter 1, section 8, where the hadith's list runs back to the Prophet's lifetime. See also Ibn Qutaybah, *ʿUyūn al-akhbār*, 1:38, for the more probably correct list attached to a different report.

125 We follow Khāliṣ, who has restored the text of this hadith from its quotation in Ibn Qutaybah, *ʿUyūn al-akhbār*, 1:215.

126 See al-Jāḥiẓ, *Al-Bukhalāʾ*, 14, lines 1–2; and *Al-Ḥayawān*, 2:149, where the speaker instead is identified as the more likely Thumāmah ibn Ashras.

127 For the longer lacunae, we include in our notes English translations of the corresponding Arabic words and phrases. "He was the best in the conjunction of . . . a million dinars . . . than that he be given . . . Someone else who . . . would . . . himself with what he posseseed."

128 "Torn to pieces" (*wa-muzziqū kulla mumazzaq*) echoes part of Q Saba' 34:19. On this phrase applied to the kingdom of Persia, see Savant, *New Muslims*, 187, 189.

129 Ibn Qutaybah cites this speech in *'Uyūn al-akhbār*, 2:233. For the use of this obscure term, see al-Jāḥiẓ, *Ḥayawān*, 4:407–8. Khāliṣ (105n5) has proposed the Arabic to this passage, based on the *Ḥayawān*. Still, the sentence does not make obvious sense, so the translation is speculative. Perhaps, contra Ibn Qutaybah, Abū Bakr's point was that the Muslims would conquer after his lifetime lands near and far, bringing into the empire even sterile, barren lands, since the term *kharisah* can mean sterile and barren lands.

130 This is not Ibn Qutaybah speaking but an unknown person he quotes. No name is legible in the manuscript.

131 Reported elsewhere, e.g., Abū Yaʿlā l-Mawṣilī, *Musnad*, 1:322.

132 The term *ahl al-bayt*, "People of the House" (or here, "People of My House"), signifies the Prophet's family.

133 I.e., the Umayyads.

134 The reference is to Matthew 8:11–12.

135 Ibn Qutaybah appears to refer here to 'Umar's efforts to ensure that new converts to Islam would be granted the same lenient fiscal status as other Muslims.

136 ". . . the Sawād that they . . . of the sons of . . . that they are good works from Khurasan . . ."

137 "An ancient poet said: 'It was enough of a failing . . .'"

138 Q Ḥujurāt 49:13.

139 Q Anʿām 6:130.

140 Q Yūnus 10:60. Ibn Qutaybah's citation of the Qur'an here differs slightly from the standard text of the Qur'an.

141 "'. . . but I did not think Saʿd was like . . . He said . . . two tribes made up of two peoples . . . together and then they both became disunited . . .'"

142 Q Ḥujurāt 49:13.

143 Literally "are filling for the measuring cup, which cannot be filled."

144 Kuthayyir ʿAzzah, *Dīwān*, 384.

145 The statement plays with the word for people (*nās*). The *nasnās* (or *nisnās*) is a figure of Arabian legend that was partially human in appearance.

146 "The human being . . . his heart."

147 "There is no shame for the man who . . . real shame lies in . . . the noble . . . the base from . . . the noble, because they liken to nobility him who . . . this being the head."

148 Ibn Shubrumah was engaging in word play here. Used one way, his descriptors flatter the man; but each has another, general sense that would apply to any person, and so the man is of little worth.

149 In §1.14.3.

150 ". . . the others became liable to revenge . . . Islam."

151 The speaker's name is not recoverable from the manuscript.

152 The point is that he was careless with his appearance, since working men rolled up their sleeves and pants.

153 ". . . of camels he will not give more . . . rulings such as the giving of a full measure . . ."

154 Quoted anonymously also in Ibn Qutaybah, *ʿUyūn al-akhbār*, 1:239.

155 Quoted anonymously in Ibn Qutaybah, *ʿUyūn al-akhbār*, 1:240.

156 The poet is Mālik ibn al-Ḥārith; see al-Sukkarī, *Sharḥ Ashʿār al-Hudhaliyyīn*, 1:238–39; Ibn Qutaybah, *ʿUyūn al-akhbār*, 1:240–41.

157 The poet is Abū l-ʿAtāhiyah: *Dīwān*, 356.

158 ". . . He followed a whim, and rode . . . Because of him, the people acquired . . . they beheld . . ."

159 ". . . that which was required is not required . . ."

160 The Arabic for "pulley" is *bakrah*.

161 Q Furqān 25:54.

162 The Arabic *muqrif* and *hajīn*, both translated here as "half-breed grade," refer to a horse sired by a non-Arabian stallion or born of a non-Arabian mare, respectively; the English "grade," referring to mixed, unknown, or unidentifiable parentage, seems the nearest equivalent for both.

163 The Arabic *taḍmīr* (and its derivatives, related to galloping) is a specialized term without an English equivalent for a specific regime of preparing a horse to race, regulating its feeding for a period beforehand to tone its muscles. See Ibn Manẓūr, *Lisān al-ʿArab*, s.v. *ḍ-m-r*, 4:491–92.

164 Our interpretation; the words are unreadable in the MS.

165 Unreadable in the MS and not traceable in other sources.

166 The words describing the horse in the Arabic rhyme with each other, rendering this one of the "wise sayings in rhymed prose" Ibn Qutaybah referred to in his introduction (see §2.1.2). Each term is thus selected to match the rhyme, and not necessarily for its purely technical connotations.

167 The source of this story may be Uqayṣir's son, Muḥammad ibn Uqayṣir al-Sulamī. See Ibn Qutaybah, *Al-Maʿānī l-kabīr*, 1:89n7.

168 References to wolves in thickets evoke Bedouin expressions for particularly fearsome wolves that hide themselves far from human settlement and allow themselves to be seen only when they are on the attack (Ibn Manẓūr, *Lisān al-ʿArab*, s.v. *gh-ḍ-w*, 15:129).

169 In *ʿUyūn al-akhbār*, 1:158, Ibn Qutaybah specifies that the poem was composed after the Battle of Ṣiffīn (36–37/657).

170 Presumably alluding to the alleged good quality in a stallion lying prone. See §2.2.4.

171 The numerical terms in this poem are translated literally from Arabic, as there are no English equivalents. Ibn Qutaybah cites this poem because its highly specialized terminology demonstrates, for him, the Arabs' unrivaled knowledge of horses. He would no doubt be pleased to know that the English language never developed so sophisticated a vocabulary as that of the Arabs!

172 The "five longs" refers to five parts of the horse that, if elongated, were deemed praiseworthy by the Arabs: the neck, the ears, the forelegs, the haunches, and forelock; "four shorts" refers to the pastern, the dock, the back, and the flanks.

173 The "six broads" are the forehead, the chest, the haunches, the thighs, the cannons of the hind legs, and the place between the ear-roots;

the "sevens" are the ears, the eyes, the shoulders, the barrel, the hamstrings of the hind legs, the bones meeting the fetlock, and the bones meeting the shoulder; and the "nines" are the bones under the eyes, the bones under the tear ducts, the cheeks, the forehead, the place between the ear-roots, the fetlocks, the veins in the forelegs, and the hind legs (Ibn Qutaybah only glosses eight of the "nines" in *al-Maʿānī l-kabīr* 1:91).

174 "Nine clothed" refers to the shoulder, the veins running from the shoulder to the end of the barrel, the forearms, the thighs, the veins in the horse's legs, and the flesh protruding at the tops of its thighs (Ibn Qutaybah glosses only six of the nine in *Al-Maʿānī l-kabīr*, 1:92); "ten longs" refers to the lips and the spaces between the eyes and the ears, between the eyes and the jaw, between the forelock and the base of the tail, between the withers and the shoulder, between the forearms and the knees, between the belly and the thigh, and between the hindquarters and backside, as well as the width of the backside (Ibn Qutaybah glosses only nine in *Al-Maʿānī l-kabīr*, 1:92); "ten shorts" refers to the spaces between the nostrils, the ears, the shoulders, the elbows, the haunches, and the withers and croup, as well as the spaces between the veins of the shoulder and the end of the barrel, between the join of the thigh and lower leg and the fetlock, between the backside and the base of the tail, and between the coronet and the hairs on the hoof; and "five talls" refers to the neck, the ears, the forelegs, the haunches, and forelock.

175 A boast of particular significance considering that the horse described lives in the desert with its Bedouin masters.

176 Literally, camels "with young or those nursing others' calves."

177 Ibn Qutaybah appears to make reference to his *Adab al-kātib*, which contains a section entitled "Bāb fī maʿrifat al-khayl wa-mā yustaḥabbu min khalqihā" ("Chapter on Horses and Their Desirable Traits")—though it does not contain any of the verses from this poem (*Adab al-kātib*, 133–40). Ibn Qutaybah does narrate and gloss the poem in the lengthy section on horses in his *Al-Maʿānī l-kabīr*, 1:91–92.

178 Lacuna in the original.

179 The poem is attributed to the Umayyad-era Kūfan poet al-Kumayt in al-Marzūqī's *Al-Azminah wa-l-amkinah*, 140.

180 That is, the Arabs.

181 The poet is Usayd ibn al-Ḥalāḥil.

182 We understand this verse to mean that the camels will not travel in the daytime during the period mentioned (as does Ibn Qutaybah's gloss following this poem). The phrase *awlajat sawālifahā* literally means "they take in the backs of their necks." Verbs related to the root *w–l–j* are used in reference to animals (particularly gazelles) concealing themselves during times of intense heat (Ibn Manẓūr, *Lisān al-ʿArab*, s.v. *w–l–j*, 2:398–99).

183 The Arabic *al-qalb* (literally, "heart," translated here as Scorpionis) can refer to a number of different stars.

184 Here Ibn Qutaybah appears to be defending Ḥātim's poetry against detractors who might claim Ḥātim erred in citing a star (Capella) with the wrong constellation (the Pleiades). Ibn Qutaybah posits that Ḥātim justifiably mentioned both stars together on account of their conjoined movements, thus showing Ḥātim's sound astronomical knowledge.

185 Possibly al-Aswad ibn Yaʿfur; see Ibn Qutaybah, *Al-Anwāʾ*, 71.

186 In al-Aswad ibn Yaʿfur's *Dīwān*, 34, the verse appears differently, starting: "You were born under Ḥādī l-Najm, burning the sky around it."

187 That is, the traveler to the king (the traveler was, in the case of this story, ʿAbīd ibn al-Abraṣ) was doomed, as if he set out under a bad star, referring to the ill omens associated with Aldebaran.

188 It rises on February 25.

189 The tents are erected for shade.

190 The expression contrasts winter and summer: Canopus coincides with the beginning of winter, the Pleiades with the beginning of summer. The proverb alludes to the risks of forcing young camels to stop suckling at the beginning of winter (i.e., after the rise of Canopus). See al-Marzūqī, *Al-Azminah wa-l-amkinah*, 1:392–93, and al-Ḥimyarī, *Shams al-ʿulūm*, 10:6488, for interpretations of these rhyming expressions.

191 Ibn Qutaybah writes the month as *ayyār*, the equivalent to May in the solar calendar. When plotting the rise of stars, he naturally prefers the solar calendar to the Muslim lunar calendar, which is not fixed to the risings of stars.

192 Malik, *Al-Muwaṭṭaʾ*, 1:199.

193 The poem is elsewhere ascribed to al-Raḥḥāl, not Jirān al-ʿAwd.

194 Q Qamar 54:19. Ibn Qutaybah only partially cites the verse here: it refers to a wind sent by God to smite unbelievers.

195 The verses are missing in the MS: we have inserted them from a nearly identical parallel passage in Ibn Qutaybah's *Al-Anwāʾ*, 175.

196 This story concludes a tale about the medical benefits of camel urine. The man suffered from severe ulcers on the neck (*khanāzīr*, scrofula), and he visited a Bedouin who agreed to cure him on condition that the man concealed the details of the Bedouin's method (which involved a mixture of camel urine and leaves of the *Salvadora* shrub). When the man returned to his town and refused to divulge the secret treatment, ʿAbd Allāh ibn Masʿūd instructed him to disclose it, seemingly in the public interest. For the complete anecdote, see al-Dīnawarī, *Al-Mujālasah wa-jawāhir al-ʿilm*, 5:368, and for a translation, see the Note on the Text, p. <?>. This story is not part of Ibn Qutaybah's meteorological section but rather was probably the conclusion of a now-missing section of *The Excellence of Arab Learning* on the Bedouin's unique medical knowledge.

197 Salm ibn ʿAmr ibn Ḥammād.

198 The Muʿāwiyah in this anecdote is the Caliph Muʿāwiyah ibn Abī Sufyān; Hind (bint ʿUtbah) was his mother.

199 This anecdote appears to have been imperfectly transmitted in the MS with the effect of reversing the meaning. In *ʿUyūn al-akhbār*, 1:223, Ibn Qutaybah relates a fuller version on the slightly different authority of Jamīʿ ibn Abī Ghāḍir: "Al-Zibriqān used to say that among his young boys the one he hated the most was the 'little pigeon-breasted male' who looked as if he was peering out of his hole, and when people asked him 'Where is your father?' he would growl in their faces, saying 'What do you want with my father?' Whereas the most

beloved of his boys was the one with a long foreskin, a pure white mien, broad haunches, and a foolish deportment who obeyed his uncle and defied his mother, and, when asked 'Where is your father?' he replied, 'With you!'"

200 The word *kadhdhāb* (translated here as "Calumniator") is a pejorative term for al-Mukhtār al-Thaqafī, opponent of the Umayyads in Iraq.

201 Mujazzaz could tell that the sleepers were related: Usāmah was Zayd ibn Ḥārithah's son.

202 The poem has been variously attributed to al-Maʿlūṭ (Ibn Qutaybah, *ʿUyūn al-akhbār*, 1:149), Sawwār ibn al-Muḍarrab (al-Jāḥiẓ, *Al-Ḥayawān*, 3:440) and Juḥdur al-ʿUklī (Ibn ʿAbd Rabbihi, *Al-ʿIqd*, 5:414).

203 The divination derives from the resemblances between the trees' names and words for separation: desert poplar (*gharab*)/distance (*gharb*); moringa (*bān*)/depart (*bāna*).

204 The word *injidhām* (from the same root as the name Judhām) means separation or cutting of ties.

205 Crow (*ghurāb*)/absence (*ghurbah*). The nickname Ḥātim derives from the verb *ḥatama*, "to necessitate/prescribe."

206 The type of arrow described here is a *qidḥ*, an unfletched arrow used as a throwing stick in the *maysir* game of chance. *Maysir* was reportedly played as a form of lots by which players competed over portions of camel meat, as referenced in al-Rāʿī's poem here. Ibn Qutaybah's *Al-Maysir wa-l-qidāḥ*, 27-32, details the subject.

207 Q Aḥqāf 46:4.

208 The poet is Labīd ibn Rabīʿah.

209 The meaning of *ghuwayrah* in the MS is uncertain: it seems to be a copyist's error, and the intended term was either *juwayrah* (little stream/waterway) or *ghuwayr* (little vale or little cave). A version of this story recorded by Ibn Durayd has *juwayrah* (*Taʿlīq min Amālī Ibn Durayd*, 103).

210 Qutaybah refers to the considerable military services he rendered to the two previous caliphs, ʿAbd al-Malik ibn Marwān and al-Walīd ibn ʿAbd al-Malik.

211 The MS has *ʿilm* (knowledge), which we have corrected to *ḥilm* (equanimity) for the sake of the meaning, following the same anecdote in Ibn Qutaybah's *ʿUyūn al-akhbār*, 3:106.

212 In other citations of this anecdote, the retainer is identified as Jarīr ibn Yazīd (Ibn Qutaybah, *ʿUyūn al-akhbār*, 1:92).

213 Abū Tammām al-Ṭāʾī. The poem is in praise of Khālid ibn Yazīd ibn Mazyad al-Shaybānī (Abū Tammām, *Dīwān*, 1:405–22).

214 Two verses from Abū Tammām's poem preceding the line "Thus the Arabs . . ." (Abū Tammām, *Dīwān*, 1:421) are not in the MS, leaving an awkward transition. The lines note how noble deeds, when strung into poetry, serve their master in war and peace, but "if a man's noble deeds have no poems to escort them, / They will never spread nor gain renown. / Thus the ancient Arabs . . ."

215 A sobriquet referencing their generosity.

216 The anecdote implies that Najdah's power in Arabia at the time was comparable to that of Ibn al-Zubayr and Ibn al-Ḥanafiyyah.

217 See above, §1.8.15.

218 Q Shuʿarāʾ 26:84. The "chosen companion" is Abraham.

219 Q Zukhruf 43:44.

220 The reading in Zuhayr, *Dīwān*, 44, is *juḥidū*, rendering the line "noble and magnanimous in hardship."

221 The Umayyad aristocrat ʿAbd al-ʿAzīz ibn Marwān.

222 Instead of the word *kuhūl* (men) recorded in the MS, Zuhayr (*Dīwān*, 54) reads *budāt* (Bedouin), pairing it with *ḥadar* (settled folk).

223 A reference to a year of warfare when a tribe is aware of impending raids and hence does not allow its animals to pasture freely for fear of capture.

224 To underscore Harim's generosity, the poet commends him for having procured wine even in dire straits. Zuhayr, *Dīwān*, 54, has *khabba al-safīru* (when the leaves fall from the trees) for *ḥubba al-quṭāru* in the manuscript.

225 Q Yūsuf 12:55.

226 Other sources identify the original "Camel Snout" as Jaʿfar ibn Qurayʿ ibn ʿAwf ibn Kaʿb (see the commentary in al-Ḥuṭayʾah, *Dīwān*, 15).

227 The poet is Muḥammad ibn Mundhir.

228 Q Nūr 24:30.

229 The poet insinuates the ʿAjlān were so feeble as to lack the mettle to hazard decisive and risky acts, such as breaking a treaty.

230 The verb "be quick" (*ʿajala*) is formed from the same root as the name al-ʿAjlān.

231 See Ibn Qutaybah, *Al-Shiʿr wa-l-shuʿarāʾ*, 1:318–19.

232 Literally, "The Bāhilah were trotters [*kurāʿ*], and you've turned them into forearms."

233 The term refers to pre-Islamic Arabian warriors of legendary running prowess, who, unlike other pre-Islamic heroes, did not raid on horseback.

234 The line was actually composed by al-Akhṭal against Jarīr.

235 Ḍabbah refers here to the kin of al-Farazdaq, a poet al-Ṭirimmāḥ lampoons in this poem.

236 The name of the administrator is Taym. See the prose commentary following the poem, and, for a slightly expanded version of the story, see Ibn ʿAbd Rabbihi, *Al-ʿIqd al-farīd*, 5:293.

237 Al-Farazdaq's reference to looms appears to be a witty pun intending spears, thereby belittling the fighters. Perhaps al-Farazdaq drew this analogy from perceiving a humorous double entendre engendered by ʿĀṣim's son's infelicitous choice of some words for weapons and warriors, which also have meanings associated with weaving and cloth trade. An expanded version of the story in Ibn Qutaybah's *ʿUyūn al-akhbār*, 1:124, closes the anecdote with ʿĀṣim's response to al-Farazdaq's chide: "Farazdaq! This boy is the poet of the believers; you are the poet of the disbelievers!"

238 The *sakhbar* tree, a kind of ficus, is a euphemism for betrayal, because when the tree grows, its top begins to droop and shifts its position (Ibn Manẓūr, *Lisān al-ʿArab*, s.v. *s-kh-b-r*, 4:354).

239 According to most versions, Muʿāwiyah purchased the mantle from Kaʿb's son. Ibn Qutaybah leaves the matter vague in *Al-Shiʿr wa-l-shuʿarāʾ*, 1:155.

240 The reference to forgiveness could alternatively mean Ibn ʿAbbās exhorted the learning of Islamic-era Hijazi poetry, since it is like

authentic pre-Islamic verse but is forgiven since it was composed by Muslims.

241 "Non-Arabic piety" appears to be a reference to ascetics or hermits who shunned the recitation of poetry (see al-Jāḥiẓ, *Al-Bayān*, 1:202).

242 The poet is al-Aḥwaṣ al-Anṣārī.

243 This group of thinkers, *aṣḥāb al-qiyās*, refers to those who follow methods of analogical reasoning (*qiyās al-ghā'ib ʿalā l-shāhid*) developed in Arabic theological thought from Greek philosophical precedents.

244 This word identifying Easterners is mostly effaced in the MS, but is likely *ʿAjam*.

245 The anecdote from which this poem is derived ascribes the verses to Abū Dhu'ayb's cousin Khalid (see al-Madā'inī, *Majmaʿ al-amthāl*, 3:181–82).

246 The following poem has been ascribed to Kuthayyir ʿAzzah, Ḥātim al-Ṭā'ī, and Dhū l-Iṣbaʿ al-ʿAdwānī, among others.

247 The poet is Dhū l-Iṣbaʿ al-ʿAdwānī.

248 The poem is attributed to either Abū Tammām, Diʿbil ibn ʿAlī l-Khuzāʿī, al-Ṣūlī, or an unknown poet.

249 The poet is al-Akhṭal.

250 The poet is Ṣāliḥ ibn ʿAbd al-Quddūs.

251 The poet is al-Aḥwaṣ al-Anṣārī.

252 Q Mā'idah 5:89.

253 Al-Farazdaq.

254 Jābir ibn Thāʿlab al-Ṭā'ī.

255 The verbs for paring and fletching arrows are used metaphorically for treating someone severely or gently, respectively (see Ibn Manẓūr, *Lisān al-ʿArab*, s.vv. *r-y-sh*, 6:309–10 and *b-r-y*, 14:70).

256 The modern edition of Kaʿb ibn Zuhayr's *Dīwān* (Cairo: Dār al-Kutub), 257, reads *raḥl* (saddle) instead of *rijl* (foot), as in the MS. The more common transmission of this line thus reads: "A saddle set down by God cannot be moved."

257 Two versions of this statement are attributed to Aktham, and the MS contains an imperfect amalgamation of both. One reads *tathabbatū fa-inna aḥzam al-farīqayn al-rakīn* (Stand firm: the most resolute

side is the steadfast); the other opens with *lā talbathū wa-lā tusriʿū fa-inna* . . . (Neither tarry nor hurry, for the most resolute side is the steadfast). See Ibn al-Athīr, *Al-Kāmil fī l-taʾrīkh*, 1:623.

258 The MS likely records this aphorism in error. The same set of sayings is recorded in Ibn Qutaybah's *ʿUyūn al-akhbār*, 1:126, where the second statement of the Bedouin reads *kam min mīta ʿillatuhā ṭalab al-ḥayāt*. The translation here follows this version.

259 The MS records this saying incorrectly; the translation here follows the version: *ʿīy ṣāmit khayr min ʿīy nāṭiq* (Ibn Sallām, *Al-Amthāl*, 44).

260 That is, your dignity and your religion.

261 The saying as reported in the MS copies directly from a poem of Ṣāliḥ ibn ʿAbd al-Quddūs. The line was derived from an older prose aphorism with slightly amended wording, adding some pronouns: *yad tashujj wa-ukhrā minka taʾsūnī* (*You* smash my skull with one hand, and nurse *me* with the other). See Abū ʿUbayd al-Bakrī, *Faṣl al-maqāl fī sharḥ Kitāb al-Amthāl*, 428.

262 As the manuscript is unclear, we have reconstructed this aphorism from Ibn Ḥadīd, *Sharḥ Nahj al-balāghah*, 3:159.

263 The precise meaning of this aphorism is unclear.

264 I.e., his heart and tongue.

265 The precise meaning is unclear. Perhaps "value the gifts that God has given you and thank Him for them."

266 Most collections of aphorisms render this saying with a slightly different wording: *al-iqtiṣād yunmī l-yasīr* (see al-Qāḍī al-Quḍāʿī, *Treasury of Virtues*, 10).

267 That is, inquire about your companion before setting off with him, and about the neighbors before buying a house.

268 Ibn Qutaybah uses "Rūm" to describe Alexander and his language in this passage. Ibn Qutaybah and his contemporaries used this term to mean, variously, classical Greece, Rome, and Byzantium, depending on the context, though they sometimes used "Yūnān" to specify ancient Greece alone, as in the beginning of this paragraph.

Glossary

This glossary includes the names of the many Arab peoples mentioned in *The Excellence of the Arabs*. These groups have often been labeled “tribes,” and in Ibn Qutaybah’s day, many writers considered the tribal organization of Arab society to be a unique trait that distinguished Arabs from other peoples of the world. Arab tribalism, however, is not as straightforward as Ibn Qutaybah, his peers, and many subsequent commentators have assumed. The idea that all Arabs are members of one pan-Arabian family tree of interrelated tribes is almost certainly a fiction of Abbasid-era writers who forged elaborate explanations in order to fit Arab groups into cohesive Arab genealogies. The Arabic terms for “tribe” are also manifold and could be used to describe groups of variable size and social cohesion. Moreover, research into Arabian populations, ancient and modern, also demonstrates that tribal composition is fluid and that members of one tribe do not always act in concert. The size and effectiveness of tribal unity thus fluctuate over time, and dividing Arabia into fixed tribal divisions oversimplifies the contours of its society. “Tribe” also carries connotations of primitivism in English, and to label all Arabs as “tribesmen” might play into modern prejudices about tribes and Arabs. For these reasons, we have chosen to eschew “tribe” in the glossary, and refer instead to the name by which lineage groups were commonly known. Large lineage groups, such as the Tamīm, are composed of subgroups, such as the Bahdalah and the Dārim, and we have defined them as they were codified by Muslim genealogists in the third/ninth century.

The Arabic definite article “al-” as well as the Arabic letters *hamzah* and *ʿayn* have been disregarded in the ordering of entries. Often-used terms such as Mecca and Medina are not cross-referenced.

al-ʿAbbās ibn Mirdās al-Sulamī (d. between 18/639 and 35/656) poet of the Sulaym lineage group.

Abbasids dynasty of caliphs (132–656/750–1258), named after their ancestor al-ʿAbbās ibn ʿAbd al-Muṭṭalib ibn Hāshim, an uncle of the Prophet.

ʿAbd Allāh ibn ʿAlī ibn Waththāb al-Madanī unknown figure. The two manuscripts of *The Excellence of the Arabs* record his name differently: Kurd ʿAlī's edition reads it ʿAbd Allāh ibn ʿAlī; the Cairo manuscript has ʿAlī ibn ʿAbd Allāh, also unknown.

ʿAbd Allāh ibn al-Ḥārith [*ibn Nawfal ibn al-Ḥārith ibn ʿAbd al-Muṭṭalib*] (d. after 80/699–700) Qurayshī hadith transmitter of the generation after Muḥammad; nephew, via his mother, of the Umayyad caliph Muʿāwiyah.

ʿAbd Allāh ibn Judʿān pre-Islamic Meccan trader of the Ṭaym ibn Murrah clan of Quraysh; renowned in Arabian lore as one of Mecca's richest men.

ʿAbd Allāh ibn Khāzim al-Sulamī (d. 73/692–93) a widely remembered governor of Khurasan under the Umayyads.

ʿAbd Allāh ibn Masʿūd see Ibn Masʿūd.

ʿAbd Allāh ibn al-Mubārak (d. 181/797) hadith transmitter, scholar, and merchant; studied with the most important jurists of his day, including Abū Ḥanīfah, Sufyān al-Thawrī, and Mālik ibn Anas.

ʿAbd Allāh ibn Rawāḥah (d. 8/629) Medinese Companion of the Prophet Muḥammad; being literate, he was one of Muḥammad's official secretaries, and, with Ḥassān ibn Thābit (q.v.) and Kaʿb ibn Mālik (q.v.), is counted among the three official poets of the Muslim community. Killed at the Battle of Mu'tah.

ʿAbd Allāh ibn Zuhayr minor hadith transmitter of uncertain identity; Hadith scholars disagree on the form of his name (possibly Zuhayr ibn ʿAbd Allāh). In the one hadith narrated by him, he appears as a Companion of the Prophet.

ʿAbd al-ʿAzīz ibn Abī Bakrah hadith transmitter from the generation after the Prophet's lifetime. Son of Abū Bakrah (q.v.).

ʿAbd al-Ghaffār al-Khuzāʿī author of a famous poem describing horses; a treatise entitled the *Book of Horses* (*Kitāb al-Khayl*) usually attributed to Abū ʿUbaydah (q.v.) is sometimes ascribed to him or his son Muḥammad.

ʿAbd al-Malik ibn Ḥamīd non-Arab client of the Arabian Bāhilah (q.v.); acquired high rank in the early Abbasid regime as secretary and confident of the Caliph al-Manṣūr (q.v.), who gave him control of the western quarter of Baghdad.

ʿAbd al-Malik ibn Marwān (r. 65–86/685–705) fifth caliph of the Umayyad dynasty and key figure in the development of state structures, ideologies, and institutions for the caliphate.

ʿAbd al-Munʿim grandson of Wahb ibn Munabbih (q.v.), and a commonly cited transmitter of his grandfather's lore.

ʿAbd al-Muṭṭalib ibn Hāshim paternal grandfather of the Prophet Muḥammad; when Muḥammad was orphaned as a child, ʿAbd al-Muṭṭalib cared for him.

ʿAbd al-Qays large Arabian lineage group, settled in al-Baḥrayn (q.v.) in pre-Islamic times.

ʿAbd al-Raḥmān son of ʿAbd al-Munʿim (q.v.) and great-grandson of Wahb ibn Munabbih (q.v.).

ʿAbd al-Raḥmān ibn Abān son of, and hadith transmitter from, Abān, who was a jurist of Medina.

ʿAbd al-Raḥmān ibn al-Azhar Companion of the Prophet from whom al-Zuhrī (q.v.) transmitted hadiths.

ʿAbd al-Raḥmān ibn Khālid possibly the hadith transmitter ʿAbd al-Raḥmān ibn Khālid ibn Yazīd al-Qaṭān, from Wāsiṭ, who died in 251/865–66.

ʿAbd al-Wārith ibn Saʿīd (d. 180/796–97) minor Basran hadith transmitter of the early Abbasid period.

ʿAbdah ibn al-Ṭabīb pre-Islamic "brigand poet" (Ar. *ṣuʿlūk*), remembered in the lore both for thieving and for singing fine poetry; survived into the Islamic period, converted to Islam, and reportedly participated in early Muslim campaigns in Iraq.

Abrahah Christian king of Ethiopian origin in south Arabia in the middle of the sixth century AD; in Islamic literature he is named as the leader of a Yemeni expedition against Mecca in the year of Muḥammad's birth, ca. AD 570.

Abraham (Ar. Ibrāhīm) the Abraham of the Bible, who in Islamic sacred history founds or reforms the monotheistic cult of the Kaaba in Mecca. Father to Isaac (through his wife Sarah) and Ishmael (through his concubine Hagar).

Abū ʿAmr ibn al-ʿAlāʾ (d. 154/771 or 157/774) famous early lexicographer, grammarian, Qurʾan reader, and expert on poetry; active in Basra, he taught most of the scholars of the subsequent generation.

Abū l-ʿAtāhiyah (d. 210/825 or 211/826) poet best known for his ascetic poetry and acclaimed as one of the leading "modern poets" (*muḥdathūn*) of the Abbasid era. His given name was Abū Isḥāq Ismāʿīl ibn al-Qāsim ibn Suwayd ibn Kaysān.

Abū Bakr (r. 11–13/632–34) Muḥammad's father-in-law and Islam's first caliph. A wealthy Qurayshī merchant before Islam; reported to be the first convert to Islam, or one of the first.

Abū Bakrah [Nufayʿ ibn Masrūḥ] Companion of the Prophet, and hadith transmitter; enslaved in pre-Islam and manumitted by the Prophet. He reportedly died in the same year as al-Ḥasan, the son of ʿAlī (q.v.), ca. 49/669–70 (al-Ḥasan's death date is variously reported).

Abū Dhuʾayb [al-Hudhalī] (d. ca. 30–35/650–55) pre-Islamic poet of the Arabian Hudhayl (q.v.); survived into the Islamic period and participated in several Muslim conquests; some report that he died on campaign during the caliphate of ʿUthmān (q.v.), either in North Africa or Turkey.

Abū Dulaf [al-Qāsim ibn ʿĪsā l-ʿIjlī] (d. between 225/840 and 228/843) poet, musician, litterateur, military commander under the Caliph al-Amīn (r. 193–98/809–13), and governor under the Caliph al-Muʿtaṣim (r. 218–27/833–42).

Abū Ghāḍir (fl. first/seventh century) likely a sobriquet of ʿUrwah al-Fuqaymī (also known as Abū Ghāḍirah), a member of the Tamīm lineage group (q.v.) and a contemporary of the Prophet.

Abū Ghassān possibly Yazīd ibn Ziyād (fl. mid second/eighth century), member of the early Abbasid movement and the chamberlain of the first Abbasid caliph, al-Saffāḥ (r. 132–37/750–54).

Abū Ḥajjār Abjar ibn Jābir (d. early first/seventh century) a Christian of the northeastern Arabian ʿIjl ibn Lujaym (q.v.) who lived into the early

Islamic period. He did not convert to Islam, but his son Ḥajjār did; Abjar is remembered in Arabic lore as giving wise advice to Ḥajjār on the eve of his conversion.

Abū Ḥanbal Jāriyah ibn Murr (fl. mid-sixth century AD) pre-Islamic poet from the Ṭayyi' (q.v.).

Abū Ḥātim [*Sahl ibn Muḥammad al-Sijistānī*] (d. ca. 255/869) Sunni philologist and specialist of Arabian poetry; teacher of many Iraqi scholars, including Ibn Qutaybah.

Abū Jaʿfar al-Manṣūr (r. 136–58/754–75) second Abbasid caliph and founder of the new Abbasid capital, Baghdad.

Abū Jahḍam ʿAbbād ibn Ḥuṣayn (d. early second/eighth century) Basran nobleman-warrior of the Tamīm (q.v.); participant in many key political events occurring in southern Iraq during the early Umayyad Caliphate.

Abū Malīl leader of the Thaʿlabah (q.v.) mentioned in pre-Islamic lore; father of Bujayr and ʿIfāq (q.v.).

Abū l-Minhāl (d. 106/724–25) Basran hadith transmitter who settled in Mecca.

Abū Mūsā l-Ashʿarī (d. uncertain, possibly 42/662) Companion of the Prophet and prominent military leader during the early Islamic conquests; one of the two arbitrators, alongside ʿAmr ibn al-ʿĀṣ (q.v.), tasked with settling the dispute over the caliphate between ʿAlī and Muʿāwiyah (qq.v.) in 37/657.

Abū Mūsā l-Shahawāt see Shahawāt.

Abū Muṣʿab al-Zubayrī [*ʿAbd Allāh ibn Muṣʿab ibn Thābit*] (d. 184/800) Meccan aristocrat of the late Umayyad and early Abbasid era, confidant of the Abbasid caliph al-Mahdī and father and grandfather of Muṣʿab al-Zubayrī and Zubayr ibn Bakkār, respectively, two of the most important early historians of the Quraysh.

Abū l-Najm al-ʿIjlī (d. ca. 120/738) Umayyad-era poet celebrated for *rajaz*-style verse about Bedouin life and praise poems of the Umayyad elite. Also known for his poetic rivalry with al-ʿAjjāj (q.v.), part of a wider political rivalry between the Muḍar (q.v.) and Rabīʿah factions in the Umayyad era.

Abū Nuʿaym [al-Faḍl ibn Dukayn ibn Ḥammād] (d. 219/834) transmitter of hadith from al-Aʿmash (q.v.) and al-Thawrī (q.v.).

Abū Sufyān [ibn Ḥarb ibn Umayyah] (d. ca. 32/653) prominent Meccan merchant of the Qurayshī clan ʿAbd Shams; chief opponent of Muḥammad but converted to Islam just prior to Muḥammad's conquest of Mecca. Father of Muʿāwiyah (q.v.), the first Umayyad caliph.

Abū Tammām al-Ṭāʾī (d. 231/845) celebrated Abbasid court poet and poetry anthologist; originally a Damascene Christian, Abū Tammām converted to Islam and feigned Arab identity by claiming descent from the Ṭayyiʾ (q.v.).

Abū ʿUbaydah Maʿmar ibn al-Muthannā (d. 210/825) non-Arab client of the Taym (q.v.); one of the most important early Arabic philologists and scholars of pre-Islamic Arab history, he was among the first to record his scholarship in book form.

Abū Zayd al-Anṣārī (d. 214 or 215/830–31) grammarian and lexicographer.

Abū Zayd al-Ṭāʾī (d. ca. 10/632) pre-Islamic horseman and poet known as Zayd al-Khayl (Zayd of the Horses); a member of his clan's delegation to Muḥammad, he converted to Islam and received a new nickname, Zayd al-Khayr (Zayd of Goodness).

ʿĀd legendary southeast Arabian people; mentioned in the Qurʾan as the people to whom God sent the prophet Hūd; they rejected Hūd's message and God destroyed them by a violent wind.

adab term connoting education, ethics and culture; byword for the repertoire of general literary knowledge and social etiquette necessary for an educated individual to succeed in Abbasid society and government service.

ʿAdī a son of Ḥātim al-Ṭāʾī (q.v.), Companion of the Prophet, and follower of ʿAlī ibn Abī Ṭālib (q.v.).

ʿAdī ibn Zayd [ibn Mālik ibn al-Riqāʿ] (d. ca. 99–101/717–20) Umayyad-era praise poet.

al-Aghlab al-Rājiz [ibn ʿAmr al-ʿIjlī] (fl. early seventh century AD) pre-Islamic poet considered by several Muslim specialists to be one of the foremost composers in the *rajaz* (q.v.) style.

Aḥmad ibn al-Khalīl possibly Aḥmad ibn al-Khalīl ibn Maymūn al-Yamānī, who transmitted from al-Aṣmaʿī (q.v.).

al-Aḥnaf ibn Qays (d. ca. 67/687) a nobleman of the Tamīm (q.v.), he settled in Kufa during the early Umayyad era; proverbial in Arabic literature for his equanimity and leadership.

al-Ahtam ibn Sumayy al-Tamīmī (fl. late sixth century AD) a pre-Islamic member of the Tamīm (q.v.); his son, ʿAmr ibn al-Ahtam, was a Companion of the Prophet Muḥammad.

al-Aḥwaṣ al-Anṣārī (d. 110/728–29) Umayyad-era Medinese aristocrat and poet famous for his carousing in Medina; his poetry reflects the luxurious and sometimes libertine aspects of his society, as well as the indignant pride of his people.

ʿĀʾishah (d. 58/678) favored wife of the Prophet Muḥammad and daughter of Abū Bakr, the first caliph. Frequently cited as a source of hadiths. She fought the fourth caliph, ʿAlī ibn Abī Ṭalib (q.v.), in 36/656 during the early Muslim community's First Civil War.

ʿAjam term connoting non-Arabs; in Ibn Qutaybah's text the word refers to peoples from further east whom we might call "Iranians," though this was not a term Ibn Qutaybah himself would have used since a specifically "Iranian" identity was the product of later times.

al-ʿAjjāj [ʿAbd Allāh ibn Ruʾbah] (d. 97/715) celebrated Umayyad-era Iraqi poet famous for composing almost all his poetry in the *rajaz* (q.v.) meter. Also known for his poetic rivalry with Abū l-Najm al-ʿIjlī (q.v.).

al-ʿAjlān ibn ʿAbd Allāh ibn Kaʿb ibn Rabīʿah ibn ʿĀmir ibn Ṣaʿṣaʿah nomadic central Arabian lineage group.

al-Akhṭal [Ghiyāth ibn Ghawth ibn al-Ṣalt] (d. ca. 92/710) Christian Arabic poet of the Taghlib (q.v.) who together with Jarīr and al-Farazdaq formed the famous poetic triad of the Umayyad period; in the poetic jousts between Jarīr and al-Farazdaq (qq.v.), he sided with the latter.

ʿAkk an Arabian lineage group that lived on the Red Sea coast of south Arabia (Tihāmah) at the dawn of Islam; genealogists disagreed over whether it belonged to the "Northern" or "Southern" Arab lineage.

Aktham ibn Ṣayfī l-Tamīmī (d. ca. 8/630) a legendary pre-Islamic Arabian sage whose lifespan is variously reported as between 130 and 300 years, making him one of the celebrated *muʿammarūn* (long-livers).

ʿAlī ibn Abī Ṭālib (d. 41/661) first cousin of the Prophet, fourth caliph, and husband of the Prophet's daughter Fāṭimah. The Shiʿah regard him as the first Imam.

ʿAlī ibn al-Ḥusayn ibn ʿAlī ibn Abī Ṭālib (d. 94/712 or 95/713) great-grandson of the Prophet, regarded as the fourth Imam of the Twelver Shiʿah; also known as "Adornment of the Worshippers" (Zayn al-ʿĀbidīn).

Allies (Ar. *Anṣār*) the Medinese clans al-Aws and al-Khazraj, who were the first clans to convert to Islam; in 1/622 Muḥammad emigrated to Medina and established the first Muslim polity there.

ʿAlqamah ibn Hawdhah (d. early first/seventh century) pre-Islamic Arabian nobleman and leader of the "Sons of the Camel Snout" (q.v.), part of the Saʿd subgroup of the Tamīm (q.v.); he reportedly lived into the Islamic era.

ʿAlqamah ibn ʿUlāthah [al-ʿĀmirī] (d. ca. 20/640) pre-Islamic Arabian nobleman-warrior, converted to Islam and became a prominent political figure. Best known in Arabic literature for his acerbic rivalry with his kinsman ʿĀmir ibn al-Ṭufayl (q.v.).

al-ʿAmālīq legendary people; Muslim genealogists linked them to the descendants of Noah and considered them among the first inhabitants of south Arabia.

al-Aʿmash [Sulaymān ibn Mihrān al-Asadī] (d. 148/765) Kufan hadith transmitter and Qurʾan reader of Persian descent.

ʿĀmir name of several lineage groups in pre-Islamic Arabia, the largest being the ʿĀmir ibn Ṣaʿṣaʿah, a powerful clan of the Qays ʿAylān (q.v.), who settled in central Arabia (Najd) and expanded into Ṭāʾif in northwest Arabia (the Hijaz).

ʿĀmir ibn Hawdhah (fl. early seventh century AD) pre-Islamic Arabian nobleman; leader of the "Sons of the Camel Snout" (q.v.), part of the Saʿd subgroup of the Tamīm (q.v.).

ʿĀmir ibn al-Ṭufayl (d. ca. 7/628), renowned pre-Islamic warrior and poet; participated in many of the most famous conflicts recorded in pre-Islamic Arabian lore; lived into the first years of the Islamic period, but did not convert and reportedly opposed Islam's spread into central Arabia.

ʿĀmir ibn al-Ẓarib al-ʿAdwānī (fl. sixth century AD) pre-Islamic Arabian sage. Lore connects him to Mecca and notes a number of his practices, such as abstinence from alcohol, which coincide with later Islamic law.

ʿAmīrah ibn Juʿal al-Taghlibī (fl. sixth century AD) obscure pre-Islamic Arabian poet (his name is variously recorded); his surviving poems are mostly lampoons composed against his own Taghlib (q.v.) kinsmen.

ʿAmr ibn al-ʿĀṣ Companion of the Prophet, leader of the invasion of Egypt in 19/640, and one of the two arbitrators appointed at Ṣiffīn in 37/657 to settle the dispute over the caliphate between ʿAlī and Muʿāwiyah (qq.v.).

ʿAmr ibn Hind, "the Burner" (r. ca. AD 554–70) Lakhmid ruler of al-Ḥīrah, Sasanian vassal, and military leader in the Sasanian-Byzantine frontier conflict. The various explanations for his nickname, "the Burner," include a story that he avenged the death of one of his brothers by ordering the immolation of ten prisoners from the Ḥanẓalah (q.v.).

ʿAmr ibn Kulthūm (fl. sixth-century AD) pre-Islamic leader of the Jusham clan of the Taghlib (q.v.); he composed one of the great pre-Islamic odes (*muʿallaqah*).

ʿAmr ibn Maʿdīkarib [*Abū Thawr*] (d. after 16/637) poet and leading figure of the Yemeni Zubayd; earned great acclaim in the Muslim victory over the Sasanians at al-Qādisiyyah (14/635 or 16/637).

ʿAmr ibn Saʿīd [*al-Ashdaq*] (d. 69–70/688–90) Meccan aristocrat of the Umayyad clan, renowned for his eloquence; governor of Mecca during the caliphate of Muʿāwiyah (q.v.); attempted to become caliph himself during the Second Civil War when he seized Damascus, but was killed by the Caliph ʿAbd al-Malik ibn Marwān (q.v.).

ʿAmr ibn ʿUtbah [*ibn Farqad al-Sulamī l-Kūfī*] (d. ca. 29/649–650) martyr credited with a variety of ascetic ideas and practices.

ʿAmr ibn Wudd [*al-ʿĀmirī*] pre-Islamic Arab hero reportedly killed by ʿAlī ibn Abī Ṭālib (q.v.) at the Battle of the Ditch in 5/627 when the pagan Meccans besieged Muḥammad and his followers in Medina.

ʿAnazah major branch of the Rabīʿah, based in northern and central Arabia at the dawn of Islam.

Anushirvan see Khosrow Anushirvan.

ʿArafāt hill outside Mecca where the rituals of the second day of the hajj pilgrimage are held.

arāk the tree *Salvadora persica*, still today popularly known as "the toothbrush tree."

Ardashīr [ibn] Bābak (r. AD 226–41) Arabic name for the founder of the Sasanian dynasty in Iran.

Aristotle (Ar. Arisṭū) considered the outstanding and unique representative of philosophy by most Arabic-language philosophers, who sometimes call him simply "the Philosopher."

Arpachshad (Ar. Arfakhshad) son of the biblical Shem, who was son of Noah. Muslim enthnogenesis made heavy use of Noah's line.

Arṭāh ibn Suhayyah (d. 86/705 or later) early Islamic poet of satire and praise, the latter dedicated to the Umayyad caliph Muʿāwiyah (q.v.).

arzan a tree with a hard wood.

Asad a large lineage group of the Muḍar (q.v.); "Northern Arabs" who resided in central Arabia (Najd); featured in numerous tales of pre-Islamic Arabian warring.

Asad ibn ʿAbd Allāh [al-Qasrī] (d. 120/738) Umayyad governor of Khurasan (r. 106–9/724–27 and 117–20/735–38).

al-Asʿar ibn Ḥumrān al-Juʿfī an unidentified poet.

al-Aʿshā, Maymūn ibn Qays (d. after 3/625) one of the most celebrated pre-Islamic poets, known for itinerancy and his interaction with important political groups on the Arabian-Iraqi frontier. He lived into the very early Islamic period, but reportedly did not convert.

Aʿshā Bāhilah ʿĀmir ibn al-Ḥārith (fl. sixth century AD) pre-Islamic poet primarily known for his elegies, which Muslim anthologists much esteemed.

al-Ashbān a term with multiple interpretations, including the name used for the pre-Islamic rulers of Spain and Italy, or an Iranian people near Isfahan.

ʿaṣīdah a porridge made with wheat flour and clarified butter, cooked into a paste thick enough to be chewed.

ʿĀṣim ibn al-Ḥadathān (d. ca. early second/eighth century?) an obscure figure reportedly important in certain Kharijite (q.v.) groups and in fighting during the Second Civil War.

al-Aṣmaʿī Abū Saʿīd ʿAbd al-Malik ibn Qurayb (d. 213/828) Basran lexicographer and narrator of anecdotes about Arabia; attended the court al-Rashīd (q.v); his teachings, particularly on the specialized vocabulary of different fields, were compiled into books by his students and subsequent generations of scholars.

al-Aswad ibn Yaʿfur (d. ca. AD 600) leader of the Tamīm (q.v.) on the Arabian-Iraqi frontier in the generation before Islam; also famed for his eloquence and poetry.

al-ʿAttābī Kulthūm ibn ʿAmr (d. 208/823 or 220/835) praise poet, secretary, and courtier, associated with the Barmakids (q.v.) and the Caliphs al-Rashīd (q.v.) and al-Maʾmūn (q.v.); a famed prose stylist, he read Persian and composed several books on *adab* (q.v.) and lexicography.

Aws ibn ʿAbd Allāh ibn Buraydah [al-Marwazī] transmitter of hadith from Buraydah (q.v.), his grandfather.

ʿAwsajah ibn Mughīth [al-Qāʾif] Arabian diviner of unknown date whose memory appears to be preserved only in the anecdote Ibn Qutaybah reports about his divination skills.

Ayyūb ibn Sulaymān (fl. first half of the second/eighth century) son of the Umayyad caliph Sulaymān ibn ʿAbd al-Malik (q.v.).

Āzar Abraham's father according to the interpretation of Q Anʿām 6:74. Early Muslim exegetes also knew the biblical name of Abraham's father, Terah (Ar. Tāriḥ), and suggested varied interpretations to reconcile the two names.

Azd one of the major subgroups of the Kahlān (q.v.); one of the major branches of the "Southern Arabs," the Azd were originally from central Yemen; groups claiming kinship to Azd were spread widely across Arabia at the dawn of Islam.

Babel (Ar. Bābil) the city of Babylon as well as the country of Babylonia (q.v.), according to ancient Arab writers. The city's ruins lie some fifty-four miles due south of Baghdad on the Euphrates.

Babylonia home to the ancient Babylonian Empire (18th–6th c. BC) that at its height stretched from the Persian Gulf to Syria.

Badr a town near Medina; site of Muḥammad's first victory in battle over the nonbelieving Meccans in 2/624.

Baghīḍ ibn ʿĀmir leader of the Tamīm (q.v.) in the early seventh century AD, converted to Islam but remained in Arabia; during the caliphate of ʿUmar (q.v.), Baghīḍ and another Arabian notable, Zibriqān ibn Badr (q.v.), were the subjects of a famous poetic duel between al-Ḥutayʾah (q.v.) and Dithār ibn Shaybān.

Bahdalah ibn ʿAwf a large subgroup of the Tamīm (q.v.).

Bāhilah a large subgroup of the Qays ʿAylān (q.v) who resided in north-eastern Arabia at the dawn of Islam.

Bāhilah ibn Aʿṣur see Bāhilah.

Bahrāʾ a large subgroup of the Quḍāʿah (q.v.) who resided on Arabia's northern Red Sea coast at the dawn of Islam.

Bahrām Gūr (r. AD 420–38) Sasanian king; ascended the throne with the help of the Lakhmid (q.v.) king al-Mundhir I following the assassination of his father Yazdagird I (r. 399–420).

al-Baḥrayn region in eastern Arabia (much larger than modern-day Bahrain).

Bakr ibn Wāʾil ancient confederacy in central, east, and (later) north Arabia, belonging to the Rabīʿah ibn Nizār "Northern Arabs."

Balkh an important city of well-irrigated oases located on major trading routes in northern Afghanistan, and a center of Buddhism and Zoroastrianism. The Barmakids (q.v.) were originally from Balkh.

al-Barājim a lineage group related to the Ḥanẓalah ibn Mālik (q.v.).

al-Barīṣ a source of water near Damascus; either the late antiquity name for Damascus's main river, al-Baradā, or al-Ghūṭah, the oasis on the south of Damascus, formed by the river.

Barmakids originally Buddhists from Balkh (q.v.), they served the first five Abbasid caliphs. For reasons that still remain obscure al-Rashīd (q.v) deposed the Barmakids in 187/803, imprisoning and executing many of them.

bashām a fragrant tree.

Basra garrison town and port city near the head of the Persian Gulf founded in 17/638 during the Islamic conquests of southern Iraq. A major intellectual center in early Islamic times.

Bedouin nomadic or semi-nomadic Arabic-speaking peoples originating in the Arabian Peninsula. Ibn Qutaybah and his peers romanticized them as the preservers of pure Arab cultural values.

believers (Ar. *mu'minūn*) any believers in a monotheistic God, though by Ibn Qutaybah's day, "believer" had become synonymous, as it is in the present-day, with "Muslim." (The distinction between "believer" and "Muslim" in nascent Islam remains the subject of scholarly debate.).

Bisṭām ibn Qays pre-Islamic hero and poet of the Shaybān (q.v.). His family was considered one of the three most noble and aristocratic Bedouin families, and he led his lineage group from the age of twenty.

Bujayr and ʿIfāq famous horsemen and sons of Abū Malīl (q.v.) mentioned in pre-Islamic battle poetry. They were reportedly killed by Bisṭām ibn Qays (q.v.).

Bukayr ibn al-Akhnas [*al-Sadūsī*] (fl. late first/seventh century) Kufan hadith transmitter.

Buraydah Companion of the Prophet who participated in the conquests in Khurasan and died during the reign of Yazīd ibn Muʿāwiyah (r. 60–64/680–83). His descendants reportedly remained in the area.

Burning Ember Tribes (Ar. *Jamarāt al-ʿArab*) a set of celebrated militarized lineage groups in pre-Islamic times. The origins of the term are legendary, and the constitutent groups were debated by Muslim writers but are generally named as the Numayr (q.v.), ʿAbs, and Ḍabbah; sometimes also the Ḥarith ibn Kaʿb.

Buzurgmihr (fl. sixth century AD) a minister of the Sasanian king Khosrow Anushirvan. He was of legendary wisdom and virtue and is credited with many wise precepts in Middle Persian (Pahlavi) and Arabic literature.

caliph (Ar. *khalīfah*) Qur'anic term indicating "successor, substitute, replacement, deputy," adapted for the political head of the Muslim community after the Prophet's death in 11/632.

caliphate the politico-religious institution associated with the caliph.

client(s) (Ar. *mawlā*, pl. *mawālī*) non-Arab convert(s) to Islam. Converts to Islam notionally had kinship with those who converted them and by extension with their lineage group.

Companions Muslims who saw, met, or heard the Prophet Muḥammad personally.

Copts pre-Islamic Egyptians. In *The Excellence of the Arabs*, the Egyptians of pharaonic times specifically.

al-Dabaran the Aldebaran star in the constellation of Taurus. It rises near and soon after the Pleiades and is one of the brightest visible stars.

Ḍabbah a lineage connoting several Arabian kin groups, including the Ṣarīm ibn Saʿd ibn Ḍabbah, kin of the Umayyad-era poet al-Farazdaq (q.v.).

Daḥamah the mother of Yazīd ibn al-Muhallab (q.v.).

Dārim a subgroup of the Tamīm, descended from Zayd Manāt. At the dawn of Islam, their lands were located to the northeast of Medina.

David (Ar. Dāwūd) the prophet-king of Israel, mentioned in several places in the Qur'an, sometimes with his son and successor, Solomon.

Daws a subgroup of the Azd. In the early seventh century AD, they were widespread in Arabia, but were particularly connected with the Lakhmids (q.v.) and the history of the Arabian-Iraqi frontier.

Dhū l-Iṣbaʿ al-ʿAdwānī (fl. sixth century AD) pre-Islamic poet of legendary stature in Muslim literature, particularly celebrated for his wisdom poetry.

Dhū Qār a victory of Arabian groups allied to Bakr ibn Wā'il (q.v.) over the Sasanians in ca. AD 604–11, near al-Ḥīrah (q.v.). It was a blow to Sasanian influence in eastern Arabia and is recalled in Arabic literature as the first "Arab victory" over the Persians, and the precursor to the Islamic conquests.

Dhū l-Qarnayn figure mentioned in the Qur'an (Q Kahf 18:83–101), often equated with Alexander the Great on the basis of similarities with episodes in the Alexander Romance.

Dhū l-Rummah Ghaylān ibn ʿUqbah (d. 117/735–36) Umayyad-era Arabian poet, famous for desert descriptions composed in an archaic style.

Dhubyān a major subgroup of the Ghaṭafān (q.v.), claiming lineage from the Qays ʿAylān (q.v.); they resided to the east of Medina at the dawn of Islam.

Diʿbil ibn ʿAlī l-Khuzāʿī (d. 244 or 246/859 or 860) Abbasid-era poet famous for his pro-Alid and pro-Yemeni verses, as well as for biting satires directed against caliphs and other high-ranking figures of his time.

dinar a gold coin originally weighing approximately 4.25 grams; the basis of the caliphate's monetary system and a symbol of status and wealth. In the second/eighth century, one dinar had the value of approximately ten silver dirhams, which increased to twenty-five dirhams by the third/ninth century.

Esau (Ar. ʿAyṣaw) son of Isaac and Rebecca, brother of Jacob. Muslim genealogy identifies him as the progenitor of al-Rūm (q.v.).

Euclid (Ar. Iqlīdus) (third century BC) Greek mathematician from Alexandria celebrated as the "Father of Geometry." His books on geometry and optics were translated into Arabic during the second/eighth century and were extensively studied and developed by Muslim mathematicians.

al-Faḍl ibn Sahl [*ibn Zadhānfarūkh*] (d. 202/818) Zoroastrian convert to Islam, brother of al-Ḥasan ibn Sahl (q.v.), and famed tutor and later vizier to the Abbasid caliph al-Maʾmūn (q.v.).

fālūdh more commonly *fālūdhaj*, from the Persian *pālūdag* ("strained"), a sweet made of flour and honey.

al-Farazdaq Abū Firās Hammām ibn Ghālib (d. ca. 110/728) one of the three most famous Umayyad-era poets (along with Jarīr and al-Akhṭal [qq.v.]). He composed poetry for and about many high-ranking Muslims and caliphs and is most famous for his lifelong poetic jousts with Jarīr.

Farrāṣ one of the subgroups of the Bāhilah (q.v.).

Fārs a province of southwestern Iran and homeland to the Sasanian kings.

farsakh (from the Persian *parasang*), a distance of about four miles, or six kilometers.

Fāṭimah (d. 11/632) longest-lived daughter of the Prophet Muḥammad, wife of ʿAlī ibn Abī Ṭālib, and mother of al-Ḥasan and al-Ḥusayn (qq.v.). The Shiʿah revere her as the most excellent woman.

Fazzān a tribal group who populated the Sūdān (q.v.) and who figure in Muslim ethnogenesis.

al-Find al-Zimmānī (fl. mid-sixth century AD) pre-Islamic warrior poet who participated in the Basūs War between the northeastern Arabian Taghlib and Shaybān (qq.v.).

Galen (Ar. Jāliyanūs) (AD 129–200 or 206) Greek doctor and philosopher and author of a large corpus of medical treatises that formed the basis of medical practice in late antiquity. His works were translated into Arabic during the second/eighth century, and Muslim physicians cited him extensively.

Ghanī ibn Aʿṣur a lineage group of Northern Arabians related to the Qays ʿAylān (q.v.). They resided in north and northeastern Arabia in the century before Islam.

ghassāniyyah unidentified dish.

Ghaṭafān a northern Arabian lineage whose lands lay in Najd between the Hijaz and Shammar Mountains.

Gog and Magog figures mentioned in the Hebrew Bible, Revelation, Christian Apocrypha, and the Qurʾan in the context of the end of time. Muslim traditions associated them with a mysterious horde of Eastern peoples, kept at bay by a great wall built by Alexander the Great. Their crossing of the wall was to herald the end times.

Hadith the entire corpus of hadiths (q.v.); used to determine the exemplary practice of the Prophet.

hadith a report of something the Prophet Muḥammad said or did, including tacit expressions of approval or disapproval, consisting of the report itself as well as a list of those who transmitted it.

ḥadīth qudsī a class of Hadith reporting words spoken by God, as distinguished from prophetic Hadith, which report the words of the Prophet. *Ḥadīth qudsī* differ from the Qurʾan, as they are not considered to be inimitable, nor revealed through the medium of Gabriel, and they are not recited in the ritual prayers.

Hagar (Ar. Hājar) according to Muslim tradition, concubine of Abraham and the mother of Ishmael, the legendary ancestor of the Arabs.

hajar "town" in the epigraphic dialects of pre-Islamic south Arabia, and therefore often found in place-names, including the ancient capital Hajar in al-Baḥrayn (q.v.).

Ḥājib ibn Zurārah (d. early seventh century AD) leader of the Tamīm (q.v.) immediately prior to the rise of Islam. Arabic lore describes how he gave his bow as a pledge to Khosrow Anushirvan (q.v.) in exchange for permission to pasture his clan's flocks in Sasanian territory.

hajj the Muslim annual pilgrimage. It has pre-Islamic origins and incorporates rituals connected with Abraham, his concubine Hagar, and son Ishmael.

al-Ḥajjāj [ibn Yūsuf] (d. 95/714) famous Umayyad governor of Iraq remembered for his harsh but effective government.

Ham (Ar. Ḥām) son of Noah. Not mentioned by name in the Qur'an but possibly the unbelieving son of Noah who refused to follow his father during the Flood. He features in Muslim genealogy as a forefather of various peoples, though inferior to Noah's sons Shem and Japheth.

Hamdān an important lineage of south Arabia, originally from the fertile mountains north of Sanaa in Yemen.

Hammām ibn Qabīṣah (d. 64/684) leader of the Numayr (q.v.) and a prominent military commander during the early Umayyad period. During the First Civil War, he fought with Muʿāwiyah ibn Abī Sufyān (q.v.), and during the Second Civil War, he sided with the unsuccessful faction of al-Ḍaḥḥāk ibn Qays and was killed in battle.

Ḥanīfah ibn Lujaym a powerful subgroup of the Bakr ibn Wā'il (q.v.), resident in the eastern part of central Arabia (al-Yamāmah) in pre-Islamic times.

Ḥanīs ibn ʿAbd Allāh ibn Ḥudhāfah al-Sahmī Companion of the Prophet. Ibn Qutaybah reports that he delivered Muḥammad's letter to the Sasanian king, but other accounts name different envoys.

Ḥanẓalah ibn Mālik the largest subgroup of the Tamīm (q.v.); resided in central Arabia at the dawn of Islam.

Haram [*ibn Qaṭbah ibn Sinān* (or *Sayyār*) *ibn ʿAmr al-Fazārī*] (d. after 13/634) a judge from pre-Islamic times known for his eloquence. He reportedly accepted Islam during the Prophet's lifetime.

Harim ibn Sinān (d. ca. AD 608) one of the leaders of the Dhubyān (q.v.) in the generation before the Prophet Muḥammad, known for his settling of conflict between the Dhubyān and the ʿAbs; famously praised by the poet Zuhayr ibn Abī Sulmā (q.v.).

harīsah a thick potage made with pounded grains, minced meat, and a variety of seasonings.

al-Ḥārith ibn ʿAwf (fl. first/seventh century) a pre-Islamic warrior and leader of the Murrah. He settled two especially prominent tribal disputes and led "the Confederates" (Ar. *al-aḥzāb*) against the Prophet at the Battle of the Trench. He later accepted Islam, and Muḥammad appointed him as a leader of the Murrah.

Hārūn al-Rashīd see al-Rashīd.

Ḥarūrīs the twelve thousand men who gathered in Ḥarūrāʾ, a place near Kufa, in 37/657 to protest against the decision by ʿAlī ibn Abī Ṭālib (q.v.) to accept arbitration in his dispute with Muʿāwiyah (q.v.) over the caliphate. Ḥarūrīs are considered the first Kharijites (q.v).

al-Ḥasan (d. ca. 49/669–70) son of ʿAlī and the Prophet's daughter Fāṭimah, and according to the Shiʿah, the second Imam, after ʿAlī.

al-Ḥasan ibn Jahwar a member of the household of al-Manṣūr (q.v.), according to Ibn Qutaybah. He is otherwise unknown.

al-Ḥasan ibn Sahl (d. 236/850–51) son of a Zoroastrian convert to Islam, secretary and governor for the Abbasid caliph al-Maʾmūn (q.v.), brother of the vizier al-Faḍl ibn Sahl (q.v.), and father of Būrān, who married al-Maʾmūn.

Hāshim a clan of the Quraysh to which the Prophet and the ancestors of the subsequent Abbasid dynasty belonged.

Ḥassān ibn Thābit (d. 50–54/670–74) a Medinese poet contemporary with Muḥammad; he is considered one of the three leading poets of the first Muslim community, alongside Kaʿb ibn Mālik (q.v.) and ʿAbd Allāh ibn Rawāḥah (q.v.).

Ḥātim ibn al-Nuʿmān (fl. mid-first/seventh century) leader of the Bāhilah (q.v.) during the early Muslim era and a prominent military commander; captured Merv (q.v.) during the caliphate of ʿUthmān (q.v.) and helped rule Khurasan; backed Muʿāwiyah ibn Abī Sufyān (q.v.) in the First Civil War and became lord over northern Mesopotamia.

Ḥātim al-Ṭāʾī (fl. second half of the sixth century AD) poet proverbial for his generosity and hospitality.

ḥaysah (or *ḥays*) an Arab dish made from dates crushed and kneaded with clarified butter, and mixed with flour, bread crumbs, or skimmed, dried, and crumbled camels' milk cheese.

Hephthalites (Ar. Ḥayātilah) a steppe people from Mongolia who formed powerful kingdoms along the Oxus during the fourth or fifth centuries AD.

Herat a city and province in western Afghanistan and a part of Greater Khurasan; situated in the fruitful valley of the Hari River.

Hijaz the birthplace and spiritual center of Islam; area in the northwestern Arabian Peninsula, encompassing Mecca and Medina.

al-Ḥijr ancient commercial town in northwestern Arabia where a vast number of inscriptions have been found in Arabic, Aramaic, Thamudic, Nabatean, Minaean, Lihyanite, Hebrew, Greek, and Latin.

Hilāl ibn Muʿāwiyah al-Ṭāʾī an unidentified poet.

Ḥimyar powerful south Arabian kingdom that flourished from ca. the first century BC until the early sixth century AD, when most of south Arabia was occupied by Ethiopian armies. In the Muslim era, Ḥimyar was one of the two main divisions of the "Southern Arabs" (the other being Kahlān [q.v.]), and one of the main constituents of the Yemeni faction.

Hind ibn Abī Hālah (d. 36/656) the son of Khadījah bint Khuwaylid, Muḥammad's wife, by her first husband, Abū Hālah, and a member of the Tamīmī Usayyid clan; reportedly accepted Islam.

Hippocrates (Ar. Abqrāt) (ca. 460–370) ancient Greek doctor and philosopher, and the symbolic father of Western medicine; various works ascribed to him were translated into Arabic during the second/eighth century.

al-Ḥirmāz a subgroup of the Tamīm (q.v.), identified by the ancestor figure Ḥirmāz ibn Mālik ibn ʿAmr ibn Tamīm.

al-Ḥirmāzī ʿAbd Allāh ibn al-Aʿwar, poet in the time of al-Rashīd (r. 170–93/786–809).

Hishām ibn ʿUqbah the less-famous brother of Dhū l-Rummah (q.v.).

Hūd the earliest of the five "Arab" prophets (Hūd, Ṣāliḥ, Ishmael, Shuʿayb, and Muḥammad) enumerated in Muslim traditions.

al-Hudhalī, Mālik ibn al-Ḥārith [ibn Tamīm] (fl. early seventh century AD) a pre-Islamic warrior and poet of the Hudhayl (q.v.).

Hudhayl Arabian lineage group residing in the pre-Islamic Hijaz (q.v.); its members spread across the Middle East during the Muslim conquests.

al-Hudhayl ibn Zufar [ibn al-Ḥārith al-Kilābī] (d. after 102/720) a highborn warrior who fought for the Umayyad Caliphate during the revolt of Yazīd ibn al-Muhallab (q.v.) in 101/719 and reportedly succeeded in killing Yazīd.

Ḥumayd al-Arqaṭ [ibn Mālik] (fl. late seventh century AD) an Iraqi poet famous for his miserliness and for mocking guests in verse.

Ḥumayd ibn Thawr [al-Hilālī] (d. ca. 90/709) a poet born in the pre-Islamic period who died after the coming of Islam, apparently at an advanced age; best known for his animal descriptions.

Hunaydah bint Ṣaʿṣaʿah [ibn Nājiyyah] (mid-first/seventh century) the paternal aunt of the Umayyad-era poet al-Farazdaq (q.v.) and the wife of al-Ḥuṭay'ah (q.v.).

al-Ḥuṭay'ah (d. ca. mid-first/seventh century) poet of the Qays (q.v.) whose life spanned the dawn of Islam; an itinerant panegyrist and famous satirist mocked for his avidity, avarice, and venality.

Ibn ʿAbbās, ʿAbd Allāh (d. 68/687–88) paternal cousin of Muḥammad and the nominal ancestor of the Abbasid line; often named as a source for hadiths and exegesis of the Qurʾan.

Ibn Abī Zinād (fl. 2nd/8th century) Medinese client who was a hadith transmitter and jurist.

Ibn al-Aʿrābī, Abū ʿAbd Allāh Muḥammad ibn Ziyād (d. 231/846) Iraqi grammarian and specialist of Arabic language, poetry, genealogy, and lore; extensively cited by later authors.

Ibn Dārah, Sālim (fl. early-mid seventh century AD) poet of the pre-Islamic and early Islamic periods best known for his lampoons, one of which may have led to his death during the caliphate of ʿUthmān (q.v.).

Ibn al-Iṭnābah al-Khazrajī, ʿAmr (fl. late sixth century AD) pre-Islamic nobleman and leader of the Khazraj clan in Medina; some fragments of poetry attributed to him are preserved in Muslim collections.

Ibn Jabalah, ʿAlī l-ʿAkawwak (d. 213/828) poet of Khurasanian descent whose excessive and semi-blasphemous praise for Abū Dulaf (q.v.) reportedly prompted the Caliph al-Maʾmūn (q.v.) to order his execution.

Ibn al-Kalbī, Abū Mundhir Hishām ibn Muḥammad (d. 204/819) Iraqi author of over one hundred books on history, genealogy, and poetry, including detailed compendiums of Arab lineages and a work on pre-Islamic idols.

Ibn Laylā, ʿAbd al-ʿAzīz ibn Marwān (d. 86/705) brother of the Umayyad caliph ʿAbd al-Malik ibn Marwān (q.v.) and long-standing governor of Egypt who oversaw the early expansion of al-Fusṭāṭ, the precursor of Cairo.

Ibn Masʿūd, ʿAbd Allāh (d. 32/652–53) a Companion of the Prophet, reportedly of humble origins, known for his expertise on the Qurʾan.

Ibn al-Muqaffaʿ, ʿAbd Allāh (d. 139/756) a Persian court secretary to the early Abbasids; celebrated for translating Middle Persian texts into Arabic.

Ibn Shihāb see al-Zuhrī.

Ibn Shubrumah, ʿAbd Allāh ibn Shubrumah al-Ḍabbī (d. 144/761) a Kufan judge.

Ibn Thumāmah see Thumāmah ibn Ashras.

Ibn al-Zubayr, ʿAbd Allāh (d. 73/692) nobleman of the ʿAbd al-ʿUzzā clan of the Quraysh; son of the Companion Zubayr (q.v.); proclaimed caliph in Mecca in 64/683, but his caliphate was not universally acknowledged, and he was defeated and killed by the Umayyad caliph ʿAbd al-Malik ibn Marwān (q.v.).

ʿIjl ibn Lujaym a subgroup of the Bakr ibn Wāʾil (q.v.) who resided in north-eastern Arabia and on the Arabian-Iraqi frontier at the dawn of Islam.

Ikhshinwāz the Arabic rendering of the name or title of the Hephthalite (q.v.) king during the reign of Peroz ibn Yazdagird ibn Bahrām (q.v.).

imam from the Arabic *amma*, "to precede, to lead"; a Qur'anic term for an exemplary religious-social-political leader; it is also used for a prayer leader. Its meaning was theorized heavily in Islamic political thought, including by sectarians.

imamate the institution of rule by an imam.

'Imrān, family of the biblical Amram and his sons Aaron and Moses.

Imru' al-Qays (fl. mid-sixth century AD) a princely descendant of the leaders of the Kindah federation and the most famous pre-Islamic Arabian poet.

'Īsā ibn Yazīd ibn Bakr al-Laythī (d. 171/787–8) Medinese poetry collector and narrator of Arabian tales and hadith. Though often cited in early collections of Arabic lore, his trustworthiness as a narrator was doubted by several prominent Iraqi specialists.

Isfahan major city of the central Iranian plateau, administrative center of the Sasanian region Media and the Muslim al-Jibāl Province, and capital of several dynasties in Muslim times.

isḥal a type of tamarisk, evergreen and native to drier areas of Eurasia and Africa. Arabic lexicons note its usefulness for toothsticks.

Isḥāq ibn Rāhawayh (161/777–78 to 238/852–53) a leading scholar of Hadith and Islamic law in Khurasan and the teacher of scholars whose works became canonical, including al-Bukhārī, Muslim, Abū Dāwūd, and al-Nasā'ī.

Ishmael (Ar. Ismā'īl) prophet mentioned in the Qur'an, usually in connection with his father Abraham, brother Isaac, and nephew Jacob; counted by Arab genealogists as the ancestor of the "Arabized Arabs," also called the "Northern Arabs."

Īyās ibn Qatādah (fl. mid-late seventh century AD) a member of the Tamīm (q.v.) who settled in Basra and reportedly participated in uprisings during the Second Civil War; also narrated a small number of hadiths.

Jabābirah the kings of ancient Mesopotamia.

Jabalah ibn ʿAbd al-Raḥmān (fl. early second/eighth century) client of the Bāhilah (q.v.) and companion of the governor of Khurasan, Muslim ibn Saʿīd al-Kilābī; appointed governor of Kerman (q.v.) in 104/722–23.

Jābir ibn ʿAbd Allāh (d. ca. 78/697) a Companion of the Prophet who participated in the Prophet's campaigns and a source for many hadiths.

Jābir ibn Thaʿlab al-Ṭāʾī (fl. sixth century AD) a minor pre-Islamic Arabian poet.

Jacob (Ar. Yaʿqūb) son of Isaac in the biblical and Muslim tradition, mentioned in the Qurʾan.

Jadd ibn Qays (fl. first quarter of the first/seventh century) contemporary of the Prophet, remembered as a "hypocrite" disloyal to his fellow Muslims.

Jadīs a legendary people that Muslim genealogists linked to the descendants of Noah and considered to be, along with a related group, the Ṭasm (q.v.), the first inhabitants of central and eastern Arabia (al-Yamāmah and al-Baḥrayn).

Jaʿfar ibn Qurayʿ ibn ʿAwf ibn Kaʿb (fl. sixth century AD) pre-Islamic Arabian nobleman nicknamed "the Camel Snout" and progenitor of the eponymous clan.

Jaʿm one of the nine ancient Arab lineage groups by Ibn Qutaybah's reckoning (through Abū Ḥātim [q.v.]). The name does not feature in other traditions about the ancient Arabs.

Jamīʿ unknown, possibly the son of Abū Ghāḍir (q.v.).

Japheth (Ar. Yāfath) son of Noah. Ibn Qutaybah's description of his descendants is common to Muslim tradition.

Jarīr ibn ʿAbd Allāh (d. 51/671) an early convert to Islam, a tribal noble, unifier, and leader of the Bajīlah.

Jarīr [*ibn ʿAṭiyyah ibn Khaṭafā*] (d. 111/729) one of the three most famous Umayyad-era poets (along with al-Farazdaq and al-Akhṭal [qq.v.]). He is best known for his love poetry and lifelong poetic flytings with both al-Farazdaq and al-Akhṭal.

Jarīr ibn Ḥāzim Abū l-Naḍr al-Azdī (d. ca. 170/786–87) notable and very active Basran hadith transmitter, counted as a reliable source by most Hadith specialists.

Jarīr ibn Yazīd [*al-Bajalī*] (fl. second/eighth century) hadith transmitter and important political figure. Governor of Basra (q.v.) in 126/744. After the fall of the Umayyads in 132/750, he retained official favor with the Abbasids and served in governorships over Basra and Yemen until the reign of al-Maʾmūn (q.v.).

Jarm ibn Rayyān a subgroup of the Quḍāʿah lineage residing in northwest Arabia near the Arabian-Syrian frontier at the dawn of Islam.

Jazīrah Arabic term for northern Mesopotamia and the upper reaches of the Tigris and Euphrates in modern Syria, Iraq, and eastern Turkey.

Jesus (Ar. ʿĪsā) in the Qurʾan, "the Messiah" (*al-Masīḥ*), prophet (*nabī*), messenger (*rasūl*), the son of Mary. Although not regarded by Muslims as the son of God, the Qurʾan does refer to him as the Word of God and affirms his virgin birth and miracles.

jinn (sg. *jinnī*) spirits created from fire, believed to possess powers for evil and good.

Jirān al-ʿAwd (fl. sixth century AD) an obscure pre-Islamic Arabian poet; his poetry and stories of his love adventures are often cited in Muslim literature.

John the Baptist in the Qurʾan, the prophet who will witness the truth of a word from God. Accounts of the birth, life, and death of John were elaborated in the Muslim tradition.

Jubayr ibn Muṭʿim (d. during the caliphate of Muʿāwiyah, 41–60/661–80) Qurayshī nobleman and Companion of the Prophet.

Judhām ibn ʿAdī major "Southern Arab" subgroup of the Kahlān (q.v.); at the dawn of Islam they resided in the Red Sea coastal region of modern northern Saudi Arabia and Jordan; Judhām comprised the major population of the first Muslim settlers in Egypt.

Juḥdur al-ʿUklī (d. ca. 100/718) Umayyad-era Arabian poet. He operated as a bandit in al-Yamāmah before being imprisoned by the lieutenant of al-Ḥajjāj ibn Yusuf (q.v.).

Jurhum a legendary lineage group that Muslim genealogists counted among the "Southern Arabs"; according to the stories, the Jurhum are said to have first settled in Yemen before moving to Mecca, which is where they were living when Abraham and Ishmael migrated south to construct the Kaaba. Ishmael married into Jurhum and his descendants would be identified as the "Northern Arabs."

Juwayriyah ibn Asmā' (d. 173/789–90) Basran hadith transmitter and a student of al-Zuhrī (q.v.) and Mālik ibn Anas (q.v.).

Kaʿb ibn ʿAwf a name referring to one of two minor lineage groups whose descent is related to the "Southern Arabs."

Kaʿb ibn Mālik (d. 50–53/670–73) poet of the Khazraj in Medina and, alongside Ḥassān ibn Thābit (q.v.) and ʿAbd Allāh ibn Rawāḥah (q.v,) one of the three leading poets of Muḥammad's Muslim community. Kaʿb is perhaps best known for the story of his penance after not participating in one of Muḥammad's campaigns.

Kaʿb ibn Māmah one of the pre-Islamic leaders of the Iyād, famous in Arabic literature for his generosity.

Kaʿb ibn Zuhayr (d. ca. 50/670) son of the pre-Islamic poet Zuhayr; most celebrated for the story of his conversion to Islam, which culminated in his performing the "Mantle Ode" (*qaṣidat al-burdah*) to Muḥammad.

Kaaba God's ancient, sacred house; in Mecca.

Kahlān the name by which genealogists identified one of the two major divisions of the "Southern Arabs," the other being Ḥimyar (q.v.).

Kalīlah and Dimnah a collection of animal fables, likely originating in the Sanskrit *Panchatantra*, transmitted through Middle Persian and into Arabic via a translation ascribed to Ibn al-Muqaffaʿ in the second/eighth century. The set of moralistic stories enjoyed great popularity.

Kerman province of southeast Iran between Fārs and Sistan, ancient Carmania. Known for silk and cotton manufacture; Sirjan, Bardasir, Bam, and the port of Hormuz were its main cities in late antiquity. Conquered by Muslims between 638 and 650.

Khadījah (d. AD 619) first wife of the Prophet, first convert to Islam, and the mother of the Prophet's daughter Fāṭimah. A businesswoman before her marriage, she supported Muḥammad economically and spiritually, and is esteemed by both Sunni and Shiʿah Muslims.

al-Khafājī's shears a metaphor for sharpness. It only appears in the poem by al-Aʿshā cited by Ibn Qutaybah, and the metaphor's origin is unclear. Khafājah was a subgroup of the ʿĀmir (q.v.).

Khalaf al-Aḥmar (d. ca. 180/796) poet and transmitter of early poetry.

Khālid ibn Barmak (d. 165/781–82) a leading member of a family of viziers and administrators.

Khālid ibn al-Walīd (d. 21/642) Meccan member of Quraysh who originally warred against the Prophet Muḥammad but later converted to Islam and became one of the most celebrated military commanders of the early Muslim community. Played a key role in the conquests of Iraq and Syria.

Khallād al-Arqaṭ Ibn Yazīd al-Bāhilī (d. 120/737–38) an Umayyad-era Basran narrator of Arabian history and Arabic poetry, and a client of the Farrāṣ (q.v.); of non-Arab origins.

khāqān a title applied by Muslim geographers and historians of Ibn Qutaybah's day to the heads of the various Turkish confederations (and also, but not by Ibn Qutaybah, to other non-Muslim rulers such as the emperor of China).

Kharijites label used to describe an array of political groups in early Islam who opposed the institution of the caliphate. Their movements often involved violent secession and conflict against provincial or caliphal authorities. Late Muslim writers regard them as a distinct theological sect, though in early Islam they were diffuse and held varied sectarian and political views.

Khathʿam ibn Anmār a major subgroup of the Kahlān (q.v), whose lineage was traced to the "Southern Arabs." They resided in the area south of Mecca up to the borders of Yemen, where they acquired significant power in the generations before Islam.

Khaybar oasis approximately 150 kilometers north of Medina, famous for its wealth of date palms.

khazīrah a broth made with flour or bran and water or milk.

Khindif a lineage group of the "Northern Arabs" descended from Ilyās ibn Muḍar; they expressed their lineage through their ancestral mother, Khindif.

khosrow (Middle Persian *xusrō*) title applied generically to monarchs of the Sasanian royal family who ruled Persia before the conquests.

Khosrow Anushirvan Sasanian king, reigned AD 531–79.

Khosrow Parviz Sasanian king, reigned AD 590–628. He was the grandson of Khosrow Anushirvan (q.v.).

Khulayd ibn ʿAynayn Umayyad-era minor poet from the ʿAbd al-Qays (q.v.); he is said to have lived in al-Baḥrayn (q.v.), and most stories about him concern his poetic jousts with the famous poet Jarīr (q.v.).

Khurasan region comprising present-day northeastern Iran, Afghanistan, and parts of Central Asia; one of the richest provinces of the caliphate. The Abbasids received strong support from Khurasan when they overthrew the Umayyads; its capital, Merv, was initially the base of al-Maʾmūn (q.v.).

al-Khuraymī, Isḥāq ibn Ḥassān (d. 214/829–30) Abbasid-era poet of Soghdian origin who became famous in Baghdad.

Kilāb a major subgroup of the ʿĀmir ibn Ṣaʿṣaʿah (q.v.); initially residing to the east of Medina, they spread to Syria, where they wielded significant power in the Islamic period.

Kufa a garrison city founded in 17/638 during the conquests on the western arm of the Euphrates in the alluvial plains of Iraq. The city briefly served as the capital of ʿAlī ibn Abī Ṭālib (q.v.) when he vied for the caliphate, and remained a key center for Shiʿi Islam for centuries afterward.

al-Kumayt ibn Zayd al-Asadī (d. 128/744) Iraqi Umayyad-era poet who mastered Bedouin-style verse and whose praises for pro-Alid figures placed him in conflict with Umayyad authorities.

Kuthayyir ʿAzzah (d. 105/723) Arabian Umayyad-era poet, celebrated for his chaste, longing love poetry (a style known as *ʿudhrī*) dedicated to his beloved, ʿAzzah.

Labīd ibn Rabīʿah (d. ca. 41/661) famous pre-Islamic Arabian poet and author of one of the great pre-Islamic odes (*muʿallaqah*); converted to Islam, and several pious poems are ascribed to him.

lafītah a porridge-like *ʿaṣidah* (q.v.) made with colocynth and flour.

Lakhmids semi-nomads on the Arabian-Iraqi frontier who established a dynasty based around al-Ḥīrah; they served as vassals for the Sasanians, guarding the frontier against the Byzantines and spreading Sasanian influence into Arabia.

Lud (Ar. Lāwudh) grandson of Noah, through Shem. Mentioned in Genesis 10:22.

Maʿadd designator for a large number of central and northern Arabians before Islam; Muslim genealogists organized tribal lineages and used the name to describe the group of "Northern Arabs."

maḍīrah a sumptuous meat stew, served at banquets and celebrated in Arabic literature of Ibn Qutaybah's day.

Madyan name in the Qur'an and the Bible of the people to whom Shuʿayb (q.v.) was sent as a prophet.

Mālik Dhū l-Ruqaybah Ibn Salamat al-Khayr ibn Qushayr (fl. sixth century AD) pre-Islamic warrior of the ʿĀmir ibn Ṣaʿṣaʿah (q.v.); distinguished himself at the Battle of Jabalah, one of the most celebrated battles in pre-Islamic Arabian lore.

al-Maʿlūṭ ibn Badal al-Qaryaʿī (fl. early second/eighth century) minor Umayyad-era Arabian poet; composed chaste, longing love poetry (a style known as *ʿudhrī*).

al-Ma'mūn (r. 197–218/813–833) seventh Abbasid caliph.

Maʿn [ibn Zā'idah al-Shaybānī] (d. 152/769) aristocrat, commander under the last Umayyads, who went into hiding after the Abbasids came to power, and was pardoned by al-Manṣūr (q.v.); governor of rebellious provinces; generous patron of poets.

Manāf a subgroup of the Dārim (q.v.).

al-Manṣūr (r. 136–58/754–75) second Abbasid caliph.

Marwān ibn al-Ḥakam (r. 64–65/684–85) fourth caliph of the Umayyad dynasty and the first of the Marwānids (q.v.). Member of one of the two most powerful branches of the Umayyad family, Marwān is credited with rescuing the Umayyad hold on the caliphate during the disorder of the Second Civil War following the death of Yazīd ibn Muʿāwiyah (q.v.).

Marwānids one of the two major Umayyad clans of the Quraysh that assumed control over the Umayyad Caliphate from the Marwān ibn al-Ḥakam (q.v.) and reigned until the Umayyad collapse in 132/750.

marzubān title broadly referring to a Sasanian regional governor with responsibilities that varied at different times and locales and that often were of a military character.

Mash (Ar. Māsh) in the Qur'an, son of Noah's son Shem; in the Bible he is a grandson of Shem.

al-Masʿūdī most likely one of two grandsons of Ibn Masʿūd (q.v.), whose descendants Ibn Qutaybah lists in his *al-Maʿārif* (*Book of Knowledge*) as including two "al-Masʿūdīs," the elder being ʿAbd al-Raḥmān ibn ʿUtbah and the younger being ʿAbd al-Malik ibn Abī ʿUbaydah.

Maymūn ibn Mihrān (d. ca. 117/735) a client and leading jurist in the Jazīrah (q.v.), and collector of the *kharāj* (q.v.) tax for the Caliph ʿUmar II (r. 99–101/717–20).

maysir pre-Islamic form of gambling using arrows; players compete for portions of a slaughtered camel, usually divided into ten parts.

Mecca cultic center of the Hijaz in pre-Islamic Arabia and of the Islamic world thereafter; the birthplace of Muḥammad.

Medina the capital for Muḥammad's polity during the reign of the first three caliphs; situated about 160 kilometers from the Red Sea and 350 kilometers north of Mecca.

Merv city in what is now Turkmenistan; in early Islamic times, the capital of Khurasan (q.v.).

Minā a stopping place in the hills east of Mecca during the hajj pilgrimage; the ritual animal sacrifice is done here.

Miskīn al-Dārimī (first/seventh century) poet from Iraq. His name, *miskīn*, means "destitute," and reportedly derives from verses in which he describes himself as destitute but also asserts his worth through his personal virtue.

al-Miswar ibn ʿAbbād nobleman of the Tamīm (q.v.) and leader of the constabulary (*ṣāḥib al-shurṭah*) in Basra in the late Umayyad era; he was removed from his office during the caliphate of Yazīd ibn al-Walīd (r. 126/744) and participated in major civil disturbances and subsequent factional infighting.

Muʿāwiyah ibn Abī Sufyān (r. 41–60/661–80) founder of the Umayyad Caliphate as a hereditary dynasty; previously governor of Damascus and then all of Syria during the reigns of ʿUmar and ʿUthmān (qq.v.); a shrewd statesman, he rose to the caliphate on the platform of seeking vengeance for the assassinated caliph ʿUthmān (his kinsman).

Muḍar one of the two main divisions of the "Northern Arabs," alongside Rabīʿah. The Prophet and his family descended from Muḍar.

Mudlij a subgroup of the Kinānah, residing in northwest Arabia (the Hijaz [q.v.]) at the dawn of Islam. They were known for their augurors in the pre-Islamic period.

Muḥammad ibn ʿAlī ibn ʿAbd Allāh ibn al-ʿAbbās (d. 125/742–43) great-grandson of the Prophet's uncle al-ʿAbbās and father of the Abbasid caliphs al-Saffāḥ and al-Manṣūr (q.v.). Muḥammad was an important figure in the establishment of the Abbasid mission in the east.

Muḥammad ibn al-Ḥanafiyyah (d. 81/700) a son of the fourth caliph, ʿAlī ibn Abī Ṭālib (q.v.), through a concubine. Revolts were raised in his name.

Muḥammad ibn Juḥādah (d. 131/749) Kufan hadith transmitter, counted as a trustworthy source by a number of Hadith experts such as Aḥmad ibn Ḥanbal and Abū Ḥātim al-Rāzī.

Muḥammad ibn al-Khaṣīb ibn Ḥamzah unknown hadith transmitter whom Ibn Qutaybah also cites in his *ʿUyūn al-akhbār* (*Choice Narratives*) and *Al-Maʿārif* (*Book of Knowledge*).

Muḥammad ibn Mundhir (fl. mid-late second/eighth century) literary figure of the early Abbasid era; a companion of poets and a specialist in Arabic language and poetry; Iraqi client of the Ṣubayr ibn Yarbūʿ.

Muḥammad ibn Ṣāliḥ al-Ḍabbī unknown hadith transmitter.

Muḥammad ibn Sīrīn Abū Bakr Muḥammad (ca. 33–110/653–728) Basran scholar and hadith transmitter also renowned for Qurʾanic exegesis and dream interpretation.

Muḥammad ibn ʿUbayd perhaps Abū ʿAbd Allāh al-Hamdānī Muḥammad ibn ʿUbayd ibn ʿAbd al-Malik al-Asadī (d. 249/863–64 or 243–244/858), a reputable transmitter of Kufan origins. He transmitted hadiths directly to Ibn Qutaybah, who mentions him in his *ʿUyūn al-akhbār* (*Choice Narratives*) and *Al-Maʿārif* (*Book of Knowledge*).

Muḥammad ibn Uqayṣir al-Sulamī (fl. first/seventh century) early Muslim Arabian horse expert; a source of various anecdotes about horsemanship and horse husbandry.

Muḥammad ibn Ziyād Abū ʿAbd Allāh ibn al-Aʿrābī (d. 231/846) genealogist, transmitter of poetry, and lexicographer of the Kufan school who authored many thematic dictionaries.

Mujazzaz al-Qāʾif Ibn al-Aʿwar ibn Jaʿdah (fl. first/seventh century) Arabian diviner of the Kinānah (q.v.) and contemporary of the Prophet Muḥammad.

Mukhallad ibn Yazīd (d. ca. 100/718) son of Yazīd ibn al-Muhallab (q.v.); one of the leaders of Basra's most powerful Umayyad-era families, Mukhallad was famed for exhibiting strong leadership characteristics as a youth and acted as governor of Khurasan on behalf of his father.

al-Mukhtār al-Thaqafī (d. 67/687) under the Umayyads, leader of a pro-Alid movement, which controlled Kufa in 66–67/685–87. He claimed to be acting as the representative of ʿAlī's son Muḥammad ibn al-Ḥanafiyyah (q.v.), and his movement is often classified as an early manifestation of extremist Shiʿism.

Murrah ibn ʿAwf a subgroup of the Ghaṭafān (q.v.), residing between Mecca and Medina at the dawn of Islam.

Mūsā ibn Saʿīd al-Jumaḥī an obscure figure of the Jumaḥ clan of the Quraysh, the only record ascribed to him appears to be the story narrated by Ibn Qutaybah in *Al-Tanbīh*.

Musāwir ibn Hind (d. ca. 75/695) poet and nobleman of the ʿAbs; active in the pre-Islamic period, his alleged survival to the time of al-Ḥajjāj (q.v.) suggests a very long life.

al-Musayyab ibn ʿAlas (fl. sixth century AD) pre-Islamic Arabian poet; Muslim collectors held his verses in high esteem, though few poems survive.

Muslim literally, a person who has "submitted" to God. The term can refer to any such believer, not just Muslims, i.e., those who belong to Muḥammad's community.

Muslim ibn ʿAmr ibn Ḥaṣīn al-Bāhilī (d. 72/691) early Umayyad-era nobleman and close confident of the Caliph Yazīd ibn Muʿāwiyah (q.v.). He was killed fighting with Muṣʿab ibn al-Zubayr during the Second Civil War.

Muslim ibn Bashshār hadith transmitter, otherwise unknown.

al-Mustawrid ibn Qudāmah (fl. mid-first/seventh century) a leader of the Bāhilah (q.v.); settled in Iraq following the conquests and was one of the witnesses when the Caliph Muʿāwiyah ibn Abī Sufyān (q.v.) infamously "adopted" Ziyād ibn Abī Sufyān (q.v.).

al-Mutajarridah (fl. sixth century AD) a wife of King al-Nuʿmān ibn al-Mundhir (q.v.); famous in Arabian lore for the scandalous poem about her composed by the poet al-Nābighah al-Dhubyānī (q.v.) when he saw her partially naked.

Muṭarrif ibn Abī Khuwaylid al-Hudhalī identity uncertain.

al-Muṭṭalib ibn Abī Wadāʿah (fl. first half of the first/seventh century) rich Qurayshī Meccan merchant and contemporary of the Prophet who embraced Islam after the conquest of Mecca and transmitted a few hadiths.

Muzarrid Yazīd ibn Ḍirār (fl. early-mid seventh century AD) warrior poet and convert to Islam; brother of al-Shammākh (q.v.); their poetry and aspects of their biographies are sometimes interchanged in the sources.

al-Nābighah al-Dhubyānī (fl. late sixth century AD) celebrated pre-Islamic poet, active in both the Ghassanid and Lakhmid courts; his poetry was highly esteemed among Muslim collectors.

al-Nābighah al-Jaʿdī (d. ca. 79/698–99) poet contemporary with the rise of Islam; he converted toward the end of Muḥammad's life and was politically active during the conquests and the subsequent factionalism of the early caliphate.

Nāfiʿ ibn al-Azraq (d. 65/685) a Kharijite (q.v.) leader. During the First Civil War he joined the Ḥarūrīs (q.v.) and was imprisoned; he escaped during the Second Civil War and, until he was killed near Basra, led a notoriously violent Kharijite group that controlled much of southern Iran.

Nahd ibn Zayd a subgroup of the Quḍāʿah residing in Yemen at the dawn of Islam. Another subgroup residing on the Arabian-Syrian frontier also claimed common lineage with them.

al-Naḥīf (or *al-Nuḥayf*) nickname for the pre-Islamic figure Saʿd ibn Qurṭ of the Judhaymah, known in Arabic literature on account of his mother's disapproval of his marriage and the poetry on this topic.

Nahīk ibn Mālik ibn Muʿāwiyah (fl. first/seventh century) poet contemporary with Muḥammad; brother of one of the Prophet's Companions, Ubayy.

Nahshal ibn Dārim a subgroup of the Tamīm (q.v.) residing in northeastern Arabia at the dawn of Islam.

Nahshal ibn Ḥarrī (d. ca. 45/665) a leader of the Arabian Nahshal ibn Dārim (q.v.), warrior, and poet; born in the pre-Islamic-era, he converted to Islam and fought during the First Civil War.

al-Najāshī [*Qays ibn ʿAmr ibn Mālik al-Ḥārithī*] (fl. seventh century AD) poet celebrated for his poetic jousts with Ubayy ibn Tamīm ibn Muqbil during the caliphate of ʿUmar (q.v.); partisan of ʿAlī (q.v.) during the First Civil War; known also for his profligacy.

Najd desert plateau in the central Arabian Peninsula and home to several major nomadic groups.

Najdah al-Ḥarūrī (d. 72/691–92) leader of the Ḥanīfah (q.v.) who rose to prominence during the instability following the succession crisis after the caliphate of Muʿāwiyah (q.v.). Wrested control of much of eastern Arabia from the caliphate for almost a decade before internal strife fragmented his following, and he was killed by one of his lieutenants.

al-Namarī name usually indicating a lineage to the al-Namir ibn Qāsiṭ, a subgroup of the Rabīʿah ibn Nizār, though various lineage groups used the name too.

nasnās/nisnās strange beings possibly conceived based on sightings of monkeys or apes.

al-Nasr can refer to either a star in Lyra or three stars in Aquila.

Naṣr ibn Khālid [or Khalaf] al-Ḍabbī identity uncertain, possibly an obscure third/ninth-century hadith transmitter.

ney an end-blown flute that is a popular wind instrument.

Nizār the son of Maʿadd (q.v.) according to Muslim genealogists, and hence one of the legendary ancestors of the "Northern Arabs."

Noah (Ar. Nūḥ) Qur'anic prophet and a major figure of Muslim ethnogenesis.

Nubians peoples living in the land to the south of Egypt.

al-Nuʿmān ibn Bashīr (d. 64/684) poet and political figure from the Khazraj Medinese Companions, killed in the wars following the death of Yazīd ibn Muʿāwiyah (q.v.).

al-Nuʿmān ibn al-Mundhir (r. AD 590s–ca. AD 602) pre-Islamic king of the Lakhmids who features prominently in stories of pre-Islamic Arabia and Arab-Persian relations.

Numayr ibn ʿĀmir a major subgroup of the Qays ʿAylān (q.v.) and one of the most renowned pre-Islamic Arabian lineages; resided in northeastern Arabia and the Syrian desert at the dawn of Islam.

Nushbah ibn Ghayẓ ibn Murrah ibn ʿAwf ibn Saʿd ibn Dhubyān a subgroup of the Qays ʿAylān (q.v.).

Peroz ibn Yazdagird ibn Bahrām (r. AD 459–84) Sasanian king Peroz I. His reign was troubled by his unsuccessful war against the Hephthalites (q.v.), who defeated and captured him in ca. 469, forcing the Sasanian Empire to pay tribute; the Hephthalites defeated Peroz a second time and killed him in 484.

petty kings, period of (Ar. *al-ṭawāʾif*) in Persian history, the period between Alexander the Great and the Sasanian Empire.

pharaohs (Ar. *farāʿinah*, sg. *firʿawn*) the ancient rulers of Egypt. The Qurʾan refers to the "pharaoh" of Moses.

Pleiades (Ar. *al-Thurayyā*) in astronomy, among the star clusters nearest to the earth and most obvious to the naked eye in the night sky.

Proponents of Equality (Ar. *ahl al-taswiyah*) an ambiguous term by which Ibn Qutaybah might mean his opponents in general, or possibly a specific group that called itself by this name in opposition to Arab privilege.

Qaḥṭabah (d. 132/749) Arab general who was one of the most prominent leaders of the Abbasid movement in Khurasan. He fought against the Umayyads and was killed trying to capture Kufa. His son Aḥmad then took Kufa.

Qaḥṭān a legendary ancestor of the "Southern Arabs," and a name synonymous with Yemen in Muslim genealogy.

al-Qāsim a son of Muḥammad and his wife Khadījah who died in infancy.

Qāsim ibn Muḥammad ibn Abī Bakr al-Ṣiddīq (d. ca. 106/724–25) Medinese hadith transmitter numbered among the so-called seven jurists of Medina; grandson of the Caliph Abū Bakr (q.v.).

al-Qāsim ibn ʿUrwah Abū Muḥammad (fl. late second/eighth century) minor Baghdadi hadith transmitter.

al-Qaṭāmī ʿUmayr ibn Shuyam (d. ca. 101/719–20) poet of the Taghlib (q.v.); his biography is obscure, but his love poetry and his praises for Umayyad elites were celebrated, and he was counted among the best Umayyad-era poets.

Qaṭarī ibn al-Fujāʾah (d. 80/699–700) Kharijite (q.v.) warrior and celebrated poet and orator; the last leader of a sect of rebellious Kharijites known as the Azraqīs, he waged numerous successful wars against the Umayyads in Iran and minted coins in his own name as "Commander of the Faithful." Killed in battle.

Qays a large lineage that included the Ghaṭafān (q.v.), the Sulaym (q.v.), and the Hawāzin (q.v.), and constituted a politically powerful faction in the Umayyad and early Abbasid eras.

Qays ʿAylān one of the main branches of Muḍar (q.v.), connoting a large number of pre-Islamic Arabian groups.

Qays ibn ʿAmr ibn Mālik al-Najāshī (d. 49/669) Arabian poet of the Kahlān (q.v.), probably called by the epithet al-Najāshī (from Negus, the title of the emperors of Ethiopia) because of his Ethiopian mother. Famous for his bellicose nature.

Qays ibn ʿĀṣim (fl. sixth century AD), pre-Islamic Arabian of the Tamīm (q.v.) celebrated in many stories for his intelligence and equanimity; also remembered as one of the pre-Islamic figures who abstained from drinking wine. Tamīm traditions stress the role of Qays in the deputation of Tamīm to the Prophet, emphasizing that the Prophet was impressed by him.

Qays ibn Sāʿid unknown poet.

Qays ibn Sāʿidah possibly Quss ibn Sāʿidah (fl. ca. AD 600), a semi-legendary orator and poet known for his skill in mediation. He is said to have been a monotheist and admired by the Prophet.

quflah a tree indigenous to the uplands of the Hijaz (q.v.), distinguished by its desiccated appearance and fragrant resin. Most Arabic literary descriptions of the tree are derived from the same anecdote reported by Ibn Qutaybah.

Qurād ibn Ḥanash al-Ṣāridī pre-Islamic poet from the Ghaṭafān (q.v.).

Qurayn see ʿUmayr ibn Salmā.

Quraysh the lineage of Muḥammad, the prophet of Islam, and the lineage group of both the Umayyad and Abbasid dynasties.

Qushayr ibn Kaʿb a subgroup of the ʿĀmir ibn Ṣaʿṣaʿah (q.v.) whose lineage is traced to the "Northern Arabs."

Qutaybah ibn Muslim (d. 96/714–15) a military commander for the Umayyads in eastern Iran; he led the major Muslim conquests in Central Asia, but friction with the caliphs and factionalism within his army's ranks led him to an unsuccessful rebellion in which he was killed.

rabīkah an Arab dish resembling *ḥaysah* (q.v.) but softer. One recipe makes it from flour and a sour cheese ground together and then mixed with clarified butter and thickened fruit juice or dates.

al-Raḥḥāl (fl. sixth century AD) reportedly a companion of the poet Jirān al-ʿAwd (q.v.); some poems are variously ascribed to either figure.

al-Rāʿī (d. ca. 90/708) an Umayyad-era poet most celebrated for his poetic duels with Jarīr (q.v.), in which he and his people were notoriously lampooned.

rajaz Arabic poetic meter, the simplest and generally believed to be the oldest. It is used for short, improvised utterances, for instance at the beginning of a battle.

al-Rashīd, Hārūn (r. 170–93/786–809) the most celebrated caliph in Arabic literature, his memory is associated with later nostalgia for an Abbasid "golden age."

Rebecca (Ar. Rifqā) wife of Isaac, mother of Esau and Jacob, and daughter of Abraham's brother Nahor in Ibn Qutaybah's reporting (in contrast to Genesis, where she is the granddaughter of Nahor through a son of his, Bethuel).

al-Riyāshī al-ʿAbbās ibn al-Faraj (d. ca. 257/871) one of the leaders of philological studies in Iraq.

al-Rūm an eponym for the Greeks and specifically for the Byzantines, who called themselves Roman.

Rūmān the name of two Yemeni groups: the Rūmān ibn Ghānim and Rūmān ibn Kaʿb, related to the Dhū l-Kalāʿ and the Madhḥij lineages, respectively.

Sacred Precinct(s) (Ar. *ḥaram*; literally, "forbidden, sacrosanct") name for the holy places of Mecca and/or Medina; sometimes also used for Jerusalem.

Saʿd the descendants of Saʿd ibn Zayd Manāt ibn Tamīm, and thus a subgroup of the Tamīm (q.v.).

Saʿd ibn Naṣr unidentified hadith transmitter.

Saḥbān Wāʾil (fl. late first/seventh–early second/eighth century) an orator and poet of the Wāʾil, whose eloquence was proverbial.

Sahl ibn Muḥammad see Abū Ḥātim.

Saʿīd ibn al-Musayyib (d. ca. 94/712–13) member of the second generation of Muslims who was renowned for his intense piety and great knowledge of Hadith.

sajʿ rhythmic rhyming prose.

Ṣakhr al-Ghayy (d. late seventh century AD) "brigand poet" of the Hudhayl born in the late pre-Islamic period; famed for his daring and raids in Arabia, which he continued during Islamic times.

Salāmah ibn Jandal (fl. second half of the sixth century AD) pre-Islamic poet; very little of his poetry survives, but he was esteemed by Muslim collectors, in particular for descriptions of horses.

Ṣāliḥ one of the Arab prophets who, according to the Qurʾan, was sent to the people of Thamūd (q.v.).

Ṣāliḥ ibn ʿAbd al-Quddūs (d. ca. 158–75/775–92) early Abbasid-era Basran poet, renowned for wisdom and admonition poems; accused of heresy and executed either during the reign of al-Mahdī or al-Rashīd (q.v.).

Ṣāliḥ ibn al-Ṣaqr (fl. late second/eighth century) otherwise unknown hadith transmitter.

Sālim ibn ʿAbd Allāh ibn ʿUmar ibn al-Khaṭṭāb (d. ca. 106/724) Medinese legal authority, grandson of the Caliph ʿUmar (q.v.).

Salm ibn ʿAmr ibn Ḥammād see Salm ibn ʿAmr al-Khāsir.

Salm ibn ʿAmr al-Khāsir (d. 186/802) a Basran poet who composed panegyrics, laments, and poems about his lost fortune (which he later recovered).

Salm ibn Qutaybah (d. 149/766–67) son of Qutaybah ibn Muslim (q.v.); he held important administrative posts under the Umayyads and Abbasids.

Salmān ibn Rabīʿah al-Bāhilī (d. ca. 28–31/648–52) member of the early Muslim elite, participated in the conquests of Iraq and Syria and was appointed judge for Kufa by the Caliph ʿUmar (q.v.), during whose caliphate he campaigned in Armenia.

Salmān the Persian (al-Fārisī) (d. 35/655) prominent early Companion of the Prophet Muḥammad, governor of Ctesiphon during the caliphate of ʿUmar (q.v.), and a partisan of ʿAlī ibn Abī Ṭālib (q.v.).

Sarah (Ar. Sārah) in both biblical and Qurʾanic traditions, the wife of Abraham and mother of Isaac.

Sawād in early Islamic times, the name for the political territory of southern Iraq; used generically, the term refers to the black, arable land in a district.

Sawwār ibn al-Muḍarrab (fl. late first/seventh century) minor Umayyad-era poet of the Saʿd, resident in Iraq.

Sayf ibn Dhī Yazan (fl. second half of the sixth century AD) the leader of a successful Sasanian-supported revolt around AD 570 against Ethiopian rule in Yemen; he became the subject of an Arabic popular romance (*sīrah*).

Sayyār ibn ʿAmr ibn Jābir al-Fazārī influential friend of al-Nuʿmān III (r. AD 580–602), the pre-Islamic king of al-Ḥīrah.

Shabīb ibn Gharqadah [al-Salamī l-Bāriqī l-Kūfī] (fl. second half of the first/seventh century), transmitter of hadith and historical reports from the second generation of Muslims.

Shabīb al-Ḥarurī [ibn Yazīd al-Shaybānī] (d. 77/696–97) a partisan of the Kharijites (q.v.) who staged a rebellion during the reign of the Umayyad ʿAbd al-Malik (q.v.).

Shahawāt [Abū Mūsā] Umayyad-era client of the Quraysh and poet known best for his lampoon and praise poems and his turbulent relations with members of the Umayyad elite. His given name was Mūsā ibn Yasār; the nickname Shahawāt ("Cravings") was reportedly earned because of his oft-expressed desires for gifts and favors.

al-Shammākh [*Maʿqil ibn Ḍirār*] (d. 30/650 or after) early Islamic-era poet and participant in the conquests; his poetry describes the desert and Arabian Bedouin pursuits. Brother of al-Muzarrid (q.v.).

Shaybān one of the major subgroups of the Bakr ibn Wāʾil (q.v.); resided in northeastern Arabia and on the Arabian-Iraqi frontier at the dawn of Islam.

Shem (Ar. Sām) son of the biblical Noah.

Shuʿayb Arabian prophet mentioned in the Qurʾan who, on the basis of Q Tawbah 9:91, was understood to have lived after Hūd (q.v.), Ṣāliḥ (q.v.), and Lot.

Shuʿayb ibn Wāqid (fl. early third/ninth century) Basran hadith transmitter.

Shuʿūbī pejorative term that in premodern Arabic lexicons signals bias against Arabs and that Ibn Qutaybah uses to refer to his opponents; translated here as "Bigot."

al-Sijistānī see Abū Ḥātim.

Sind region around the lower course of the Indus (in modern-day Pakistan).

Solomon (Ar. Sulaymān) son of David and king of Israel; revered as a prophet and ideal king in the Qurʾan and Muslim tradition.

Sons of the Camel Snout a clan of the Saʿd subgroup of the Tamīm (q.v.); they trace their genealogy to a pre-Islamic progenitor usually identified as Jaʿfar ibn Qurayʿ ibn ʿAwf ibn Kaʿb (q.v.).

Sūdān (Ar. *bilād al-Sūdān*; literally, "land of the Blacks") the general name in premodern Arabic sources for the Saharan-Sahelian sector of Africa lying south of the Maghreb, Libya, and Egypt, and stretching across the continent from the Atlantic Ocean to the Red Sea.

Sufyān ibn ʿUyaynah (d. 196/811) major Meccan hadith transmitter, legal authority, and Qurʾan commentator.

Sulayk ibn ʿUmayr al-Saʿdī al-Tamīmī (d. ca. AD 605) a pre-Islamic foot soldier known for his good sense of direction.

Sulaym a large and powerful subgroup of the Qays ʿAylān (q.v.) spread across central Arabia (Najd) at the dawn of Islam.

Sulaymān [ibn ʿAbd al-Malik] (r. 96–99/715–717) seventh caliph of the Umayyad dynasty.

Sulaymān ibn ʿAlī ibn ʿAbd Allāh ibn al-ʿAbbās ibn ʿAbd al-Muṭṭalib (d. 142/759) early Abbasid prince and uncle of the first Abbasid caliphs al-Saffāḥ and al-Manṣūr (q.v.); served as governor of Basra.

Surāqah ibn Mālik ibn Jaʿsham al-Mudlajī (d. before 35/656) al-Qāʾif leader of the Kinānah, famous for his unsuccessful attempt to track Muḥammad when he emigrated from Mecca to Medina. Tradition asserts that he converted after the conquest of Mecca.

Susa ancient site in the southwest Iranian province of Khuzistan.

Suwayd ibn al-Ṣāmit pre-Islamic poet of the Aws lineage from Medina. Best known for his wisdom poems.

Taghlib bint Wāʾil an important, mostly nomadic, lineage of the Rabīʿah ibn Nizār. Before Islam, the Taghlib were within the Sasanian and Lakhmid (q.v.) sphere of influence. Often their name is written Taghlib ibn Wāʾil.

al-Ṭāʾif fortified town situated high in the mountains, approximately 120 kilometers southeast of Mecca; famous for its orchards and gardens. It was dominated by the Thaqīf (q.v.), who served as guardians of the town's shrine.

Ṭalḥah (d. 36/656) prominent Companion of Muḥammad, counted among the first eight converts to Islam and among the ten persons for whom the Prophet said Paradise was promised.

Ṭalḥah ibn ʿAbd Allāh ibn ʿAwf (d. 97/715–16 or 99/717–18) Medinese judge and legal authority.

Tamīm one of the most important lineages of "Northern Arabs"; its members inhabited much of northeast and central Arabia (Najd) at the dawn of Islam.

Ṭarafah ibn al-ʿAbd (d. mid-sixth century AD) one of the major pre-Islamic Arabian poets and author of one of the great odes (Ar. *muʿallaqah*). He was attached to the court of ʿAmr ibn Hind (q.v.) at the Lakhmid (q.v.) capital of al-Ḥīrah.

Ṭasm a legendary lineage; Muslim genealogists linked them to descendants of Noah and considered them and a related group, Jadīs (q.v.), to be the first inhabitants of central and eastern Arabia (al-Yamāmah and al-Baḥrayn).

Ṭayyi' a major Arabian lineage; genealogists connected them to the "Southern Arabs," though their lands in the century before Islam were located in northern and nothereastern Arabia. Their name, transliterated into Syriac as *Ṭayyāyē*, became the generic label by which Iraqis and the Sasanian Empire referred to all Arabians in late antiquity.

Thaʿlabah a "Northern Arab" lineage; resided near Medina at the dawn of Islam and engaged in a number of conflicts with the Prophet Muḥammad before submitting in ca. 7/628–29.

Thamūd a legendary people of ancient north Arabia, frequently mentioned in the Qur'an as one of the past peoples destroyed by God for disobeying their prophet, Ṣāliḥ (q.v.).

Thaqīf a "Northern Arab" lineage; occupied lands between Mecca and al-Ṭā'if (q.v.) at the dawn of Islam. Alongside Quraysh, members of Thaqīf constituted the most powerful political elites of the Umayyad era.

al-Thawrī [*Sufyān ibn Saʿīd ibn Masrūḳ Abū ʿAbd Allāh al-Kūfī*] (d. 161/778) prominent representative of early Islamic law, tradition, and Qur'an interpretation.

Thumāmah ibn Ashras (d. 213/828?) theologian and representative of the religious movement known as *al-muʿtazilah*, which was founded at Basra in the first half of the second/eighth century and became one of the most important theological schools of Islam. On account of his great learning and intellectual ability he was invited to the court by al-Rashīd (q.v.) and al-Ma'mūn (q.v.).

Tihāmah the area of the Red Sea coastal plain stretching from ʿAqabah in the north to Bāb al-Mandab in the south of the Arabian Peninsula, and perhaps even further along the southern Indian Ocean coast.

al-Ṭirimmāḥ (d. 110/728) eloquent poet of the Umayyad middle period who resided in Kufa and was famous for his desert descriptions.

Tubbaʿ, people of an ancient community twice mentioned in the Qur'an (Q Dukhān 44:37 and Q Qāf 50:13) as examples of peoples destroyed for shunning their prophets. Tubbaʿ himself is sometimes interpreted as a believer, and the name was regularly associated in Arabic literature with a dynasty of pre-Islamic kings of Yemen.

Ṭufayl ibn ʿAwf (d. after AD 608) one of the oldest poets of Qays (q.v.) and famous for his horse descriptions, which earned him the nickname "Ṭufayl of the Horses."

Ṭurayḥ ibn Ismāʿīl al-Thaqafī (d. 165/782) poet from al-Ṭāʾif (q.v.).

Turks used by Ibn Qutaybah and his sources as a generic ethnonym designating most if not all of the Turkic-language speaking peoples of Central Asia.

ʿUbayd ibn ʿAqīl (d. 207/822–23) Basran scholar, Qurʾan specialist, and transmitter of hadith.

ʿUbayd ibn Thaʿlabah ibn Yarbūʿ pre-Islamic leader of the Banū Ḥanīfah, legendarily connected with the establishment of Hajar (q.v.).

al-ʿUdayl ibn al-Farkh (fl. early second/eighth century) minor Iraqi Umayyad-era poet from the ʿIjl ibn Luyajm (q.v.).

ʿUhaynah (or ʿUhniyyah) one of nine ancient Arab lineages (through Abū Ḥātim [q.v.]), according to Ibn Qutaybah. The name does not feature in other popular listings of ancient Arab lineages.

al-ʿUjayr al-Salūlī [*ibn ʿAbd Allāh* or *ibn ʿUbayd Allāh*] (fl. early second/eighth century) Umayyad-era poet.

ʿUkl the descendants of ʿUkl ibn ʿAwf. The ʿUkl belonged to a confederacy called al-Ribāb, which was in alliance with Saʿd ibn Zayd Manāt, the greatest clan of Tamīm (q.v.).

ʿUmar ibn Jīlān unknown figure.

ʿUmar ibn al-Khaṭṭāb (d. 23/644) Companion of the Prophet and second caliph after Muḥammad (r. 13–23/634–44).

ʿUmayr ibn Salmā (fl. late sixth century AD) pre-Islamic member of the Ḥanīfah (q.v.); celebrated in Arabic literature along with al-Samawʾal ibn ʿĀdiyāʾ and al-Ḥārith ibn Ẓālim as one of the three "Arab Dependables" (men who kept their oaths notwithstanding any consequences). The best known of several stories about ʿUmayr's oaths is his killing of his brother Qurayn after Qurayn killed a man whom ʿUmayr had sworn to protect.

Umayyads (r. 41–132/661–750) the first dynasty to rule the Islamic world.

Umayyah ibn Abī l-Ṣalt (fl. early seventh century AD) pre-Islamic Arabian poet of the Thaqīf (q.v.); author of a number of poems with monotheistic messages.

Uqayṣir see Muḥammad ibn Uqayṣir.

Ursa Minor (Ar. Jadī l-Farqad) the Great Bear, one of the main constellations of the nothern hemisphere.

ʿUrwah al-Bāriqī [ibn al-Jaʿd ibn Abī l-Jaʿd] Companion of the Prophet and transmitter of hadith; the sources disagree on his exact name.

ʿUrwah ibn al-Ward (fl. sixth century AD) pre-Islamic "brigand poet"; a Robin Hood–like figure in pre-Islamic lore known for his self-sacrifice, many raids, and untiring generosity to the poor.

ʿUrwah ibn al-Zubayr (d. 93/711–12 or 94/712–13) son of the Companion al-Zubayr (q.v.); an eminent hadith transmitter, jurist, and pioneer of Muslim historical study.

Usayd ibn al-Ḥalāḥil (fl. sixth century AD) minor pre-Islamic Arabian poet.

ʿUtaybah ibn al-Ḥārith ibn Shihāb [ibn ʿAbd al-Qays ibn al-Kibās ibn Jaʿfar ibn Thaʿlabah ibn Yarbūʿ] a horseman of the Tamīm (q.v.), he was famous in pre-Islamic times for his valor.

al-ʿUtbī (d. 228/842) Basran poet, person possessing *adab* (q.v.), genealogist, and historian of the Umayyads who authored several books.

ʿUthmān ibn Abī l-ʿĀṣ [al-Thaqafī] (d. 51/671) a Companion of the Prophet, from al-Ṭāʾif (q.v.).

ʿUthmān [ibn ʿAffān] (r. 23–36/644–56) third caliph of Islam who ruled during the important period of the conquests and early organization of the state. He organized the now-canonical Qurʾanic codex; his death sparked the First Civil War.

ʿUthmān ibn Muḥammad ibn Ibrāhīm ibn Ḥātib al-Jumaḥī possibly ʿUthmān ibn Ibrāhīm ibn Ḥātib al-Jumaḥī (fl. mid-late first/seventh century) member of the Quraysh; resident in Medina; transmitted hadiths to some Iraqi scholars.

ʿUyaynah ibn al-Nahhās al-ʿIjlī a poet from Bakr ibn Wāʾil (q.v.) whose lifetime straddles the origins of Islam.

Wabr ibn Muʿāwiyah al-Asadī an unknown poet.

Wahb ibn Munabbih (ca. 34–110/654–728) Yemeni hadith transmitter of Persian origins; reputed for his knowledge of Christian and Jewish lore.

Wahriz (d. before AD 579) a Persian general of Khosrow Anushirvan (q.v.) active in the Yemen.

Wakīʿ ibn Abī Sūd al-Tamīmī powerful Umayyad-era military commander. He clashed with Qutaybah ibn Muslim (q.v.) in a chaotic period in Khurasan during the short reign of Sulaymān ibn ʿAbd al-Malik (q.v.); he assumed the governorship of Khurasan in 96/715 but within less than a year lost his position.

Wakīʿ [ibn al-Jarrāḥ ibn Malīḥ al-Ruʾāsī] (d. 197/812) famous Iraqi hadith transmitter.

Waʿlah al-Jarmī pre-Islamic poet.

washīqah a traveling provision of meat that is boiled and then cut into strips and dried.

Yām son of Noah, the fourth in Muslim tradition, which reports his name also as Canaan (Kanʿān), whereas in the Bible, Canaan is a son of Ham. Based on Q Hūd 11:43, some tales relate that Yām refused to enter the ark, claiming that he could save himself from the deluge by climbing to the top of the highest mountain.

al-Yamāmah the eastern part of central Arabia, identified at the dawn of Islam as the land to the east of the Najd upland region.

Yaʿrub ibn Qaḥṭān sometimes called the progenitor of the "Southern Arabs" by Arab genealogists (credit is alternatively given to his father, Qaḥṭān [q.v.]).

Yazīd ibn Abī Ziyād [Abū ʿAbd Allāh] (d. 136/753–54) a client (q.v.) who lived in Kufa.

Yazīd ibn ʿAmr [al-Maʿfurī l-Miṣrī] an unknown hadith transmitter often cited by Ibn Qutaybah.

Yazīd ibn Muʿāwiyah (r. 60–64/680–83) the second Umayyad caliph, reviled by the Shiʿah for ordering the killing of al-Ḥusayn (q.v.).

Yazīd ibn al-Muhallab (d. 102/720) son of the general al-Muhallab and his successor to the governorship of Umayyad Khurasan (q.v.); repeatedly arrested and returned to favor before being killed in a major revolt he organized against the Umayyads in Iraq.

Yemen the southwestern part of the Arabian Peninsula.

Zabbān al-ʿAdawī (fl. first/seventh century) a contemporary of the Prophet Muḥammad.

Zaghāwah a lineage that populated the Sūdān and that features in Muslim ethnogenesis.

Zamzam the sacred well of Mecca, to the east of the Kaaba (q.v.) alongside the wall where the "Black Stone" is enshrined.

Zawl a place, otherwise unidentified, mentioned by Ibn Qutaybah as being in Sanaa in Yemen.

Zayd ibn Akhzam [Abū Ṭālib al-Baṣrī al-Ṭāʾī] (d. 257/870–71) transmitter of prophetic traditions to Ibn Qutaybah.

Zayd al-Khayl see Abū Zayd al-Ṭāʾī.

Zechariah (Ar. Zakariyyāʾ) the father of John the Baptist (q.v.).

al-Zibriqān ibn Badr tribal leader and poet of the Tamīm (q.v.) and a Companion of the Prophet active in the conquests; three of his sons-in-law were governors under ʿUmar (q.v.).

Ziyād al-Aʿjam [*Ibn Salmā* or *Ibn Sulaym* or *Ibn Jābir ibn ʿAmr*] (d. ca. 125/742–43) celebrated Umayyad-era poet of the ʿAbd al-Qays (q.v.); known also for his inability to pronounce certain Arabic letters, hence his sobriquet al-Aʿjam ("the mumbler").

Ziyād ibn Abī Sufyān (d. 53/673) a prominent governor under the Umayyad caliph Muʿāwiyah ibn Abī Sufyān (r. 41–60/661–80). Muʿāwiyah tried to attach Ziyād to his own clan of the Umayyads; often referred to disparagingly as "Ziyād, the son of his [unknown] father."

al-Ziyādī probably Abū l-Ḥasan al-Ziyādī (d. 242/856), a celebrated man of letters who was appointed judge (*qāḍī*) over eastern Baghdad during the caliphate of al-Mutawakkil (r. 232–47/847–61).

al-Zubayr ibn al-ʿAwwām (d. 36/656) a prominent member of Muḥammad's community in Mecca from the ʿAbd al-ʿUzzā clan of Quraysh; competed, along with his sons ʿAbd Allāh (q.v.) and Muṣʿab, for power after Muḥammad's death.

Zuhayr ibn Abī Sulmā (d. AD 609) a pre-Islamic poet famous for his gnomic sayings and the meticulous composition of his odes, including his great ode (*muʿallaqah*).

al-Zuhrī (d. 124/742) a founder of the study of Hadith and transmitter of historical lore. A protégé of the Umayyad caliphs from ʿAbd al-Malik ibn Marwān (q.v.) to Hishām ibn ʿAbd al-Malik. He served at different periods as a judge, tax collector, and police chief.

Ẓulaym a small clan of the Ḥanẓalah (q.v.) reportedly descended from the "Northern Arabs."

Bibliography

Abū l-ʿAtāhiyah. *Dīwān*. Edited by Karam al-Bustānī. Beirut: Dār Ṣādir, 1384 [1964].

Abū l-Faraj al-Iṣfahānī. *Al-Aghānī*. 24 vols. Cairo: Maṭbaʿat Dār al-Kutub al-ʿArabiyyah, [1927–74?].

Abū Nuwās. *Dīwān*. Edited by Ewald Wagner and Gregor Schoeler. 7 vols. Wiesbaden: Franz Steiner; Beirut: Klaus Schwarz, 1958–2006.

Abū Tammām. *Dīwān bi-sharḥ al-Khaṭīb al-Tabrīzī*. Edited by Muḥammad ʿAbduh ʿAzzām. 4 vols. Cairo: Dār al-Maʿārif, 1951–65.

Abū ʿUbayd al-Bakrī. *Faṣl al-maqāl fī sharḥ Kitāb al-Amthāl*. Edited by Iḥsān ʿAbbās and ʿAbd al-Majīd ʿĀbidīn. Beirut: Dār al-Amānah, 1983.

Abū ʿUbaydah, Maʿmar ibn Muthannā. *Naqāʾid Jarīr wa-l-Farazdaq*. Edited by Anthony Ashley Bevan. 3 vols. Leiden: E. J. Brill, 1905–12.

Abū Yaʿlā l-Mawṣilī. *Musnad*. Edited by Ḥusayn Salīm Asad. 6 vols. Damascus: Dār al-Maʾmūn li-l-Turāth, 1984–86.

al-ʿAjjāj. *Dīwān*. Riwāyat ʿAbd al-Malik ibn Qurayb al-Aṣmaʿī. Edited by ʿIzzat Ḥasan. Beirut: Dār al-Sharq, [1971?].

al-Aʿshā. *Dīwān*. Notes and comments by Muḥammad Ḥusayn. [Cairo?]: Maktabat al-Ādāb, [1950?].

al-ʿAskarī. *Dīwān al-Maʿānī*. 2 vols. Cairo: Maktaba al-Qudsi, 1352 [1933].

al-Aṣmaʿī. *Al-Aṣmaʿiyyāt*. Edited by Aḥmad Shākir and Muḥammad ʿAbd al-Salām Hārūn. Cairo: Dār al-Maʿārif, 1955.

al-Aswad ibn Yaʿfūr. *Dīwān*. Edited by Nūrī Ḥamūdī al-Qaysī. Baghdad: Wizārat al-Thaqāfah wa-l-ʿIlām, 1970.

al-Azharī. *Tahdhīb al-lughah*. Edited by ʿAbd al-Salām Muḥammad Hārūn and revised by Muḥammad ʿAlī l-Najjār. Cairo: al-Mu'assasah al-Miṣriyyah al-ʿĀmmah li-l-Ta'līf wa-l-Anbā' wa-l-Nashr; al-Dār al-Miṣriyyah li-l-Ta'līf wa-l-Tarjamah, 1964–67.

Commins, David Dean. *Islamic Reform: Politics and Social Change in Late Ottoman Syria*. New York/Oxford: Oxford University Press, 1990.

Crone, Patricia. *Medieval Islamic Political Thought*. Edinburgh: Edinburgh University Press, 2004.

al-Dhahabī, Shams al-Dīn Muḥammad. *Tārīkh al-Islām wa-wafāyāt al-mashāhīr wa-l-aʿlām*. Edited by Bashshār ʿAwwād Maʿruf. 17 vols. Beirut: Dār al-Gharb al-Islāmī, 2003.

al-Dīnawarī, Abū Bakr Aḥmad. *Al-Mujālasah wa-jawāhir al-ʿilm*. Edited by Abū ʿUbaydah Mashhūr ibn Ḥasan Āl Salmān. 10 vols. Beirut: Dār Ibn Ḥazm, 1998.

Donner, Fred. *Muhammad and the Believers: At the Origin of Islam*. Cambridge, MA: Harvard University Press, 2010.

Encyclopaedia of Islam, Second Edition. Edited by P. Bearman, Th. Bianquis, C. E. Bosworth, E. van Donzel, and W. P. Heinrichs. Leiden: Brill Online, 2012.

Encyclopaedia of Islam, Third Edition. Edited by Gudrun Krämer, Denis Matringe, John Nawas, and Everett Rowson. Leiden: Brill Online, 2014.

Encyclopaedia of the Qur'ān. Edited by Jane Dammen McAuliffe. Leiden: Brill Online, 2015.

al-Farazdaq. *Dīwān*. 2 vols. Beirut: Dār Ṣādir, 1960.

Gibb, Hamilton A. R. "The Social Significance of the Shuubiya." In *Studies on the Civilization of Islam*, edited by Stanford J. Shaw and William R. Polk, 62–73. Boston: Beacon, 1962.

Goldziher, Ignaz. *Muhammedanische Studien*. 2 vols. Halle: Max Niemeyer, 1888–90.

———. *Muslim Studies*. 2 vols. Edited by S. M. Stern. Translated by C. R. Barber and S. M. Stern. Chicago: Aldine, 1967.

Ḥātim al-Ṭā'ī. *Dīwān*. Edited by ʿĀdil Sulaymān Jamāl. Cairo, [1975?].

al-Ḥimyarī, Nashwān. *Shams al-ʿulūm*. Edited by Ḥusayn ibn ʿAbd Allāh al-ʿUmarī. 12 vols. Damascus: Dār al-Fikr, 1999.

al-Ḥuṭayʾa, Jarwal ibn Aws. *Dīwān*. Edited by Nuʿmān Muḥammad Amīn Ṭāhā. Cairo: al-Khānjī, 1987.

Ibn ʿAbd Rabbih. *Al-ʿIqd al-farīd*. Edited by Aḥmad Amīn, Aḥmad al-Zayn, and Ibrāhīm al-Abyārī. 7 vols. Cairo: Lajnat al-Taʾlīf wa-l-Tarjamah wa-l-Nashr, 1940–53.

Ibn Abī l-Ḥadīd. *Sharḥ Nahj al-Balāghah*. Edited by Muḥammad Abū l-Faḍl Ibrāhīm. 18 vols. Cairo: ʿĪsā l-Bābī l-Ḥalabī, 1959–63.

Ibn Abī Ḥātim. *Tafsīr*. Edited by Asʿad Muḥammad al-Ṭayyib. 14 vols. Riyadh: Maktabat Nizār Muṣṭafā l-Bāz; Beirut: al-Maktabah al-ʿAṣriyyah, 2003.

Ibn al-Anbārī. *Sharḥ al-Qaṣāʾid al-sabʿa al-ṭiwāl*. Edited by ʿAbd al-Sallām Muḥammad Hārūn. Cairo: Dār al-Maʿārif, 1963.

Ibn al-Athīr, ʿIzz al-Dīn. *Al-Kāmil fī l-tārīkh*. Edited by C. J. Tornberg. 12 vols. Beirut: Dār Ṣādir, 1979.

Ibn al-Athīr, Majd al-Dīn. *Al-Nihāyah fī gharīb al-Ḥadīth wa-l-athar*. Cairo, 1311/1893.

Ibn Durayd, Abū Bakr Muḥammad. *Al-Ishtiqāq*. Edited by ʿAbd al-Salām Muḥammad Hārūn. Cairo: al-Khānjī, n.d.

———. *Taʿlīq min Amālī Ibn Durayd*. Edited by al-Sayid Muṣṭafā l-Sanūsī. Cairo: Maktabat al-Adab, 1992.

Ibn Ḥabīb, Muḥammad. *Al-Muḥabbar*. Edited by Ilse Lichtenstädter. Hyderabad: Maṭbaʿat Jamʿiyyat Dāʾirat al-Maʿārif al-ʿUthmāniyyah, 1942.

Ibn al-Jawzī. *Virtues of the Imam Aḥmad ibn Ḥanbal*. Edited and translated by Michael Cooperson. 2 vols. New York: Library of Arabic Literature/New York University Press, 2013.

Ibn Manẓūr. *Lisān al-ʿArab*. 15 vols. Beirut: Dār Ṣādir/Dār Beirut, 1955–56.

Ibn Qutaybah, ʿAbd Allāh ibn Muslim. *Adab al-Kātib*. Edited by ʿAlī Muḥammad Zaynū. Beirut: Muʾassasat al-Risāla Nāshirūn, 2012.

———. *Al-Anwāʾ*. Hyderabad : Dāʾirat al-Maʿārif al-ʿUthmāniyyah, 1956.

———. *Faḍl al-ʿArab wa-l-Tanbīh ʿalā ʿulūmihā*. Edited by Walīd Maḥmūd Khāliṣ. Abu Dhabi: al-Majmaʿ al-Thaqāfī, 1998.

———. *Gharīb al-Ḥadīth*. Edited by Riḍā l-Suwaysī. Tunis: al-Dār al-Tunisiyyah li-l-Nashr, 1979.

———. *Gharīb al-Ḥadīth*. Edited by ʿAbdallāh al-Jubūrī. Baghdad: Lajnat Iḥyāʾ al-Turāth al-Islāmī, [1977?].

———. *Kitāb al-ʿArab*. In *Rasāʾil al-Bulaghāʾ*. Edited by Muḥammad Kurd ʿAlī. Cairo: Lajnat al-Taʾlīf wa-l-Tarjamah wa-l-Nashr, 1954.

———. *Kitāb al-Maʿānī l-Kabīr*. Edited by Muḥammad Nabīl Ṭarīfī. 2 vols. Beirut: Dār Ṣādir, 2012.

———. *Kitāb al-Shiʿr wa-l-shuʿarāʾ*. Edited by Aḥmad Muḥammad Shākir. 2 vols. Cairo: Dār Iḥyāʾ al-Kutub al-ʿArabiyyah, 1364–66/1945–47.

———. *Al-Maʿārif*. Edited by Tharwat ʿUkāshah. Cairo, 1960. Reprint, Cairo: al-Hayʾah al-Miṣriyyah li-l-Kitāb, 1992.

———. *Al-Maysir wa-l-qiḍāh*. Edited by al-Sayyid Muḥibb al-Dīn al-Khaṭīb. Cairo: al-Maṭbaʿah al-Salafiyyah, 1924.

———. *ʿUyūn al-akhbār*. 4 vols. Cairo: Maṭbaʿat Dār al-Kutub al-Miṣriyyah, 1925–30.

Ibn Sallām, Abū ʿUbayd al-Qāsim. *Kitāb al-Amthāl*. Edited by ʿAbd al-Majīd Qaṭāmish. Damascus: Dār al-Maʾmūn li-l-Turāth, 1980.

al-Jāḥiẓ. *Al-Bukhalāʾ*. Edited by Ṭaha al-Ḥājirī. Cairo: Dār al-Kātib al-Miṣrī, 1948.

———. *Al-Ḥayawān*. Edited by ʿAbd al-Salām Muḥammad Hārūn. Cairo: Muṣṭafā l-Bābī l-Ḥalabī; Beirut: Dār Iḥyāʾ al-Turāth al-ʿArabī, 198[?].

———. *Kitāb al-Bayān wa-l-tabyīn*. 2nd edition. Edited by ʿAbd al-Salām Muḥammad Hārūn. 4 vols. Cairo: Maktabat al-Khānjī, 1960–61.

———. *Rasāʾil*. Edited by ʿAbd al-Sallām Muḥammad Hārūn. Cairo: Maktabat al-Khānjī, 1964–65.

Jirān al-ʿAwd al-Numayrī. *Dīwān*. Riwāyat Abī Saʿīd al-Sikrī [or al-Sakrī]. Cairo: Dār al-Kutub al-Miṣriyyah, 1931.

Kaʿb ibn Zuhayr. *Dīwān bi-sharḥ al-Sukkarī*. Edited by ʿAbbās ʿAbd al-Qādir. Cairo: Dār al-Kutub wa-l-Wathāʾiq al-Qawmiyyah, 2002.

Khalīl ibn Aḥmad. *Kitāb al-ʿAyn*. Edited by Mahdī Makhzūmī and Ibrāhīm Sāmarrāʾī. 8 vols. [Baghdad?]: Wizārat al-Thaqāfah wa-l-Iʿlām, 1980.

Khāliṣ, Walīd Maḥmūd. *See* Ibn Qutaybah.

al-Khaṭīb al-Baghdādī. *Ta'rīkh Baghdād*. 14 vols. Cairo: Maktabat al-Khānjī, 1931.

Kramers, J. H. and C. E. Bosworth. "Ṣulṭān." In *Encyclopaedia of Islam, Second Edition*.

al-Kumayt. *Shiʿr al-Kumayt ibn Zayd al-Asadī*. Edited by Dā'ūd al-Sallūm. 3 vols. Baghdad: Maktabat al-Andalus, 1969.

Kuthayyir ʿAzzah. *Dīwān*. Edited by Iḥsān ʿAbbās. Beirut: Dār al-Thaqāfah, 1971.

Lane, Edward William, and Stanley Lane-Poole. *An Arabic-English Lexicon*. London/Edinburgh: Williams and Norgate, 1863–93.

Mālik ibn Anas. *Al-Muwaṭṭa'*. Transmitted by Yaḥyā ibn Yaḥyā. Edited by Saʿīd Muḥammad al-Laḥḥām. Beirut: Dār Iḥyā' al-ʿUlūm, 1994.

al-Marzūqī, Abū ʿAlī Aḥmad. *Al-Azminah wa-l-amkinah*. Edited by Khalīl al-Manṣūr. Beirut: Dār al-Kutub al-ʿIlmiyyah, 1996.

al-Masʿūdī. *Murūj al-dhahab wa-maʿādin al-jawhar*. 7 vols. Edited by Charles Pellat. Beirut: Manshūrāt al-Jāmiʿah al-Lubnāniyyah, 1965–79.

al-Maydānī, Aḥmad ibn Muḥammad. *Majmaʿ al-amthāl*. Edited by Muḥammad Abū l-Faḍl Ibrāhīm. 4 vols. Beirut: Dār al-Jīl, 1987.

McAuliffe, Jane Dammen. "Abraha." In *Encyclopaedia of the Qur'ān*. Leiden: Brill Online, 2015.

Millar, Fergus. *Religion, Language and Community in the Roman Near East*. Oxford: Oxford University Press, 2013.

Miskīn al-Dārimī. *Dīwān*. Edited by ʿAbd Allāh al-Jubūrī and Khalīl Ibrāhīm al-ʿAṭiyyah. Baghdād: Maṭbaʿat Dār al-Baṣrī, 1389/1970.

al-Mufaḍḍal ibn Muḥammad al-Ḍabbī. *Al-Mufaḍḍaliyyāt*. Edited by Aḥmad Muḥammad Shākir and ʿAbd al-Sallām Muḥammad Hārūn. Cairo: Dār al-Maʿārif, 1964.

al-Quḍāʿī, al-Qāḍī. *A Treasury of Virtues*. Edited and translated by Tahera Qutbuddin. New York: Library of Arabic Literature / New York University Press, 2013.

al-Rāʿī. *Dīwān al-Rāʿī al-Numayrī*. Edited by Reinhard Weipert. Beirut: Franz Steiner, 1980.

Robin, Christian. “Abraha et la reconquête de l’Arabie déserte: un réexamen de l’inscription Ryckmans 506 = Muraygħān 1.” *Jerusalem Studies in Arabic and Islam*, 39 (2012): 1–93.

Savant, Sarah Bowen. “Naming Shuʿūbīs.” In *Essays in Islamic Philology, History, and Philosophy*. Edited by Alireza Korangy Isfahani, Wheeler M. Thackston, Roy P. Mottahedeh, and William Granara, 166–84. Berlin: De Gruyter, 2016.

———. *The New Muslims of Post-Conquest Iran: Tradition, Memory, and Conversion*. Cambridge: Cambridge University Press, 2013.

———. “Persians after the Arab Conquests.” *Annales Islamologiques*, 42 (2008): 73–91.

al-Shammākh. *Dīwān al-Shammākh ibn Ḍirār al-Dhubyānī*. Edited by Ṣālāḥ al-Dīn al-Hādī. Cairo: Dār al-Maʿārif, 1968.

al-Sukkarī, Abū Saʿīd. *Sharḥ Ashʿār al-Hudhaliyyin*. Edited by ʿAbd al-Sattār Aḥmad Farrāj. 3 vols. Cairo: Maktabat Dār al-ʿUrūbah, 1963–65.

al-Ṭufayl. *Dīwān*. Edited by ʿAbd al-Qādir Aḥmad. Baghdad: Wizarat al-ʿIlam, 1967.

Ṭurayḥ ibn Ismāʿīl al-Thaqafī. *Dīwān*. Edited by Badr Aḥmad Ḍayf. Alexandria: Dār al-Maʿrifah al-Jāmiʿiyyah, 1987.

Umayyah ibn Abī l-Ṣalt. *Dīwān*. Edited by ʿAbd al-Ḥāfiẓ al-Saṭlī. Damascus: al-Maṭbaʿah al-Taʿāwuniyyah, 1974.

ʿUrwah ibn al-Ward. *Dīwān*. Edited by Karam al-Bustānī. Beirut: Dār al-Ṣādir, 1953.

Wadie, Jwaideh. *The Introductory Chapters of Yāqūt’s Muʿjam al-Buldān*. Leiden: E. J. Brill, 1959.

Webb, Peter. *Imagining the Arabs: Arab Identity and the Rise of Islam*. Edinburgh: Edinburgh University Press, 2016.

Zuhayr ibn Abī Sulmā. *Dīwān*. Edited by ʿAlī Ḥasan Fāghūr. Beirut: Dār al-Kutub al-ʿIlmiyyah, 1988.

Further Reading

General

Bray, Julia. "Lists and Memory: Ibn Qutayba and Muhammad b. Habib." In *Culture and Memory in Medieval Islam*, edited by Farhad Daftary and Josef W. Meri, 210–31. London: I. B. Tauris, 2002.

Cooperson, Michael. "'Arabs' and 'Iranians': The Uses of Ethnicity in the Early Abbasid Period." In *Islamic Cultures, Islamic Contexts: Essays in Honor of Professor Patricia Crone*, edited by Behnam Sadeghi, Asad Q. Ahmed, Adam Silverstein, and Robert Hoyland, 364–87. Leiden: Brill, 2014.

Ibn Qutaybah. "Ibn Quteiba's *'Uyun al-Akhbar*." Translated by Josef Horowitz. *Islamic Culture*, 4 (1930): 171–98, 331–62, 487–530; and 5 (1931): 1–27.

———. *Introduction au Livre de la Poésie et des poètes*. Translated by M. Gaudefroy-Demombynes. Paris: Les Belles Lettres, 1947.

Lecomte, Gérard. "Ibn Ḳutayba." In *Enyclopaedia of Islam, Second Edition*.

———. *Ibn Qutayba: l'homme, son oeuvre, ses idées*. Damascus: Institut Français de Damas, 1965.

Lowry, Joseph. E. "Ibn Qutayba: The Earliest Witness to al-Shāfiʿī and His Legal Doctrines." In *'Abbasid Studies: Occasional Papers of the School of 'Abbasid Studies, Cambridge, 6–10 July 2002*, edited by James E. Montgomery, vol. 1. Leuven and Dudley, MA: Peeters, 2004.

Montgomery, James E. "Of Models and Amanuenses: The Remarks on the Qaṣīda in Ibn Qutaybah's *Kitāb al-Shiʿr wa-l-Shuʿarāʾ*." In *Islamic Reflections, Arabic Musings: Studies in Honour of Alan Jones*, edited by R. Hoyland and P. Kennedy, 1–47. Oxford: Gibb Trust, 2004.

al-Ṭabarī, Muḥammad ibn Jarīr. *The History of al-Ṭabarī*. 40 vols. Albany: State University of New York Press, 1985–2007.

Zakeri, Mohsen. *Sāsānid Soldiers in Early Muslim Society: The Origins of the ʿAyyārān and Futuwwa*. Wiesbaden: Harrassowitz, 1995.

On Shuʿūbism

Crone, Patricia. "Post-Colonialism in Tenth-Century Islam." *Der Islam*, 83, no. 1 (2006): 2–38.

al-Dajīlī, ʿAbd al-Ṣāḥib. *Al-Shuʿūbiyyah*. Najaf: Maṭbaʿat al-Quḍāʾ, 1960.

al-Dūrī, ʿAbd al-ʿAzīz. *Al-Judhūr al-taʾrīkhiyya li-l-Shuʿūbiyya*. Beirut: Dār al-Ṭalīʿah, 1962.

Hanna, S. A., and G. H. Gardner. "Al-Shuʿūbiyya Up-Dated: A Study of the 20th Century Revival of an Eighth Century Concept." *Middle East Journal*, 20 (1966): 335–51.

Jaffāl, Khalīl Ibrāhīm. *Al-Shuʿūbiyyah wa-l-adab abʿād wa-maḍmūnāt min al-ʿaṣr al-jāhilī ḥattā l-qarn al-rābiʿ al-hijrī*. Beirut: Dār al-Niḍāl, 1986.

Larsson, Göran. *Ibn García's Shuʿūbiyya Letter: Ethnic and Theological Tensions in Medieval al-Andalus*. Leiden: Brill, 2003.

———. "Ignaz Goldziher on the Shuʿūbiyya Movement." In *Goldziher Memorial Conference*, edited by Éva Apor and István Ormos, 151–57. Budapest: Library of the Hungarian Academy of Sciences, 2005.

Mottahedeh, Roy. "The Shuʿûbîyah and the Social History of Early Islamic Iran." *International Journal of Middle East Studies*, 7 (1976): 161–82.

Norris, H. T. "Shuʿūbiyyah in Arabic Literature." In *ʿAbbasid Belles-Lettres*, edited by Julia Ashtiany, T.M. Johnstone, J.D. Latham, R.B. Serjeant, and G. Rex Smith, 3–47. Cambridge: Cambridge University Press, 1990.

Pourshariati, Parvaneh. "The Akhbār al-Ṭiwāl of Abū Ḥanīfa Dīnawarī: A Shuʿūbī Treatise on Late Antique Iran." In *Sources for the History of Sasanian and Post-Sasanian Iran*, edited by Rika Gyselen, 201–89. Bures-sur-Yvette: Groupe pour l'Étude de la Civilisation du Moyen-Orient, 2010.

Qaddūra, Zāhiya. *Al-Shuʿūbiyyah wa-atharuhā l-ijtimāʿī wa-l-siyāsī fī l-ḥayāt al-Islāmiyyah fī l-ʿaṣr al-ʿAbbāsī l-awwal*. Beirut: Dār al-Kitāb al-Lubnānī, 1972.

Richter-Bernburg, Lutz. "Linguistic Shuʿūbīya and Early Neo-Persian Prose." *Journal of the American Oriental Society*, 94, no. 1 (1974): 55–64.

al-Sāmarrāʾī, ʿAbd Allāh Sallūm. *Al-Shuʿūbiyya: ḥarakah muḍāddah li-l-Islām wa-l-ummah al-ʿArabiyyah*. Baghdad: Dār al-Ḥurriyyah li-l-Ṭibāʿah, 1981.

Szombathy, Zoltán. "Some Notes on the Impact of the Shuʿūbiyya on Arabic Genealogy." In *Goldziher Memorial Conference*, edited by Éva Apor and István Ormos, 255–69. Budapest: Library of the Hungarian Academy of Sciences, 2005.

Index of Qur'anic Verses

Index

About the NYU Abu Dhabi Institute

The Library of Arabic Literature is supported by a grant from the NYU Abu Dhabi Institute, a major hub of intellectual and creative activity and advanced research. The Institute hosts academic conferences, workshops, lectures, film series, performances, and other public programs directed both to audiences within the UAE and to the worldwide academic and research community. It is a center of the scholarly community for Abu Dhabi, bringing together faculty and researchers from institutions of higher learning throughout the region.

NYU Abu Dhabi, through the NYU Abu Dhabi Institute, is a world-class center of cutting-edge research, scholarship, and cultural activity. The Institute creates singular opportunities for leading researchers from across the arts, humanities, social sciences, sciences, engineering, and the professions to carry out creative scholarship and conduct research on issues of major disciplinary, multidisciplinary, and global significance.

About the Translators

Sarah Bowen Savant (Harvard University, PhD 2006) is Associate Professor at the Aga Khan University in London. She is a cultural historian, focusing on early Islamic history and history writing up to 1100, with a special focus on Iraq and Iran. She is the author of *The New Muslims of Post-Conquest Iran: Tradition, Memory, and Conversion* (Cambridge: Cambridge University Press, 2013), which won the Saidi-Sirjani Book Award, given by the International Society for Iranian Studies on behalf of the Persian Heritage Foundation. Her current book project focuses on the history of books in the Middle East. With a team, she is developing digital methods to study the origins and development of the Arabic and Persian textual traditions. She has also published articles and edited volumes dealing with ethnic identity, cultural memory, genealogy, and history writing.

Peter Webb (SOAS, University of London, PhD 2014) is a British Academy Postdoctoral Fellow (2015–18) at SOAS. His research investigates Arabic literature, cultural production and communal identity in the pre-modern Middle East. The origins and evolution of Arab identity are the subject of his book *Imagining the Arabs: Arab Identity and the Rise of Islam* (Edinburgh: Edinburgh University Press, 2016); his postdoctoral fellowship and current book project study the idea of pre-Islam (*al-Jāhiliyyah*) in Muslim imaginations, exploring the ways in which Muslim communities have memorialized, mythologized, and reconstructed the pre-Islamic past. In addition to articles and book chapters on Arabic literature and history, Peter has also prepared a critical edition and translation of al-Maqrīzī's "Arab Brigands" (Bibliotheca Maqriziana, Brill, forthcoming in 2017). Prior to his academic career, Peter was a solicitor at Clifford Chance LLP.

The Library of Arabic Literature

For more details on individual titles, visit www.libraryofarabicliterature.org

Classical Arabic Literature: A Library of Arabic Literature Anthology
Selected and translated by Geert Jan van Gelder (2012)

A Treasury of Virtues: Sayings, Sermons, and Teachings of ʿAlī, by al-Qāḍī al-Quḍāʿī, with the *One Hundred Proverbs* attributed to al-Jāḥiẓ
Edited and translated by Tahera Qutbuddin (2013)

The Epistle on Legal Theory, by al-Shāfiʿī
Edited and translated by Joseph E. Lowry (2013)

Leg over Leg, by Aḥmad Fāris al-Shidyāq
Edited and translated by Humphrey Davies (4 volumes; 2013–14)

Virtues of the Imām Aḥmad ibn Ḥanbal, by Ibn al-Jawzī
Edited and translated by Michael Cooperson (2 volumes; 2013–15)

The Epistle of Forgiveness, by Abū l-ʿAlāʾ al-Maʿarrī
Edited and translated by Geert Jan van Gelder and Gregor Schoeler (2 volumes; 2013–14)

The Principles of Sufism, by ʿĀʾishah al-Bāʿūniyyah
Edited and translated by Th. Emil Homerin (2014)

The Expeditions: An Early Biography of Muḥammad, by Maʿmar ibn Rāshid
Edited and translated by Sean W. Anthony (2014)

Two Arabic Travel Books

Accounts of China and India, by Abū Zayd al-Sīrāfī

Edited and translated by Tim Mackintosh-Smith (2014)

Mission to the Volga, by Aḥmad ibn Faḍlān

Edited and translated by James Montgomery (2014)

Disagreements of the Jurists: A Manual of Islamic Legal Theory, by al-Qāḍī al-Nuʿmān

Edited and translated by Devin J. Stewart (2015)

Consorts of the Caliphs: Women and the Court of Baghdad, by Ibn al-Sāʿī

Edited by Shawkat M. Toorawa and translated by the Editors of the Library of Arabic Literature (2015)

What ʿĪsā ibn Hishām Told Us, by Muḥammad al-Muwayliḥī

Edited and translated by Roger Allen (2 volumes; 2015)

The Life and Times of Abū Tammām, by Abū Bakr Muḥammad ibn Yaḥyā al-Ṣūlī

Edited and translated by Beatrice Gruendler (2015)

The Sword of Ambition: Bureaucratic Rivalry in Medieval Egypt, by ʿUthmān ibn Ibrāhīm al-Nābulusī

Edited and translated by Luke Yarbrough (2016)

Brains Confounded by the Ode of Abū Shādūf Expounded, by Yūsuf al-Shirbīnī

Edited and translated by Humphrey Davies (2 volumes; 2016)

Light in the Heavens: Sayings of the Prophet Muḥammad, by al-Qāḍī al-Quḍāʿī

Edited and translated by Tahera Qutbuddin (2016)

Risible Rhymes, by Muḥammad ibn Maḥfūẓ al-Sanhūrī

Edited and translated by Humphrey Davies (2016)

A Hundred and One Nights

Edited and translated by Bruce Fudge (2016)

The Excellence of the Arabs, by Ibn Qutaybah
Edited by James E. Montgomery and Peter Webb
Translated by Sarah Bowen Savant and Peter Webb (2017)

Scents and Flavors: A Syrian Cookbook
Edited and translated by Charles Perry (2017)

Arabian Satire: Poetry from 18th-Century Najd, by Ḥmēdān al-Shwēʿir
Edited and translated by Marcel Kurpershoek (2017)

In Darfur: An Account of the Sultanate and Its People, by Muḥammad ibn ʿUmar al-Tūnisī
Edited and translated by Humphrey Davies (2 volumes; 2018)

War Songs, by ʿAntarah ibn Shaddād
Edited by James E. Montgomery
Translated by James E. Montgomery with Richard Sieburth (2018)

Arabian Romantic: Poems on Bedouin Life and Love, by ʿAbdallah ibn Sbayyil
Edited and translated by Marcel Kurpershoek (2018)

Dīwān ʿAntarah ibn Shaddād: A Literary-Historical Study, by James E. Montgomery (2018)

Stories of Piety and Prayer: Deliverance Follows Adversity, by al-Muḥassin ibn ʿAlī al-Tanūkhī
Edited and translated by Julia Bray (2019)

Tajrīd sayf al-himmah li-stikhrāj mā fī dhimmat al-dhimmah: A Scholarly Edition of ʿUthmān ibn Ibrāhīm al-Nābulusī's Text, by Luke Yarbrough (2019)

The Philosopher Responds: An Intellectual Correspondence from the Tenth Century, by Abū Ḥayyān al-Tawḥīdī and Abū ʿAlī Miskawayh
Edited by Bilal Orfali and Maurice Pomerantz
Translated by Sophia Vasalou and James E. Montgomery (2 volumes; 2019)

The Discourses: Reflections on History, Sufism, Theology, and Literature—Volume One, by al-Ḥasan al-Yūsī
Edited and translated by Justin Stearns (2020)

English-only Paperbacks

Leg over Leg, by Aḥmad Fāris al-Shidyāq (2 volumes; 2015)

The Expeditions: An Early Biography of Muḥammad, by Maʿmar ibn Rāshid (2015)

The Epistle on Legal Theory: A Translation of al-Shāfiʿī's Risālah, by al-Shāfiʿī (2015)

The Epistle of Forgiveness, by Abū l-ʿAlāʾ al-Maʿarrī (2016)

The Principles of Sufism, by ʿĀʾishah al-Bāʿūniyyah (2016)

A Treasury of Virtues: Sayings, Sermons, and Teachings of ʿAlī, by al-Qāḍī al-Quḍāʿī with the *One Hundred Proverbs* attributed to al-Jāḥiẓ (2016)

The Life of Ibn Ḥanbal, by Ibn al-Jawzī (2016)

Mission to the Volga, by Ibn Faḍlān (2017)

Accounts of China and India, by Abū Zayd al-Sīrāfī (2017)

A Hundred and One Nights (2017)

Disagreements of the Jurists: A Manual of Islamic Legal Theory, by al-Qāḍī al-Nuʿmān (2017)

What ʿĪsā ibn Hishām Told Us, by Muḥammad al-Muwayliḥī (2018)

War Songs, by ʿAntarah ibn Shaddād (2018)

The Life and Times of Abū Tammām, by Abū Bakr Muḥammad ibn Yaḥyā al-Ṣūlī (2018)

The Sword of Ambition, by ʿUthmān ibn Ibrāhīm al-Nābulusī (2019)

Brains Confounded by the Ode of Abū Shādūf Expounded, by Yūsuf al-Shirbīnī, with *Risible Rhymes* by Muḥammad ibn Maḥfūẓ al-Sanhūrī (2 volumes; 2019)

The Excellence of the Arabs, by Ibn Qutaybah (2019)

Light in the Heavens: Sayings of the Prophet Muḥammad, by al-Qāḍī al-Quḍāʿī (2019)